The BBC Asian Network

Gurvinder Aujla-Sidhu

The BBC Asian Network

The Cultural Production of Diversity

Gurvinder Aujla-Sidhu
De Montfort University
Leicester, UK

ISBN 978-3-030-65766-6   ISBN 978-3-030-65764-2   (eBook)
https://doi.org/10.1007/978-3-030-65764-2

This Palgrave Macmillan imprint is published by the registered company Springer Nature Switzerland AG.
The registered company address is: Gewerbestrasse 11, 6330 Cham, Switzerland

ACKNOWLEDGEMENTS

I am indebted to the BBC interviewees who gave up their time to contribute to this study. My aim in this book is to narrate their experiences of working for the BBC producing content specifically for minority audiences. The interviews took place in 2015–2016 as part of my PhD research, and I began writing this book in 2019. I was still writing it when the Covid-19 pandemic impacted the UK and the world in 2020. During this period, George Floyd was killed, and the subsequent Black Lives Matter global protests have profoundly influenced media organisations to make changes to their diversity commitments. It has forced all institutions in the UK to look at their staff, their policies, and their plans to embed or bring "diversity" to the fore in order to better serve their clients or buyers. Simultaneously, there is a demand from the audiences for stronger and more nuanced understanding of racial discrimination, prejudice, and an end to the erasure and absence of content that examines the histories of minority communities, specically Black history. I work in a university which had been trying to address inequality in undergraduate attainment outcomes prior to 2020, but Covid, and George Floyd, has brought structural inequalities to the fore, and since then De Montfort University has been trying to address them.

Naturally the BBC along with other media organisations has also tried to address the issues that Black Lives Matter protests have raised. Therefore, I have sought to use the latest diversity statistics and their most recent strategic plans to address the issues, which were released in May and June 2020.

I am also grateful for the feedback from the anonymous reviewers, which has helped to improve how the content is structured. I want to thank my colleagues in the Media Discourse Centre at De Montfort University, especially Professor Stuart Price and Ben Harbisher. Thank you also to Professor Tim Wall and Dr Anamik Saha for their feedback, guidance, and recommendations. Furthermore, I would like to thank colleagues and friends at the MeCCSA Radio Studies Network and the Ecrea Radio Studies section who have offered ideas and support at conferences and workshops where I presented aspects of this work.

Thanks also to Max Hanska, Margaret Montgomery, and Rinella Cere for their support, and the team at Palgrave Macmillan who have helped answer many questions along the way. Finally, to my family—my husband and kids for well just putting up with me!

An earlier version of some of the research outlined in Chapters 4 and 6 appears in *The Radio Journal Studies in Broadcast Media and Audio*, Vol. 18: 1 Producing Diversity in BBC Radio and Aujla-Sidhu, G. (2017), and How to serve British Asian communities? The dilemmas facing the BBC. *Radio Journal: International Studies in Broadcast and Audio*, Vol. 15 Issue 1 May 2017.

CONTENTS

LIST OF FIGURES

CHAPTER 1

Introduction

INTRODUCTION

Despite the existence of diversity strategies, initiatives, and targets to improve the number of ethnic producers, presenters, journalists, writers, and editors across all broadcast media, the UK radio industry continues to fail to reflect the breadth and range of communities living in the UK (Ofcom 2019a). The damning findings from the Office for Communications (Ofcom), the UK government-approved regulatory and competition authority, come during a period of sustained activity within media organisations pertaining to diversity and inclusion initiatives. All broadcasters have set themselves targets to enhance the on-air reflection of minority groups: disabled, ethnic, LGBT, and correspondingly, the recruitment of staff from these groups. The assumption being that to create high-quality programmes that reflect the diverse lives of people living in Great Britain, the media workforce also ought to be drawn from a range of ethnic and social classes (Ofcom 2019b, p. 4). Media organisations have been compelled to scrutinise the representation of their audiences because they need to remain relevant in response to strong competition from streaming services such as Netflix and Amazon. It is also morally the right thing to do—to acknowledge and represent the lives of people who consume radio and television in the UK. The BBC has made a concerted effort behind the scenes to enhance media content depicting minority ethnic communities, their lives, and their concerns. Furthermore, as a public-funded

© The Author(s), under exclusive license to Springer Nature Switzerland AG 2021
G. Aujla-Sidhu, *The BBC Asian Network*,
https://doi.org/10.1007/978-3-030-65764-2_1

organisation, with a public service remit, the BBC has been forced to demonstrate that it creates content for *all* audiences and that minority ethnic listeners consume its output.

Research about ethnic media has tended to focus on how the media serve their audience and what role they perform, whereas less is known about the conditions ethnic media producers labour under, their careers trajectories, and the politics of representation (Cottle 2000; Husband 1994). This book aims to provide an understanding of how minority ethnic journalists create media content featuring diverse audiences whilst working to a public service remit and tries to offer the voice of primarily ethnic staff working in radio production at the BBC Asian Network (a digital ethnic-specific radio station). The following chapters focus on how the work by this group of staff contributes to the construction of a distinctive ethnic audience for the BBC and the challenges, barriers, and conflicts that have emerged as a consequence of the BBC's strategic attempts to make the BBC Asian Network relevant for young British Asian listeners. Studying the media production of ethnic staff is important because it offers an alternative lens through which to view the production process which is often structured to cater for a wide general population. Through in-depth interviews, BBC staff outlined the difficulties and challenges they face producing content for their target listener, and they offer an insight into the internal production culture within BBC Radio. The interviews also reveal how the gatekeeping system limits the dissemination of original journalism about the British Asian communities because the BBC ignores or marginalises the expertise of minority ethnic journalists working at the BBC Asian Network. Instead, journalists find that content that emphasises difference or focuses upon the Muslim communities in the UK is more likely to be cherry-picked by other teams to air on other BBC programmes. What also emerged is that although the radio station was established 16 years old in 2002, there is confusion and resistance among some staff to serve third- and fourth-generation British Asian listeners as directed by senior management.

The material for this study was gathered through in-depth interviews with a range of BBC employees: editors, producers, and presenters, who either work at or previously were employed at the BBC Asian Network. The data collection took place between December 2014 and March 2016. A production studies approach combined with a grounded theory framework was applied for the analysis. This method presents an insight into the internal production and decision-making process within the BBC and offers an understanding of how the BBC as a public service broadcasting (PSB) tries to articulate and manage issues pertaining to race and ethnicity at a time when diversity and inclusion is at the top of the agenda. Production studies have tended to focus upon the film and television sectors as opposed to radio which is a ubiquitous medium but is often overlooked within media research. Moreover, there are few studies that specifically focus upon the experiences of minority ethnic media workers, in this instance, British Asian producers, editors, and presenters. There are some exceptions; Simon Cottle's (1997) seminal study of ethnic employees working in the BBC television found that minority programme producers worked within staid, unadventurous, hierarchical, and bureaucratic constraints and that minority staff appeared to have wholeheartedly embraced BBC conventions of creating programmes with high production values that offered a mainstream framing of ethnicity and race as opposed to producing programmes solely directed at minority audiences. His interviews with producers illustrated how in the 1990s BBC management were already questioning if British Asians required separate specific content or if they were an integral part of British life and history under the umbrella notion of "multiculturalism." Cottle's work offers a critical insight into programme making within the BBC.

Similarly, this book utilises the testimonies of ethnic staff and examines how they try to create and entice an "imagined community" of listeners to the BBC, and it looks at the differences between the staff in how they conceptualise and visualise British Asian identity (Anderson 2012). The interview material revealed a divide between two groups of minority ethnic staff at the BBC Asian Network; some of the older British Asian staff members believe the BBC should focus on older listeners and offer a more robust and authentic articulation of British Asian identity. In contrast, younger staff composed of third- or fourth-generation British Asians born and raised in Britain appeared at ease focusing on a younger listener and articulating a more ambiguous vision of British Asian identity.

The BBC annually spends around 7.3 million pounds on entry-level talent schemes which seek to place people into roles in TV/Radio production, national and local journalism, engineering, software engineering, business management, and legal, to broaden the representation of minority groups (BBC 2018b, p. 4). However, the BBC radio workforce is composed of just 9 per cent of minority ethnic staff (Ofcom 2019b, p. 8). Previous research into the ethnic composition of the media workforce has questioned the emphasis upon targets and numbers, suggesting they give an illusion of change as opposed to enacting actual change because such figures can often include non-production roles (Campion 2005). Thirty years after Cottle's work, and thirteen years after Campion's study of ethnic producers, this study looks at contemporary diversity and inclusion strategies in the BBC and the structural inequalities, gatekeeping, and internal cultures from the point of view of the staff experiencing them.

The BBC Asian Network

The BBC Asian Network is the only digital radio station within the BBC that specifically caters for British Asians and as such plays a significant role in the mixed radio ecology in the UK. The station is directed to appeal to British Asian listeners (people with South Asian roots/heritage such as Pakistani, Indian, Bangladeshi, and Sri Lankan communities) through the provision of speech and music. A BBC review in 2015 indicated that the station reached 15.1 per cent of the UK's Asian adults per week, thus indicating that the BBC Asian Network plays a key role in attracting and driving minority audiences to the wider BBC (BBC Trust 2015, p. 18). The broadcaster struggles to attract Black, Asian, and minority ethnic viewers and listeners to its main output. BBC 1 and BBC 2 tend to attract white middle-class viewers with ABC1[1] profiles, at 54 per cent and 57 per cent, respectively (Ofcom 2019c, p. 31). Analysis of BBC Asian Network listeners shows that they are primarily aged between 25 and 44 years of age and tend to be male (Barratt 2017, p. 2). An earlier listener analysis conducted in 2016 demonstrated that the BBC Asian Network had a record reach among C2[2] profiles, a group composed of skilled manual labourers (Eustace 2016, p. 2). Therefore, the social origins of BBC Asian Network listeners are summarised as primarily C2DE, which refers to those working in either skilled or unskilled roles, retired, casual, or unemployed, although there is an acknowledgement that people from other social groups also listen, particularly those in AB (professional groups).

The BBC Asian Network originated from minority radio programming created by BBC Local Radio to cater for the UK's Asian communities in both Leicester and Birmingham in the late 1970 and 1980s. The programmes were later constructed into a regional radio service for the

---

[1] National Readership Survey (NRS) social grades are a system of demographic classification used in the UK.

[2] NRS social grades are a system of demographic classification used in the UK.

Midlands on AM frequency in 1988, which was later broadcast nationally via the Sky satellite. In 2002, the station was re-launched as a national digital radio station alongside 1Xtra and 6 Music. Director General Greg Dyke directed 1Xtra and the BBC Asian Network to appeal to audiences who felt underserved by the BBC's existing services (Gardam 2004). 1Xtra was initially conceived as being a service for Black British youth; however, the station which emphasises urban music also has a strong appeal among non-minority listeners (BBC Trust 2015, p. 10). The BBC Asian Network has a unique remit within the BBC's portfolio of radio stations because it offers an equal split of speech and music at 50/50. The BBC's other national radio stations are either speech-based, such as 5 Live and Radio 4, or a mixture of speech and music, such as Radio 2 and Radio 1. The speech content on the BBC Asian Network includes news bulletins, documentaries, and phone-in/debate programme. In this manner, the station offers a unique national platform for minority voices to articulate their concerns. Their voices and viewpoints are given prominence on the station and often a story may emerge on the BBC Asian Network but may be shared with other BBC programmes as part of institutional efforts to make diverse journalism central to the core business of the BBC. The remit set by the former BBC Trust emphasises:

> A strong focus on accurate, impartial, and independent news and current affairs, together with debate, entertainment, and culture relevant for a modern British Asian audience. The music played should include a broad range of South Asian-influenced music, with a particular emphasis on new and live music and British Asian artists. During the day an extensive playlist should form the backbone of the schedule, while weekend programmes should focus on more specialised areas. (BBC Trust 2016, p. 2)

The Service Licence promotes the idea that the station can appeal widely to all British Asians through information and music. No other BBC station is as explicitly defined by the target audience, for example, explicit Asian programming for British Asian listeners. The station is also encouraged to enable listeners to "interact and communicate with each other and the station" in order to create a community of listeners (BBC Trust 2016, p. 2). A similar public service broadcasting (PSB) is SBS (Special Broadcasting Service) Radio in Australia, which produces audio content in 74 languages aimed at non-English-speaking communities and CBC Radio in Canada, which offers programming in both English and French plus eight other indigenous languages. These services target several minority communities, whereas the BBC Asian Network is specifically tasked with serving the British Asian population in the UK.

The BBC has a history of producing content in non-English for people living aboard through the Empire Service and Overseas Service. Khamkar (2017) has noted that although the BBC historically produced Asian language radio through the World Service, it was only in the late 1960s that it began to create content aimed at the Asian migrant community in the UK. Early programmes for immigrants from South Asia included on BBC 1"*In Logon Se Miliye*" 1965, translated as "Let me introduce you to these people," "*Apna Hi Ghar Samajhiye*" 1967 (Make Yourself at Home), and *Nai Zindagi Naya Jeevan* 1968–1982 (New life). These programmes were broadcast in Hindustani[3] by volunteers or presenters who migrated to the UK and sought to appeal to both Indian and Pakistani viewers in equal measure. The programmes are described by Malik (2002, p. 57) as "classic public service broadcasts" because they tried to integrate newly arrived Asian immigrants into Britain with practical advice, education, and some entertainment. In keeping with the PSB ethos, the goal was to educate the audience in conversational English which the BBC recognised as being a challenging task. Programme editor of *Make Yourself at Home*, David Gretton, described the Indian and Pakistani industrial immigrants as "illiterate" in an interview about the new programme (Gretton 1965). Malik (2002) has argued that the BBC thought South Asians required guidance on how to integrate due to greater perceived cultural differences with the majority population. In contrast, African and Caribbean migrants were considered to have traditions and customs which were closer to "English" culture. Media historian, David Hendy, has studied BBC archives to document one hundred years of the broadcaster's existence. He suggests that Asian content was purposely "ghettoised on the schedules" because it was broadcast at times when the majority audience were less likely to listen or watch TV (Hendy n.d.). Meaning immigrant audiences were treated by the broadcaster as being separate and distinct from the majority audience. The fact that the early programming on ITV and BBC situated minorities as immigrants become problematic in the 1970s and 1980s when the second and third generations of British Asians were increasingly born in Britain.

---

[3] Hindustani is the dialect of Hindi used in Delhi and is the lingua franca throughout India.

Unlike the early integration programmes, The BBC Asian Network is aimed at British Asians who are born and raised in the UK. The presentation is largely in English; the music is a mix of foreign language *Bollywood*, *Bhangra*, and classical music alongside urban and British Asian music featuring British Asian artists. The remit places a strong emphasis upon news and current affairs involving and pertaining to Britain's minority communities and music. Stories about the British Asian communities are also shared with other programmes within the BBC to help them enhance their reflection of British Asian audiences. Therefore, the emphasis upon news and speech about the British Asian communities ought to make the station strategically significant within the BBC's portfolio of radio stations. However, in its eighteen-year history as a national BBC radio station, it has faced a proposed closure in 2010 and enacted a few editorial strategies to evolve the output to remain relevant to the changing British Asian listener. Equally, listener figures have fluctuated, due in part, to the different strategies enacted by BBC management and the external press coverage related to the proposed closure in 2010. Since 2018 listener figures have dipped to 519,000 RAJAR[4] (Q4 2019). One challenge is attracting third- and fourth-generation listeners in the digital media era, where fewer young people listen to radio combined with the popularity of streaming services such as Spotify (Ofcom 2019c). In 2010 the BBC recommended the closure of the BBC Asian Network due to the high production cost contrasted with low listener figures in 2009/10. The BBC argued that the money saved could be reinvested to produce and deliver content to Asian audiences through a range of BBC television and radio services. 6 Music was also selected for closure as part of a cost-saving exercise that was enacted due to a government-imposed freeze on the licence fee in 2008. The recommendation to close the BBC Asian Network was rejected by the BBC Executive in 2011 because a review of the station recognised the service attracted diverse South Asian listeners who are "typically less well served by other BBC radio services" and that the music and original news and speech programming were "highly valued" by listeners (BBC Trust 2012, p. 3). The BBC Trust noted that the BBC Asian Network made a strong contribution to help deliver the BBC's public purposes (see Royal Charter 2016).

[4] Radio Joint Audience Research Limited was established in 1992 to operate a single audience measurement system for the radio industry in the UK. Its fieldwork operations in 2020 were delayed due to the coronavirus pandemic, so this book uses data primarily from 2019.

In 2011 the station was reprieved but was forced to reduce running costs by cutting staff and presenters and offering longer shows on the station. Listeners emphasised they wanted the BBC to provide a radio station aimed specifically at British Asian audiences (BBC Trust 2012, p. 3). In 2012 a new reduced schedule and presenter line-up was unveiled. The aim was to provide fewer but longer programmes, especially in off-peak periods. Distinctive content including the religious programming and drama were axed because these genres were considered to appeal to a limited number of listeners and had a greater production cost attached to them. The review also enabled the BBC Asian Network to focus upon listeners aged 25 to 45 years of age and retain its "friend of the family" editorial strategy, which sought to appeal the average Asian household. In 2016 the remit for the BBC Asian Network was further amended to allow the station to focus specifically upon younger listeners, third- and fourth-generation British Asians. The various editorial strategies are examined in Chap. 5 in further depth.

ETHNIC MEDIA

Although the BBC was the first public service provider to include programming for British Asian audiences, Channel 4 also focused on the same diaspora when it was first established. In 1982, Channel 4 included magazine programmes such as Eastern Eye and Black on Black in the main schedule; these historic programmes offered explicit recognition of the existence of minority communities in the UK. The growth in Asian radio services in the UK has been incremental, due in part, to the regulation of broadcasting in the UK. Commercial or independent radio was not permitted until 1973. The early radio stations emphasised geographical communities as opposed to communities of interest or minority communities. The first Asian station was Sunrise Radio in London established in 1989 on medium wave; it later began broadcasting nationally across the UK via DAB.[5] Sunrise was the first 24-hour Asian radio station and continues to offer music, news, and entertainment from South Asia, broadcasting in English, Hindi, Urdu, and Punjabi. It is signed up to RAJAR and is the most listened to Asian radio station in London, with 318,000 listeners (RAJAR, Q4 2019). Other notable Asian radio stations include Sabras

---

[5] DAB is digital and a standard way to broadcast digital radio services in many countries around the world, especially in the EU.

Radio in Leicester, launched in 1995, Asian Sound Radio in Manchester, and Radio XL in Birmingham.

Alongside Asian radio, there exists ethnic television and print media which cater specifically for British Asians. Lay and Thomas (2012) mapped ethnic media in London. They found that 175 media organisations catered for minority communities, 49 exclusively focused on the Asian communities, reflecting the different languages spoken by Indian, Pakistani, Sri Lankan, and Tamil communities. Their study also found that clear generational differences exist; some services were aimed at second and third generations whose interests differ from their parents and grandparents who may have migrated to the UK. Minority editors or publishers explained their role is to offer an alternative to mainstream media and to also foster "cultural unity and identity" (Lay and Thomas 2012, p. 376). Ethnic media offer minority communities the provision of information and news in a range of languages and connections to culture, music, and arts. Yu and Matsaganis (2019, p. 24) suggest that ethnic media contribute to the construction of communities, through the prominence upon culture, and thus they work to strengthen people's cultural and ethnic identities.

Ethnic media is broadly defined as media produced by minority staff specifically for a racial or linguistic community, and it tends to emerge when a community requires a "voice" (Matsaganis et al. 2011, p. 76). There are many variations of ethnic media organisations; some hire staff who are members of the ethnic community living in a town or city serving local communities, whilst others belong to larger worldwide media organisations serving an audience living in different parts of the world. Ethnic producers tend to have expert knowledge about the audience they serve and, in theory, are better equipped to voice the concerns of minority communities with authority. On occasions this representation can highlight the parallel existence of minorities living in cities or countries. Ethnic media are able to provide new groups with information to support their settlement and articulate experiences of inequality or injustice which adversely impact minority communities. However, Yu (in Yu and Matsaganis 2019) has highlighted the unique paradox faced by ethnic media; if they publish or broadcast in non-English, these media are unable to access mainstream audiences and, consequently, they are also not heard by the majority audience. This means a number of services can exist in a silo and that the needs of their listeners/viewers are not understood by the majority population.

Whilst careers in mainstream media can be described as relatively stable, ethnic media is characterised by change, and as such, the sector heavily relies upon volunteers and low-paid staff who are willing to work long hours to produce information (Brown 2005). Sreberny (2005, p. 446) has suggested that ethnic media organisations in the UK enable minority audiences "to direct the gaze backwards, inwards and all around" because these services acknowledge the history of migrant communities, their interests, music, and cultures and allow people to possess a space outside of the public sphere.

In contrast, mainstream media is defined as media produced by and produced for the majority or mainstream population. In the UK this refers to organisations such as ITV, Sky, Bauer Media, Global media group, and the BBC. They are all expected to reflect minority communities both on-air and within their workforce. Bauer media has been urged by Ofcom to "urgently address" the lack of diversity among its workforce, where just 3 per cent of staff are from minority ethnic backgrounds (Ofcom 2019b, p. 24). Although the BBC fares better, Ofcom found just 9 per cent of the 34 million people who listen to BBC radio each week are from a minority ethnic background (Ofcom 2019b, p. 4). The British Asian population in the UK is estimated to be approximately 3.7 million, making it by far the largest ethnic group in the country. Within this context, it is perhaps unsurprising that a publicly funded radio service exists specifically for South Asian audiences. This also makes the BBC Asian Network unique, an ethnic-specific service that operates within the parameters of the BBC public service remit.

BRITISH ASIAN COMMUNITIES

A considerable number of British Asians migrated to the UK from South Asia in the post-war years for largely economic reasons following the formal decolonisation of British India and latterly in the 1970s from East Africa. In Britain, the term "Asian" refers explicitly to people whose families migrated from countries such as India, Bangladesh, Pakistan, and Sri Lanka or those who have mixed race heritages pertaining to these countries. There exist a number of differences within and among each of these groups, and there are also differences that exist between them and the majority population of the UK. Although the terminology "Asian" implies homogeneity, it is in fact a contested term. The construction of "British Asian" as a singular identity means that the media and politicians have created and defined Asian identity to label groups of different people together. Shohat and Stam (2014, p. 10) argue terminology such as Black or Asian works to privilege "Whiteness" because it centres the group thus making everyone else the "rest" and therefore, implicitly, inferior. Furthermore, the identity that is envisaged is frequently constructed through a Eurocentric lens and preserves historical stereotypes. It is argued that because British Asian communities have membership of former colonised countries, the media, state, and education system depict stereotypes, prejudices, and racism as an outcome of the post-colonial experience (Brunt and Cere 2010). This means minority communities are narrowly showcased by the media and imagined through restricted out-of-date parameters. Ali et al. (2006, p. 7) argued that "British Asian" connotes a culture that is "static, patriarchal and authoritarian, in contrast to British/Western culture, with its gleaming (post) modernity," meaning that British Asians are considered collectively to be traditional or old-fashioned. Kaur and Kalra (in Sharma et al. 1996, p. 219) argue that British Asian is "over-used and poorly defined" and seeks to represent an arguably large ethnic cultural category in Britain. The use of terms such as Black, Asian, or BAME (Black, Asian, and minority ethnic) are used in post-colonial societies to convey notions of shared cultures but the terms also encompass difference and otherness (Gillespie 1995).

Through the in-depth interviews ethnic staff explained how they create a distinctive minority audience for the BBC Asian Network. Fitzgerald and Housley (2007) suggest that audiences are imagined by the media because the programme makers work to unite disparate groups of people on the basis that they share similar concerns or interests. Moreover, Ang (1991, p. 28) suggests that public service broadcasters have a different relationship with their audience compared to commercial media because the relationship is characterised by a "pervasive sense of cultural responsibility and social accountability." This perspective is somewhat idealistic as increasingly the BBC is under pressure to justify the licence fee and its existence in both economic and social terms and improve the representation of minority staff within the institution.

THE BBC

The sheer scope and size and history of the BBC mean it plays a unique role in the cultural and public life of Britain. As an organisation the BBC is considered to be the best-funded model of PSB (Freedman et al. 2018). The BBC's public service role commitments make the broadcaster distinct. In this book public service broadcasting (PSB) is understood as the goal to deliver high-quality programme content for all citizens, impartial news provision alongside information, educational programming, and entertainment within a mixed schedule. Lowe and Martin (2013, p. 20) define public service broadcasting as a means to provide "services" "to groups that are not attractive in commercial terms." In other words, public service broadcasting is expected to provide "niche market failure" content for minority audiences alongside popular programmes. There are three significant perspectives in the debate about the need for public service broadcasting: first, within a neo-liberal society public service broadcasting is unnecessary and unwelcome; second, that there is a need for PSB to provide niche content for unserved or unprofitable audiences; and third, that there is a duty to provide broadcasting free from the desire for profit that focuses on providing audiences with information for the society and culture in which they live. The BBC embodies the third approach: independent from the state, but publicly funded to provide a range of high-quality programmes for all audiences. PSB also situates the audience as "citizens" as opposed to consumers because citizens have rights and obligations, including the right to representation and inclusion within society, whereas consumers have interests and needs which the media can monetise (Syvertsen, 1999, 2004). However, as an institution the BBC is also inherently associated with promoting British culture, values, and norms (Creeber 2004). Lotz (in Freedman et al. 2018, p. 46) believes this poses the greatest challenge for the BBC because it is expected to "serve the full citizenry of a diverse nation while simultaneously creating a common culture." BBC employees are likely to be middle class, and consequently, the BBC is criticised for largely catering for middle-class audiences at the expense of young people and minority ethnic audiences (Hesmondhalgh, in Deery and Press 2017; Lacey 2018). Mills (2016, p. 33) has argued that the prospective employees' class and educational background influence their chances of employment in the BBC. In fact, a number of scholars have argued that as an institution the BBC has struggled to evolve from its historical goals that portrayed a singular image of the nation (Carter and McKinlay 2013; Creeber 2004: Malik 2013).

The BBC has a public purpose to serve, reflect, and represent diverse communities in the UK and their way of life to its audience (*Royal Charter* 2016). The expectation is that the BBC offers an accurate reflection of communities and recruits people from ethnically diverse and other minority backgrounds. Consequently, since the publication of the 2016 *Royal Charter*, issues relating to diversity and inclusion within programme making and recruitment have gained greater agency within the BBC. However, commercial media and other critics portray the BBC as being an exception to business norms due to the secure funding which allows the organisation to grow in influence and size (De Bens and Cees 2007). The Royal Charter sets out the scope and scale of the broadcaster and is the constitutional means by which the institution is granted power editorial independence from the government.

The charter renewal process in 2016 embraced criticisms of the organisation including that the BBC has "special privileges" and set out new public purposes and emphasised "distinctiveness" in terms of programme output (Department for Culture, Media and Sport 2016, p. 28). The former culture secretary John Whittingdale was described during the negotiations as being hostile to the BBC and the licence fee (Nickerson 2016). The BBC is the largest radio operator in the UK, and the Department for Culture, Media and Sport has noted that its strength in radio lies in the "editorial quality" (Gardam 2004, p. 35). The 2016 Royal Charter also introduced a new governance structure and replaced the BBC Trust with a Unitary Board, onto which the government can appoint four non-executives directly. The Unitary Board has an oversight of the BBC's mission and public purposes as outlined in the Charter. This allows the state to exert indirect influence and, consequently, it is unrealistic to believe the BBC is completely free from the influence of politics and, inevitably, business interests.

> To continue to be successful in the future, and to merit its special privileges and substantial public funding, the BBC needs to stand apart from other broadcasters, distinguishing itself from the market. This will become increasingly important as choice and competition continue to proliferate, viewing habits evolve, audiences' fragment, and consumer and citizen expectations expand. The government will therefore: embed distinctiveness in the BBC's overall mission (Department for Culture, Media and Sport 2016, p. 28)

It is notable that the government considers the licence fee and a mandate to serve all audiences to equate to "special privileges," and it is implied that the BBC should be grateful for this. There is also an expectation on part of the government and commercial media that public service content ought to be worthy and attract niche audiences who are unserved by commercial media. This is also referred to the "market failure" model, which forces public service providers to serve audiences that commercial media deems as not profitable and are considered less worthy. The White Paper outlined that the BBC needs to ensure that it produces material for diverse communities and clarified that being "served" does not simply mean that people consume content, but that they get value from the BBC (Department for Culture, Media and Sport 2016, p. 29). Distinctiveness and its definition are vague. The White Paper sets out that it ought to mean every service within the BBC (online, radio, and TV) should be "substantially different to other providers" in terms of genre, the quality, level of innovation, risk taking, and creative ambition (Department for Culture, Media, and Sport 2016, p. 32). However, when public service creates an innovative and popular programme, for example, *The Great British Bake Off*, it is expected to relinquish the format to commercial media. This contradiction is specific to public service broadcasting; commercial operators do not face similar criticisms.

In 2018 the BBC ran a series of focus groups to better understand the internal culture within the BBC pertaining to race and ethnicity and the impact this has on the career progression of ethnic minority employees. It is acknowledged that whilst number of new ethnic employees hired is around 14 per cent each year, on average 15 per cent of ethnic minority staff leave the organisation, making these figures above the BBC Radio average (Ofcom 2019b, p. 8). Employees from minority ethnic groups are under-represented across all roles within BBC Radio (Ofcom 2019b, p. 8). Across the BBC (TV and Radio), 13 per cent of the workforce is classed as being Black, Asian, or from a minority ethnic group. Whilst the representation of minority staff within the BBC is broadly in keeping with the ethnic composition of the UK population, but regional television and radio newsrooms located in ethnically diverse cities and regions have low numbers of minority ethnic staff.

Labour Studies in Media

It is suggested that successive governments have advantaged the cultural or creative industries and deemed it as significant to create jobs and wealth (Mayer 2011). Initially, the terminology creative was used to describe artistic activities such as furniture making, theatre, and dance alongside newer digital technology roles. Thirteen sectors including advertising, the arts, crafts, fashion, and television and radio are included as comprising the "creative industries." As a result, cultural workers have been situated as being not only highly skilled but also possessing collaborative and economic skills. However, most of these industries remain largely dominated by white middle-class employees (Hesmondhalgh and Saha 2013; O'Brien et al. 2016). Hesmondhalgh (2019) has argued that the ideological and structural framework of the creative industries enables inequality within employment to exist. He suggests the sector is characterised by insecurity, freelancing, and project-based work, and people are often recruited due to their social networks which reinforce class, gender, and ethnic hierarchies. There is a significant under-representation of people from working-class origins working in the creative industries due in part to a high number of short-term contract roles, an emphasis upon freelance work, and low or no salary (O'Brien et al. 2016, p. 117). The impact of these normative entry methods means only people with financial resources or a wealthy family who can support them can enter the media industries (Hesmondhalgh and Baker 2011, p. 116).

This study examines specifically the conditions in which ethnic staff work to a public service remit in the BBC. Similar work by Campion (2005) who interviewed one hundred programme makers across the broadcast industry revealed there was an emphasis upon staff to accentuate the "strangeness" of minority communities in order to make programmes appealing for general or mainstream audiences (Campion 2005, p. 27). Saha (2018) has strongly argued that ethnic employees are hired by media organisations to fulfil diversity targets and address their coverage of minority issues. However, his work finds that ethnic staff are forced to conform to methods of production that work to commoditise diversity and depict ethnic communities using stereotypes or as "other." Moreover, he contends that diversity schemes contribute to the maintenance of "institutional whiteness" in the media because minorities are recruited specifically to increase the visibility of minorities, but they can be placed onto fixed-term contracts or posts where they are unlikely to be promoted (Saha 2018, p. 18). In this way, according to Hall (in Morely and Chen 1996, p. 471), they are a "segregated visibility," present and visible but not part of the principal decision-making.

Research on media production has called for the fair representation of minority ethnic staff in organisations because historically they have lacked opportunities to work in the media sector. It is also assumed that the participation of employees from a range of backgrounds will positively influence the representation on screen of minority communities. When minority staff are able to produce content that enables them to articulate their histories and lived experiences, this is referred to as "intraculture" and the broadcaster becomes the platform for deliberation (Butsch, cited in Ross and Nightingdale 2003, p. 117).

DATA COLLECTION

Thirty former and current BBC employees were interviewed between December 2014 and February 2016: fifteen women and fifteen men. At the time of the interviews, half of the employees occupied senior roles within the BBC, such as editors, heads, or senior journalists. The other fifteen were in junior or entry-level roles such as broadcast journalists, producers, and some were talent on-air presenters. Twenty-three of the interviewees were British Asian and were either first, second, or third generation. All the interviewees had experience of producing media content for British Asian listeners, meaning they were all "grounded" in the production process (Strauss and Corbin 1998). Interviewing was used as the research method to examine BBC staff's personal and professional experiences of producing and delivering content for minority audiences whilst working within the parameters of a public service remit. Some interviewees were contacted via email and others via social media. Their perspectives illuminate the internal culture at the BBC Asian Network and reveals how minority staff negotiate external forces: political, social, and economic to produce material for and represent British Asian listeners. Similar studies of production also use in-depth interviews as the primary research method because this technique contributes to the development of a description of a social group, institution, and the culture or way of life (see Campion 2005; Cottle 1997; Hesmondhalgh and Baker 2011; Matsaganis and Katz 2014; Saha 2018). The voices and perspectives of the BBC staff offer the opportunity to "thicken" the description or knowledge of institutions. A semi-structured approach was selected because it allowed different questions to be posed to staff who occupied different roles within the BBC.

My previous roles as broadcast journalist within the BBC between 2004 and 2012 meant I was knowledgeable about some of the working practices at the BBC Asian Network and had an understanding of the listener they are trying to serve. Ganga and Scott (2006, p. 2) define "insider" research as "social interviews conducted between researchers and participants who share a similar cultural, linguistic, ethnic, national and religious heritage." For this study the insider was connected by shared knowledge of journalism practices and ethnically to some of the interviewees. This extra knowledge meant I could probe and ask questions that someone else may not. There was however a need to be objective and to leave my individual experiences to one side because what the researcher brings to the study can influence what is seen (Charmaz 2014). Significant changes had taken place at the BBC and the BBC Asian Network since my departure. Primarily, after the station was saved from closure the budget was reduced and staff headcount was halved, meaning longer shows, shared programming, and a new editorial strategy. This offered the starting point for the interviews.

All interviewees were offered the option of anonymity, enabling them to talk openly and freely; however, most interviewees occupying senior roles authorised the use of their names and titles. Some of the latter interviews took place during the highly controversial Charter Renewal process in 2015 and 2016 and, as such, some interviewees were worried about their jobs. Anonymised interviewees have been given a generic South Asian pseudonym and a vague job title to conceal their identity. Their quotes used throughout the book have been carefully evaluated in order to avoid revealing people's real identity, thus specific situations or references to stories that may identify them have been removed.

PURPOSE OF THIS BOOK

This book examines the experiences of minority staff within BBC and looks at how they work to create and construct a distinctive minority community of listeners for the BBC. Chapter 2 concentrates on the BBC and looks at the principal goals of public service broadcasting to see how they underpin the delivery of the BBC Asian Network output. The chapter questions if the structures of the institution, missions, and culture within the BBC influence how ethnic viewpoints are showcased by the BBC. The chapter specifically explores how British Asian identity is envisaged by the BBC and, correspondingly, how programme producers represent this community back to the audience. Notions of framing, stereotyping, and Eurocentrism are examined with reference to programme making. In particular, the issue of universality is critically examined in light of the BBC mandate to serve ethnic and regional audiences whilst also showcasing a common British culture.

Chapter 3 seeks to critically evaluate the premise that British Asians are reflected in the media and the press through notions of difference and otherness. A number of scholars have argued that minority ethnic communities are showcased in the media with an emphasis upon their difference (Campion 2005; Moylan 2013; Saha 2018). This chapter focuses on the growing significance of the British Asian community in the UK and their increasing importance to the BBC and other media organisations as a potential audience. In addition, there is examination about why some British Asian communities are depicted more favourably than others—for example, Muslim communities are more likely to be showcased negatively compared to Indian Sikh and Hindu communities in the UK.

The career progression and retention of ethnic minority media workers is examined in Chap. 4. Utilising interview material gathered for this study alongside the BBC's key findings from internal focus groups, its socio-economic survey combined with the BBC's diversity data, the chapter illuminates some of the issues ethnic staff face. The interviews reveal differences exist between the older and young ethnic staff due to their generation, education, and level of integration into British life. Increasingly, ethnic journalists who are recruited tend to be "integrated" and whilst this is not problematic for the BBC, some older ethnic staff find it challenging because these journalists can lack sufficient knowledge about the communities they will serve. It is unclear if ethnic journalists must possess specialist cultural knowledge alongside their practical journalism skills to gain employment at the BBC Asian Network or if knowledge pertaining to British Asian communities is in fact secondary.

The station was established to combat the chronic lack of British Asian representation across the BBC, but it has struggled to secure the intended listening community due to fierce competition within the Asian radio sector. Chapter 5 offers an overview of three different editorial strategies enacted at the station and takes a close look at the proposed closure of the BBC Asian Network in 2010. What emerges is that a singular service for all British Asians is unable to entice some of the target listening community because it is too simplistic to expect Asian people to listen to the station simply because they are Asian. Some of the interviewees called for a deeper nuanced understanding of Asian communities so that programme content can be shaped accordingly.

Normative journalism practices and gatekeeping are scrutinised in Chap. 6. BBC staff describe how they experience the gatekeepers and commissioners and adapt their ideas and pitches accordingly. Their perspectives reveal the complex challenges and tensions that have been created through an organisational pressure on ethnic journalists to share their "diverse" journalism across BBC programmes and platforms. The producers are keenly aware that content pertaining to Muslim communities in the UK is more likely to be selected by story commissioners across the BBC because issues relating to race, ethnicity, and religion are understood and showcased within a restricted framework which tacitly promotes "otherness," conflict, and terrorism (Flood et al. 2011).

What underlies this study is that British Asian identity is continuously evolving and adapting. In response to the changing Asian community, the BBC has revolutionised how it frames ethnic content, which was historically referred to as "immigrant programmes" (Hendy n.d.). Therefore, Chap. 7 looks at how the BBC has revolved the language offer on the Asian Network by introducing blended language (a hybrid of English and a South Asian language such as Hindi) presentation for specific linguistic programmes. In addition, there is a focus upon how the senior leadership in the BBC perceive the target listener; "the common denominator is Britishness, not Asian-ness, its Britishness" (Former Controller, Bob Shennan 2015). The BBC Asian Network does not aim to promote Asian culture and, instead, concentrates upon trying to depict on-air a British Asian lifestyle, whilst also trying to connect distinctive religious and community groups who share a similar colonial history and the experiences of living in Britain into a distinct community of listeners.

Chapter 8 concentrates upon the music policies at the BBC Asian Network and assesses how the station playlist has adapted in response to changing tastes among the target listeners. The station is tasked with finding and nurturing new and emerging British Asian artists, and although this is clearly defined in the station's remit, some staff have strong opinions over what music genres deserve airtime. The former head of Programmes, Mark Strippel, highlighted that the station should not be stereotyped as simply offering *Bhangra* and *Bollywood* music. There is an examination of how normative BBC music policies enable the marginalisation of specialist and "foreign music" and how British Asian artists are relegated to the BBC Asian Network (Wall and Dubber 2009; Saha 2012). BBC staff also raise their concerns about the genres that selected for the playlist within the context of wider challenges facing the radio industry, reducing listening hours among younger listeners, competition from streaming and podcast services, and difficulties in matching the context to the target audience.

Chapter 9 looks at the future prospects of the Asian Network and outlines the BBC's new diversity and inclusion strategies for radio and television. Contemporary developments in broadcasting and changes within the BBC are assessed with reference to changing audience habits. The chapter concludes by summarising the key findings from the study.

References

Ali, Nasreen, Virinder S. Kalra, and S. Sayyid, eds. 2006. *A Postcolonial People, South Asians in Britain*. London: Hurst & Co.

Anderson, Benedict. 2012. *Imagined Communities: Reflections on the Origin and Spread of Nationalism*. Revised edition. London: Verso.

Ang, Ien. 1991. *Desperately Seeking the Audience*. London/New York: Routledge.

Barratt, Flossie. 2017. BBC Station Performance Report BBC Asian Network UK – 6 Month Weight. *BBC Marketing and Audiences*. http://downloads.bbc.co.uk/radio/commissioning/BBC_Asian_Network_Final_for_Commissioning.pdf. Accessed 12 Oct.

BBC. 2018a. Reflecting the Ethnic Diversity of the UK within the BBC Workforce. A Report on Career Progression and Culture for BAME Staff at the BBC. http://downloads.bbc.co.uk/mediacentre/bame-career-progression-and-culture-report.pdf. Accessed 12 October.

———. 2018b. Reflecting the Socio-Economic Diversity of the UK within the BBC Workforce. A Report on Career Progression and Culture at the BBC. http://downloads.bbc.co.uk/mediacentre/socio-economic-diversity.pdf. Accessed 12 October.

BBC Trust. 2012. BBC Asian Network Service Licence Review 2012. http://downloads.bbc.co.uk/bbctrust/assets/files/pdf/regulatory_framework/service_licences/radio/2012/asian_network_may12.pdf. Accessed 12 October.

———. 2015. BBC Trust Service Review 2015. *BBC Trust*. http://downloads.bbc.co.uk/bbctrust/assets/files/pdf/our_work/music_radio/music_radio.pdf

———. 2016. BBC Asian Network Service Licence (Aug) 2016. *BBC Trust*. http://downloads.bbc.co.uk/bbctrust/assets/files/pdf/regulatory_framework/service_licences/radio/2016/asian_network_aug16.pdf. Accessed 12 Oct.

Bob Shennan. 2015. Face to face interview, 11 November.

Brown, D. 2005. *Ethnic Minorities, Electronic Media, and the Public Sphere: A Comparative Approach*. Cresskill: Hampton Press.

Brunt, Rosalind, and Rinella Cere. 2010. *Postcolonial Media Culture in Britain*. Basingstoke: Palgrave Macmillan.

Campion, Mukti. 2005. *Look Who's Talking Cultural Diversity Public Service Broadcasting and the National Conversation*. Oxford: Nuffield College Oxford.

Carter, Chris, and Alan McKinlay. 2013. Cultures of Strategy: Remaking the BBC, 1968–2003. *Business History* 55 (7): 1228–1246.

Charmaz, C. 2014. *Constructing Grounded Theory*. 2nd ed. Thousand Oaks: Sage.

Cottle, Simon. 1997. *Television and Ethnic Minorities: Producers' Perspectives*. Aldershot: Avebury, https://www.bbc.co.uk/programmes/p06d0gws.

Cottle, S, eds. 2000. Ethnic Minorities and the Media: Changing cultural boundaries. Maidenhead: Open University Press.

Creeber, Glen. 2004. "Hideously White" British Television, Glocalization, and National Identity. *Television and New Media* 5 (1): 27–39.

'David Gretton Interviewed by Sandra Harris'. 1965. *BBC Radio News*, https://www.bbc.co.uk/programmes/p06d0gws

De Bens, Els, and Hamelink J. Cees, eds. 2007. *Media Between Culture and Commercialisation*. Bristol: Intellect.

Deery, June, and Andrea Press, eds. 2017. *Media and Class, TV Film and Digital Culture*. New York/London: Routledge.

Department for Culture, Media and Sport. 2016. A BBC for the Future: A Broadcaster of Distinction. CM 9242. Government. https://www.gov.uk/government/uploads/system/uploads/attachment_data/file/524863/DCMS_A_BBC_for_the_future_linked_rev1.pdf

Eustace, Mathew. 2016. BBC Asian Network Live Listening Performance Q1 2016 (6 Month Weight). *BBC Marketing and Audiences*. http://downloads.bbc.co.uk/commissioning/site/asian-network-indie-rajar-summary-q1-2016.pdf. Accessed 12 Oct.

Fitzgerald, Richard, and William Housley. 2007. Talkback, Community and the Public Sphere'. *Media International Australia* 122 (1): 150–163. https://doi.org/10.1177/1329878X0712200118.

Flood, Chris, Stephen Hutchings, Galina Miazhevich, and Henri Nickels. 2011. Between impartiality and ideology. *Journalism Studies* 12 (2): 221–238. https://doi.org/10.1080/1461670X.2010.507934.

Freedman, Des, Trine Syvertsen, Vana Goblot, Mark Thompson, Jon Thoday, Amanda D. Lotz, Tess Alps, Patrick Barwise, Jennifer Holt, and Matthew Powers. 2018. *A Future for Public Service Television*. Cambridge: Goldsmiths Press.

Ganga, Deianira, and Sam Scott. 2006. Cultural "Insiders" and the Issue of Positionality in Qualitative Migration Research: Moving "Across" and Moving "Along" Researcher–Participant Divides. *Forum Qualitative Social Research* 7 (3). https://www.qualitative-research.net/index.php/fqs/issue/view/4

Gardam, Tim. 2004. Independent Review of the BBC's Digital Radio Services. http://news.bbc.co.uk/nol/shared/bsp/hi/pdfs/19_10_04_digital_radio.pdf. Accessed 12 Oct.

Gillespie, Marie. 1995. *Television, Ethnicity and Cultural Change*. London/New York: Routledge.

Hendy, David. n.d.. https://www.Bbc.Com/Historyofthebbc/100-Voices/People-Nation-Empire/Make-Yourself-at-Home. https://www.bbc.com/historyofthebbc/100-voices/people-nation-empire/make-yourself-at-home

Hesmondhalgh, David. 2019. *The Cultural Industries*. 4th ed. London: Sage.

Hesmondhalgh, David, and Sarah Baker. 2011. *Creative Labour, Media Work in Three Cultural Industries*. Milton Park: Routledge.

Hesmondhalgh, David, and Anamik Saha. 2013. Race, Ethnicity, and Cultural Production. *Popular Communication* 11 (3): 179–195.

Husband, Charles. 1994. *A Richer Vision*. London: Unesco.

Khamkar, Gloria. 2017. *The Evolution of British Asian Radio in England: 1960–2004*. Bournemouth University. http://eprints.bournemouth.ac.uk/29335/

Lacey, Kate. 2018. Radio's Vernacular Modernism: The Schedule as Modernist Text. *Media History* 24 (2): 166–179.

Lay, Samantha, and Lisa Thomas. 2012. Ethnic Minority Media in London: Transition and Transformation. *Media, Culture and Society* 34 (3): 369–380.

Lowe, Gregory Ferrell, and Fiona Martin, eds. 2013. *The Value of Public Service Media*. Nordicom.

Malik, Sarita. 2002. *Representing Black Britain, Black and Asian Images on Television*. London: Sage.

———. 2013. "Creative Diversity": UK Public Service Broadcasting After Multiculturalism. *Popular Communication* 11 (3): 227–241.

Matsaganis, M.D., and V.S. Katz. 2014. How Ethnic Media Producers Constitute Their Communities of Practice: An Ecological Approach. *Journalism* 15 (7): 926–944.

Matsaganis, M.D., V.S. Katz, and S. Ball-Rokeach. 2011. *Understanding Ethnic Media Producers, Consumers, and Societies*. Thousand Oaks: Sage.

Mayer, Vicki. 2011. *Below the Line Producers and Production Studies in New Television Economy*. Durham: Duke University Press.

Mills, Tom. 2016. *The BBC Myth of a Public Service*. London: Verso.

Morely, David, and Kuan-Hsing Chen. 1996. *Stuart Hall Critical Dialogues in Cultural Studies*. London: Routledge.

Moylan, Katie. 2013. *Broadcasting Diversity, Migrant Representation in Irish Radio*. Bristol: Intellect.

Nickerson, James. 2016. BBC Charter Renewal: Culture Secretary John Whittingdale Reveals Shake up of Broadcaster in White Paper. *CityAM*, 12 May 2016, sec. Business. https://www.cityam.com/bbc-charter-renewal-culture-secretary-john-whittingdale-announces-in-white-paper/

O'Brien, Dave, Daniel Laurison, Andrew Miles, and Sam Friedman. 2016. Are the Creative Industries Meritocratic? An Analysis of the 2014 British Labour Force Survey. *Cultural Trends* 25 (2): 116–131.

———. 2019a. 'Diversity and Equal Opportunities in Radio Monitoring Report on the UK Radio Industry'. https://www.ofcom.org.uk/__data/assets/pdf_file/0022/159421/diversity-in-radio-2019-report.pdf

———. 2019b. Diversity and Equal Opportunities in Television – Monitoring Report on the UK-Based Broadcasting Industry. Research report. UK: Ofcom. https://www.ofcom.org.uk/__data/assets/pdf_file/0028/166807/Diversity-in-TV-2019.pdf

———. 2019c. Media and Nations. https://www.ofcom.org.uk/__data/assets/pdf_file/0019/160714/media-nations-2019-uk-report.pdf

———. 2019d. Diversity and Equal Opportunities in Radio 2019, In-Focus Report on the Main Three Broadcasters. https://www.ofcom.org.uk/__data/assets/pdf_file/0032/159386/in-focus-report.pdf

Rajar Q4 2019. retrieved from https://www.rajar.co.uk/docs/2019_12/2019_Q4_Quarterly_Summary_Figures.pdf

Ross, Karen, and Virginia Nightingdale. 2003. *Media and Audiences, New Perspectives*. Maidenhead: Open University Press.

Royal Charter for the Continuance of the British Broadcasting Corporation. 2016. https://www.gov.uk/government/uploads/system/uploads/attachment_data/file/564457/Updated_Framework_Agreement_1.11.2016.pdf

Saha, Anamik. 2012. Locating MIA: "Race", Commodification and the Politics of Production. *European Journal of Cultural Studies* 15 (6): 736–752.

———. 2018. *Race and the Cultural Industries*. Cambridge: Polity.

Sharma, S., John Hutnyk, and Ashwani Sharma. 1996. Dis-Orienting Rhythms, The Politics of the New Asian Dance Music. London: Zed Books.

Shohat, Ella, and Robert Stam. 2014. *Unthinking Eurocentrism Multiculturalism and the Media*. 2nd ed. Routledge: Abingdon.

Sreberny, Annabelle. 2005. 'Not Only, But Also': Mixedness and Media. *Journal of Ethnic and Migration Studies* 31 (3): 443–459.

Strauss, Anselm, and Juliet Corbin. 1998. *Basics of Qualitative Research, Techniques and Procedures for Developing Grounded Theory*. Thousand Oaks: Sage Publications.

Syvertsen, Trine. 1999. The Many Uses of the Public Service Concept. *Nordicom Review* 1 (99): 5–12.

———. 2004. Citizens, Audiences, Customers and Players a Conceptual Discussion of the Relationship between Broadcasters and Their Publics. *European Journal of Cultural Studies* 7 (3): 363–380.

Wall, Tim, and Andrew Dubber. 2009. Specialist Music, Public Service and the BBC in the Internet Age'. *The Radio Journal: International Studies in Broadcast and Audio Media* 7 (1): 27–47.

Yu, S. Sherry, and M.D. Matsaganis. 2019. Ethnic Media in the Digital Age. New York: Routledge.

CHAPTER 2

Public Service Versus the Politics of Representation

The UK has a mixed media ecology that includes public ownership chiefly, the BBC and private ownership; ITV, Channel 4, and Sky. Although discussions about the concentration of private ownership are prevalent, there is also concern about the special position of the BBC as a public and cultural institution in public life and its involvement in politics, identity, and cultural belonging. Therefore, it is unsurprising that a wealth of regulation and policies exist to restrict media organisations. The media is considered to possess significant political, cultural, and social power because it plays an important role in the production and reproduction of social relations (Freedman 2008, p. 6). Some of the issues that emerge from the study of media organisations are the concern over who owns and controls the media, the potential impact this has on democracy, and how this influences the viewpoints disseminated by the media.

The government established the BBC as an independent media corporation with a public service remit to ensure that it would provide high-quality broadcasting and cater to a range of tastes and interests. The motivation behind this unique media model was the desire, on part of the government, to control media technologies to limit the potential impact the content could have on audiences. Furthermore, the government wanted to ensure that media content enriched society through the provision of education, news, and information and to promote people's democratic obligations. From its inception, the broadcaster has behaved as a public body acting in the national interest (Puttnam 2016, p. 16). The public service broadcasting (PSB) model has underlying principles of intervention at its core because the institution is expected to contribute and sustain the well-being of society and showcase a common culture. These interventions include guarantees by the BBC to air a range of high-quality programmes, provide news and current affairs content that is objective and balanced, whilst reflecting all groups in society and promoting the notion of "Britishness." Tracey (1998, p. 18) suggests that "public broadcasting is above all else a structure of ambition" because it is used to define society and structures.

The PSB model is emblematic of a pluralist media model that aims to ensure that a range of perspectives are articulated and behaves as a channel that connects private life with the state to create a climate where citizens are informed. Unanimous agreement over the definition of public service broadcasting is lacking. Instead, several competing definitions exist within different legislations that describe the aims and goals of PSB often, contradicting each other (Syvertsen 1999, 2004). This is due in part to the historical development of the BBC and its goals which has resulted in the definition of "public service" as one that focuses upon the outcomes or results. Tambini and Cowling (2004, p. 57) suggest that PSB is "ideologically ambivalent" because balancing public provision and regulation of such organisations poses difficulties for governments because, although they want such organisations to be successful, they simultaneously seek to restrict their size and influence. This book focuses on public service broadcasting in the UK enacted through the BBC. Lowe and Martin's (2013) definition is applied in the book; they describe public service content as something produced for "groups that are not attractive in commercial terms," specifically audiences that commercial operators choose to ignore because they are not considered profitable. The BBC tends to view the audience as a public of citizens as opposed to consumers. However, the Office for Communications (Ofcom), the UK government-approved regulatory and competition authority, uses both citizen and consumer interchangeably when referring to the BBC, even though each term has a distinct meaning.

Freedman (2008, p. 149) had defined PSB as a model that rejects market definitions and produces content for an audience assumed to consist of citizens, who share a broad range of interests and are simultaneously culturally diverse. Freedman (2019) does, however, question if public service models are effective in scrutinising and holding power to account, due to their close relationship with elites and the state. Syvertsen (1999) acknowledges that PSB is forced to operate within parameters set by the state and society and, therefore, the content reflects the dominant ideology in society. This chapter seeks to examine how hegemonic views influence how race and ethnicity is viewed within the BBC. Public service goals are examined with reference to how they may influence the way race and diversity is addressed. In addition, this chapter tries to understand how the BBC's internal structures and policies shape and direct the articulation of race and identity. The BBC plays a significant role in Britain's cultural and social life; therefore, the way race is treated and disseminated is important. In light of fragmenting audiences, the organisation has been forced to work harder to engage minority audiences. One problem the BBC has had to overcome is its own inconsistent history, missions, and objectives, alongside growing opposition to the existence of a licence fee.

The contemporary BBC has faced significant problems concerning its size, scope, mission, and funding (Lowe and Martin 2013; Mills 2016). The role and position of public service broadcasting in the UK has shifted, and increasingly, the BBC is expected to use its funding to provide authentic content for a breadth of communities and perspectives, recruit from diverse sections of the public, and financially support schemes such as the Local Democracy Reporter Scheme (employees are funded by the BBC but work in the local press). Tracey (1998) has documented the declining role of public service broadcasting in the UK and suggests that the BBC is undergoing an assault on its existence, and core purposes, largely due to political ideologies which have advantaged economic principles in the creative sector. Successive post-war governments sought to advantage the creative and cultural sectors in order to create wealth and new jobs in the wake of the declining tertiary sectors (Mayer 2011; Randle 2015). One consequence of this has been inequality in access in terms of employment and increasingly an emphasis upon efficiency and profit over innovation and artistic freedom.

SERVING THE PUBLIC INTEREST: CITIZENS AND CUSTOMERS

The BBC has always been distinct from other broadcasters due to the legitimacy secured through the endeavour to promote citizenship and the common good, which also makes it appear superior to commercial media, which is depicted as being focused upon money and ratings (Syvertsen 1999). Although producing popular programme content has never been an explicit BBC priority, it is precisely, because the broadcaster competes with commercial media, that it must justify its relevance via engagement with the core audience. Historically, radio listeners were essentially invisible to programme makers and as such were conceived as being an audience of public citizens. A good citizen is someone who performs their civic duties and can be portrayed by the media an exemplar of national culture (Butsch 2008, p. 7). Citizens have de facto rights and obligations, which includes the right to representation and inclusion within society. Tracey (1998) has noted that because the BBC has positioned the audience as citizens, it is thus forced to demonstrate it is serving them adequately. Ang (1991) suggests it is far simpler for commercial media to serve their audience because they only need to ensure people are watching or listening. In contrast, PSB have a responsibility to ensure citizens are educated, informed, and served, and this is far harder to evaluate because it is difficult to measure increased awareness in people as opposed to measuring the number of viewers.

The Pilkington Report (1962) criticised the BBC's approach to producing content that is in the "public interest" arguing the broadcaster was paternalistic choosing what the institution thought was good for the audience. Thus, the audience was positioned by the broadcaster as passive and receptive. The concept public interest is synonymous with the national interest and is difficult to define because it is often determined in context. The Pilkington Report defined public interest as a duty or obligation on the part of the media to acknowledge that public have the freedom to choose from a variety of programmes (1962, p. 17,18). In contrast, Dawes (2017) poses that both "public service" and "public interest" from their inception have been associated with "public control" as opposed to private enterprise. He contends that private enterprise was deemed to be problematic by the government; therefore, the BBC emerged as a monopoly institution founded in the national interest and accountable to the government, through a politicisation of the institution itself (Scannell and Cardiff 1991).

A key goal of PSB is to serve the citizen and depict a vision of public life through content that reflects the nation's communities and articulate diverse spectrum of public opinion. However, critics argue that the BBC provides media content through a middle-class lens (Creeber 2004; Lacey 2018). It is recognised that the existence of the BBC has elevated the media content of commercial operators and as such Scannell (1989, p. 136) has argued that PSB has fundamentally contributed to the "democratisation" of modern life, in its private and public forms. Moreover, he rejects the viewpoint that the broadcaster imposes social control or hegemonises culture, arguing that the value of the BBC is that it provides mixed programmes for national audiences and caters for all equally, whilst it minimises the privatisation of information and culture for only those audiences who can afford to pay.

EDITORIAL INDEPENDENCE

A fundamental pillar of public broadcasting is its independence from vested interests (e.g. advertisers) and power structures (e.g. governments) because an independent or "free" media is considered to be a key mechanism through which democracy operates. This also enables the media to be critical of institutions or structures of power without reprisals. This enables the production of programmes that are best able to serve the audience because they are produced from within a structure of independence (Tracey 1998). Tracey (1998, p. 31) also acknowledges it is vital that public broadcasting supports independent-minded programme makers to create programmes which are "good in their own terms." It is important that the media does not simply present the views of the state or the owner and that it is able to be critical. Although the government has initiated media policies and established regulation for media organisations, it is unwilling to legislate what types of content are permissible. Freedman (2008) suggests non-intervention into the minutiae of broadcasting, and publishing is a key principle of pluralist governments that permit the dissemination of critical, popular ideas from mainstream and marginal groups.

However, Tom Mills (2016) has critiqued the size, position, and role of the BBC in UK culture. Mills outlines the premise that the BBC has failed to express the voice of ordinary citizens, favouring the dissemination of voices in power and, therefore, has in effect silenced the audience. This contributes to his overall argument that the BBC is not independent from politics, power structures, and corporate interests and is in fact embedded with the "complex networks of power and influence"(Mills 2016, p. 136). Furthermore, he presents the case that politics and the media industries have become professionalised, pointing to the number of media workers who become PR consultants or advisors to politicians and the number of politicians who were formerly journalists. Mills (2016) also recognises that the introduction of market economic policies within the institution has further eroded the BBC's independence.

Similarly, Gunaratnam (2003) makes the case that the media articulate race issues by reflecting prevailing political beliefs through which there is an emphasis upon integration of minority communities. Moreover, Gunaratnam argues that these views on race and ethnicity are grounded in western perspectives of colonialism and she describes this type of knowledge as being "unstable ... rather than universal and timeless" (2003, p. 13). There is a clear paradox between the political motivation to control and assimilate minority communities' and the state's desire to achieve social cohesion and positive race relations. Definitions of race and ethnicity can work to construct and impose identities upon minority communities. Yu's (2016) study of minority ethnic journalists working in ethnic media found that they bought their unique identity and perspectives into the newsroom and, as such, influenced the production and framing of news. Yu also asserts that there are two types of identity co-existing for minority audiences, the identity which ethnic communities self-identify with and the identity which is socially constructed and prescribed to them.

Freedman (2019, p. 205) has questioned the governance structure of the BBC and suggests it is a "compromised version of a potentially noble ideal" because the existing frameworks result in the institution being embedded and implicated within elite networks of power. This has an impact upon the BBC's ability to scrutinise and challenge power. Freedman's argument mirrors critiques set out by others: Christians et al. (2009) and Mills (2016) that the BBC as an organisation is firmly aligned with and part of the social, political, and cultural elites in society.

The UK media model has been defined by scholars in a few ways; however, Hallin and Mancini's (2004) work is particularly significant in this area; they describe Britain as having a liberal model. They define the liberal framework as one that emphasises "objectivity" and political neutrality. There is some evidence, however, that a "corporatist" model of media is in existence within the UK because the media including the BBC tends to cooperate on matters of national welfare as dictated by the government. Christians et al. (2009) have critiqued the notion that news and information within a PSB model is presented with objectivity, accuracy, and fairness, outlining that the normative working methods of journalists and news media mean that they do not only report on activities in society but support and strengthen them. Furthermore, these normative values in public service do not guarantee that the media discourse covers the genuine issues in society, for example, poverty or marginalisation of minority communities. Therefore, they pose that public broadcasting that is subject to government rules and regulations pertaining to its purpose and mission and the position of the organisation in relation to the state is problematic (Christians et al. 2009, p. 130). In particular they note that less powerful groups and their voices and alternative views are either absent or marginalised in the mainstream version of events because these perspectives tend to challenge the dominant view set out by the structures of power. The *raison d'etre* for the BBC Asian Network is to present the unheard voices and perspectives of British Asian audiences not only on the radio station but also across the BBC. There is less focus in research on how public service broadcasters consciously or unconsciously reflect political aspirations and policy as the de facto normative viewpoint in society. Despite the weaknesses outlined, PSB is considered to be a preferable model to commercial media because it tries to unite audiences, has an inclusive approach, and is able to frame public discussion in terms of what serves the general good (Curran and Seaton 1997, p. 336).

OBJECTIVE NEWS AND CURRENT AFFAIRS

Public service broadcasting is also associated with the commitment for accurate and impartial news and due prominence in the coverage of public affairs. The notion of impartiality and balance is central to the work of the BBC because it is generally accepted that impartiality offers the highest editorial standards. The broadcaster has been expected to provide the public with a range of distinctive news, information, and entertainment material from its inception. Historically, the BBC was the only institution that could perform these objectives, but due to media proliferation, a number of commercial and alternative media platforms can also perform these functions. PSB is often seen to set standards whilst also contributing "to the cultural resources of society rather than merely offering what is profitable" (Curran and Seaton 1997, p. 335). High editorial standards are ambiguous to define, and yet they are a significant aspect of public service broadcasting because they imply excellence and quality across programme making. News and current affairs content presented in a balanced manner means that the information imparted is useful and enables the audience to make up their own mind about the issues. As a consequence, a number of scholars agree that the BBC's journalism is a core element of PSB commitments and is at the heart of the organisation's intellectual core (Born 2004).

Thus, in this manner PSB contributes to the sustenance and growth of the public sphere. The public sphere is an influential theoretical framework within media and communication studies because it is the place where journalism has the potential to improve the quality of public life through the provision of information. The conceptualisation of Habermas's public sphere is idealised; ownership of the press and media in the UK is concentrated and diversity within broadcast news and programme content is questionable. Historically, Habermas modelled the public sphere on ancient Greek societies, where men from privileged backgrounds came together to discuss and debate political and economic affairs. The weakness with Habermas's earlier work was that women, the disabled, and poor were excluded from participation within the political processes of that time. It is important within a modern sphere that diverse voices are incorporated, but it is also evident that these perspectives remain peripheral. Ethnic media which publish or broadcast in non-English lack a connection to the wider media ecology and, consequently, the public sphere. This means they are able only to speak to and be heard by minority audiences but not the majority population. Yu (2019) consequently argues that the issues, inequality, and prejudices faced by these communities remain unacknowledged (Yu and Matsaganis 2019). In response to their marginalisation from the public sphere some groups have established alternative media or counter publics which offer a perspective that stands in opposition to the dominant hegemony in society.

It is widely acknowledged that audiences tend to trust PSB, particularly the news and current affairs programmes (Ofcom 2019a, p. 11). Although social media is increasingly used as a source of news, BBC 1 remains the most used news source among adults (Jigsaw Research 2019, p. 2). Bakir and Barlow (2007, p. 12) have argued the key role of the media is to be "social glue" and "serving as a prerequisite for forming self-identity." The notion that trust is a social glue has also been endorsed by sociologists from Simmel (1908) to Durkheim (1964), the central argument being that without trust people would be unable to arrive at the shared goals that form the basis of any community (Bakir and Barlow 2007). With almost one hundred years of experience of producing news and media content, the BBC draws on this reputation. However, Hall et al. (2013) and Born (2004) acknowledge that norms such as objectivity and balance mean that BBC news output is heavily reliant upon official sources who maintain the hegemonic perspective and thus fail to acknowledge the voicepoints of ordinary people.

Questions about the BBC's bias, objectivity, and balance have been posed in reference to the coverage of the 2016 EU Referendum in the UK. Virdee and McGeever (2018, p. 1813) suggest that racist rhetoric became "normalised in elite political discourse and practice and everyday life," and this was articulated as logical or "common sense" in line with the media's normative practice of reflecting political objectives. They argue that this legitimised anti-Muslim racism and had cemented the idea that Islam is "in some sense incompatible with modern British values of tolerance and diversity" (Virdee and McGeever 2018, p. 1813). Ibrahim and Howarth (2020, p. 233) accuse the BBC of using the notion of impartiality and objectivity as a tool to "de-racialise and distance race in its diverse workforce" in order to maintain a cultural hegemony on race which is problematically grounded in the history of Empire and colonialism. The Naga Munchetty impartiality ruling in July 2019, where the female British Asian presenter was found to have breached impartiality rules after speaking about her experiences of racism on-air, was criticised by Ofcom for a lack of transparency. The ruling was over-turned by the Director General, but an Ofcom investigation ruled that the initial decision "created a perception that the BBC had misunderstood the requirements of due impartiality as they relate to racism"; it urged the broadcaster to support staff to challenge controversial viewpoints that have little support or are not backed by facts (Ofcom 2019a, b, c, p. 17). Ibrahim and Howarth (2020) suggest the BBC was uncomfortable with Munchetty's experience of racism occurring in a post-colonial context and because knowledge originating from lived experiences is deemed to be subjective and thus does not adhere to what is permissible knowledge within the organisation.

UNIVERSALITY: AUDIENCES AND PROGRAMME CONTENT

The BBC and other public service broadcasters historically focused upon addressing their national population as a community or mass. The principle of universality has two key aims; first to reach all audiences in terms of geography and to have universality of appeal (in terms of interest and taste). As a consequence, the BBC showcases a range of entertainment, literature, drama, and music on-air. There is also an expectation that programme producers are innovative and take risks. Georgina Born's (2004) extensive ethnographic study of the BBC noted that provision of a range of programmes such as talks, sports, drama, religion, light entertainment, and music from the outset was due in part because the broadcaster realised that to survive it needed a mass audience to be popular. Therefore, Malik (2013) suggests that PSB has sought to appeal to different ethnic groups utilising the principle of universality as a means by which to celebrate difference. The historic Asian Programmes and African-Caribbean units within the BBC and Channel 4 were designed to appeal directly to Black and Asian communities as part of the universal offer.

The BBC's historical radio programming emphasised the notion of mixed programming; the schedule was purposely varied to include highbrow music which was placed with lighter or less intellectual programmes to educate audiences whilst also discouraging them from having the radio on in the background. The act of listening to radio was considered by the broadcaster to be a serious commitment, and the public was thus expected to focus and pay attention to content so that they could hear ideas and voices or music they may not otherwise chosen to consume (Loviglio and Hilmes 2013, p. 17). Lacey (2018, p. 168) has proposed that the creation of early radio schedules was an institutional response to managing continuous transmission and should be understood as a discrete "institutional address to a listening public." Her examination of historic radio schedules reveals that although the audience was imagined collectively as citizens through a middle-class lens, throughout the day individual programmes addressed singular listeners: women, men, children, student, festival attender, and so on. Later, the BBC split its services into three distinct stations that divided the population into categories, the intellectuals were offered the Third Programme, The Home Service was the middlebrow station that sought to offer a mix, and at the lower end the Light Programme was for those from lower socio-economic groups. The radio schedule and effectively radio stations existed to maximise the audience; they achieved this by the ability to complement the daily routine of people's lives with relevant style of programme and music, for example, news in the breakfast show. The emphasis upon defined or alternative musical tastes was also catered for within the context of specialist music shows.

However, the principle has been critiqued notably by Goodwin (in Savage et al. 2019) who describes the concept as being an "anachronistic" because it has worked to restrict how the BBC addresses new opportunities and challenges in the digital era. It is evident that the PSB can be characterised within narrow parameters and that critics would like the BBC to concentrate upon audiences which are less profitable or niche.

Born and Prosser (2001) have argued that public service media should be allowed to produce

> the entire range of broadcast genres, thereby meeting a wide range of needs and purposes through the trinity of information, education, and entertainment. The aim here is that [Public service media] should be truly popular, both as a value in itself... [and] in order to draw audiences. (Born and Prosser 2001, p. 676)

Defenders of PSB want it to be judged as a media service in its own right and not as a method to fix gaps or as a means through which content is created for minority ethnic audiences. The contemporary BBC is in a precarious position; if it does not create popular programmes, it is accused of "market failure," but if it successfully competes, it is charged with abusing its privileged position. In Born's view, the BBC has a pivotal role within the media ecology because it plays an important part in informing people. However, she acknowledges audiences are not always happy because "BBC's journalistic culture remains vulnerable to charges of elitism" due to the tendency to value "serious" content over entertainment programmes (Born 2004, p. 278, 379). A 2019 review of BBC News by the regulator Ofcom found some audiences believe the news concentrates on "representing a white, middle class and London-centric point of view that is not relevant to their lives" (Ofcom 2019a, p. 4). Moreover, audiences criticised the "lack of diversity in the stories that the BBC covered" (Ofcom 2019a, p. 21). Georgina Born has questioned the terminology "diverse," arguing there are a few meanings, and that they are commonly confused; in terms of representation, she argues it is imperative that programmes first and foremost reflect the tastes and interests of diverse social groups, but it is also important that diverse employees are enabled to make programmes and represent their own interests and identities (2004, p. 380). Her argument is that diversity in terms of mixed programming has been the most neglected aspect of diversity because this enables experimentation and innovation across all genres.

The Puttnam report (2016) recognised there is little agreement on the need for PSB. The report contends that public service is an ambiguous concept and is measured in terms of genre rather than in terms of individual programmes. This risks relegating public service "to discrete programmes, rather than outlets or remits" (Puttnam 2016, p. 22). In other words, the BBC may be expected to focus upon so-called niche market failure programmes leaving commercial media free to pursue audiences through popular programmes.

Investment into original programmes by public service providers, including ITV, Channel 5, Channel 4, and the BBC amounted to £2586 million in 2018, with the BBC spending £815 million (Ofcom 2019b, p. 7). Moreover, a review of the BBC highlighted concerns that the BBC is not producing content for younger audiences. This audience is considered to be fundamental to the future success of the BBC, without their engagement in terms of viewing and listening support for the licence fee could be further eroded and this will undermine the BBC's ability to deliver its missions (Ofcom 2019c, p. 10). Netflix reaches approximately two-thirds of 15- to 24-year-olds each week and YouTube reaches 42 per cent, whereas the BBC iPlayer reaches just 26 per cent of this age group (Ofcom 2019c, p. 12).

REFLECT ALL COMMUNITIES (NATIONAL CULTURE)

The Royal Charter stipulates that the BBC's fourth public purpose is to "reflect, represent and serve the diverse communities":

> In doing so, the BBC should accurately and authentically represent and portray the lives of the people of the United Kingdom today and raise awareness of the different cultures and alternative viewpoints that make up its society. (DCMS 2016, p. 5)

Critics argue the BBC has not focused enough reflecting people from the UK regions, whereas a larger body of research (Cottle 2000; Moylan 2013, Shohat and Stam 2014; Saha 2018) is critical of the poor representation of minority ethnic groups by the media. There are two key problems, settled minority communities tend to be portrayed through narrow or racialised stereotypes, and coverage of new migrant groups is often framed negatively to reflect the government's hostile agenda (Bloch and Solomos 2010). Research examining how minority communities are represented has tended to focus upon the racialised or stereotyped representations of ethnic minorities on-air, for example, as out of work young people or as problematic immigrants (Van Dijk 1992; Bourdieu 1993; Cottle 2000; Campion 2005; Malik 2008). Malik (2008) and Campion (2005) outline that the media seek to homogenise minority communities around narratives of asylum seekers, black gang culture and gun crime, the war on terror or simply the strangeness of some minority cultures. Consequently, Malik (2008, p. 348) argues that the tropes presented in the media are preoccupied with emphasising difference and this can endanger a liberal democracy because the implication is that the sense of belonging is dependent upon the individual's cultural identity, capital, and race. Furthermore, research also reveals that some "audiences are turning away because they don't see themselves on the BBC" or that they feel they are inauthentically portrayed by the BBC (Ofcom 2019c, p. 8). Race, as noted earlier, is a social construct and the BBC is judged on how it reinforces and illustrates minority groups whilst it also draws upon its ideologies of nation building and national identity. Ibrahim and Howarth (2020) conclude the values and missions of the organisation are at odds with each other. Furthermore, migrant cultures within PSB are appraised by standards established by the West, and as a consequence, the way the BBC tackles diversity is inherently conservative and dated (Campion 2005; Moylan 2013, Shohat and Stam 2014). Although Ofcom's annual report of the BBC is critical of how the BBC as an organisation has responded and measured its achievements pertaining to diversity and inclusion, it does note that the British Asian population in the UK tends to hold positive opinions about how the BBC delivers this public purpose (Ofcom 2019c, 15). It is implied that other settled groups such as African-Caribbean and African communities do not feel adequately reflected by public service.

Promotion of the nation or national culture poses complex problems for the BBC which is tasked to serve the full citizenry of the country which is the "greatest challenge" for PSB (Amanda Lotz in Freedman et al. 2018, p. 46). The BBC is criticised for only reflecting the views of the majority, white middle-class population in the output (Creeber 2004; Hesmondhalgh and Saha 2013; Ofcom 2019a, b, c) at the expense of other groups.

> People from lower socio-economic groups rate the BBC less favourably than average across all aspects of representation and portrayal, while those in higher socio-economic groups tend to be more favourable towards the BBC overall compared to the UK average. (Ofcom 2019c, p. 15)

The Ofcom report also raised concerns that the methodology used by the BBC for identifying dissatisfaction among the audience does not allow the BBC to identify the groups that are being underserved. This suggests that the broadcaster struggles to achieve this public purpose. Globalisation has challenged the concept of identity because the movement of people and their interaction with the host nation has meant that identity is unable to remain stable and the same. The Parek Report (2000) blamed multiculturalism for the segregation of some minority communities. One consequence has been that politicians and the media have moved away portraying positive examples of multiculturalism and instead emphasised a political ideology that promotes integration. Titley (2014, p. 251) has argued that the contradictory pressure on PSB to reflect and represent the diversity of the audience on the one hand, whilst also promoting national cohesion leaves PSBs "implicated and uneasily positioned" alongside the state. This argument is echoed by others (Christians et al. 2009; Hall et al. 2013; Mills 2016) that the media articulates the voice of the dominant political and cultural elites at the expense of ordinary citizens. Therefore, it is hardly surprising that, in the UK, subscription for foreign television services is higher amongst minority audiences (Ofcom 2013) and that BBC 1 and BBC 2 have the oldest viewing profiles in research conducted by Ofcom.

Malik (2008 2013) has critiqued how the BBC and Channel 4 have moved from a position that emphasised multiculturalism to creative diversity. She suggests that a consequence of increased competition and reduced regulation has enabled the broadcasters to move from catering for distinct minority audiences to the curation of content that aims to integrate minority issues within a mainstream agenda. This move fails to give adequate coverage and examine in depth issues faced by communities because they are framed and angled with Eurocentric perspectives.

INSTITUTIONAL PROCESSES AND THE BBC ASIAN NETWORK

The BBC's role as the principal provider of news and current affairs is long established, making it popular with audiences over providers such as Sky, ITV, or Channel 4. However, it is apparent that the broadcaster has a lot of work to do to achieve its four public purposes: provide impartial news and information, to support learning for people of all ages, show the most creative, highest quality, and distinctive output, and reflect and represent diverse communities. Public service broadcasting should be the place where people learn about the lives of other communities. Studies of media production tend to concentrate on how media organisations work and pay less attention to examining social power and conflict in the process of production and what impact this has on the final media product. Saha (2018) contends that institutional and societal imperatives demand that visibly minority staff both blend in and conform to conventional working methods. Therefore, he argues that diversity and inclusion targets to increase minority ethnic staff numbers are meaningless because people are hired to demonstrate organisational inclusiveness, but the ideological function of diversity initiatives contribute to sustaining and maintaining "institutional whiteness" (Saha 2018, p. 88). Organisations also tend to work towards matching or exceeding the percentage of specific racial groups within their staff numbers to correlate to the size of ethnic groups in society. However, Hall (in Morely and Chen 1996) has also argued that diversity schemes do not work, and instead many ethnic staff end up being the "segregated visibility," present within the media, perhaps on short-term contracts or in roles that lack editorial power. The Ofcom 2019 Annual Report on the BBC also expressed a concern over how the BBC presents its workforce figures and the details on the diverseness of its workforce.

Most of the staff working at the BBC Asian Network are British Asian. The key reason for the establishment of the BBC Asian Network was to offer a platform for Asian culture and music and to challenge racialised stereotypes. The station is mandated to have a strong focus upon on news and current affairs, to produce high-quality, original, and challenging programmes. It is therefore a unique national radio station within the BBC's portfolio and is clearly defined by the audience it seeks to serves. Content for speech programmes should recognise the "diversity of the British Asian population in terms of geography, interests, ethnicity, and religion" (BBC Trust 2016, p. 4). There is clear acknowledgment in the remit that the lived experiences of British Asians vary according to where they reside, their background, and their faith. The news content however can often showcase stories that present a negative image of some communities, for example, terrorism, and is in stark contrast to programme content which emphasises and celebrates British Asian culture. According to Joy *(not her real name)*, a daytime producer, the role of the station is to showcase the "best of the different Asian cultures in the UK, which breathe life into British culture." She explained that the staff achieve this by showcasing South Asian music and by crafting programmes that include a wealth of "cultural references" to Asian lifestyles in order to create "a deeper under-standing" of British Asian history and heritage (Joy, producer 2015). Media research has acknowledged the weaknesses in the representation of diverse communities, and this type of content is not available elsewhere on the BBC. BBC Asian Network presenter, Noreen Khan outlined how the station is unique:

> [...] I think because we are distinctive, and quite unique. There's no other radio station that caters for this many different communities and there's probably over four million South Asians in the UK. So, we are catering for a large chunk of that so-called minority. (Presenter, Noreen Khan 2015)

BBC Radio has made a concerted effort to improve the representation of minority groups on-air across all stations and programmes. In contrast, commercial radio is still primarily focused upon recruitment of diverse staff as opposed to the on-air coverage of diverse audiences. The BBC Asian Network journalists and programme producers are tasked with sourcing original news stories about the British Asian communities. These stories are pitched to the rest of the BBC, and some are commissioned by other departments such as Breakfast, Radio 4, or Newsnight. This means that the issues are presented to majority audiences alongside minority listeners. This move enables the BBC to combat criticism that it does not reflect minority audiences across the output and demonstrates that the broadcaster is attempting to offer a reflection of the breadth of communities in the UK. However, the interviews revealed content that features the Muslim community is more likely to be commissioned over the other Asian communities (see Chap. 6). Saha (2018) suggests that the mainstreaming of diversity issues into general programming has had a negative ideological impact upon minority ethnic audiences because this type of content elides discussion of structural inequalities such as racism, lack of opportunities, or prejudices in programming. There is instead a tendency within the media to imply these ideas are anachronistic. Crucially, the stories that are pitched by staff from the BBC Asian Network only get selected if they have a wide appeal. As a consequence, minority ethnic staff recruited into roles across the cultural industries, including journalism, adopt the conventional working methods, practices, and institutionalised processes. This includes pitching material that reinforces racialised stereotypes in order to get it commissioned something that Saha (2018, p. 106) describes as the "marketised version of diversity." In other words, the BBC offers a portrayal that emphasises "integration" and gives a positive view of people's lives but critically ignores inequality of opportunity or racism. Diversity is thus used by the media to promote integration and contributes to the drive across the media to demonstrate efficiency in the knowledge economy. However, as outlined institutional imperatives, power frameworks, media regulation, and the close allegiance with the state means that ethnic staff within the BBC are consciously and unconsciously urged to reproduce content that reinforces "difference" and "otherness." A number of issues such as societal attitudes, internal BBC perspectives, and other discourses shape and influence the behaviour of producers and the representation of the BBC Asian Network listeners (Freedman 2008). The manner in which the BBC management imagine the target audience influences the mode of address used for the audience.

History of the BBC Asian Network

As discussed in Chap. 1, the national BBC Asian Network emerged from a daily Asian programme broadcast on BBC Radio Leicester in the late 1970s. At the time, the BBC was the only place for British Asians to hear Bollywood news, entertainment, and music because no other ethnic broadcast media had been established. Owen Bentley, who was the Station Manager at Radio Leicester, outlined why he introduced Asian programmes:

> My aim then was to capture this audience so that we could convert them to listening to Radio Leicester. What is the best way to do this? to produce some programmes that are going to attract them. This is a short-term measure. (Former Station Manager, BBC Radio Leicester, Bentley 2015)

During this period Leicester had become home to immigrants from Kenya and Uganda, simultaneously the National Front movement was also very strong. Owen Bentley explained he did have fears about adding Asian content to Radio Leicester, "I worried about it to some extent but thought we should do it anyhow. But the backlash was tiny. There were a few nasty people who wrote and complained. But there was no groundswell against the programme."

The popularity of the Asian show at BBC Radio Leicester encouraged BBC West Midlands (BBC WM) to establish daily Asian programme on their medium wave frequency. In October 1988, the two regions combined their resources to jointly create seventy hours of Asian-specific content for listeners in the two regions. Primarily the largest two ethnic groups, Pakistani audiences in the West Midlands and Gujarati Indians in the East Midlands, were targeted. At this stage, the presenters were community members who volunteered their time and were paid nothing or very little. Kamlesh Purohit worked at the BBC Asian Network, he is currently Deputy Managing editor at BBC Radio Leicester, and he recounted listening to BBC Radio Leicester in the 1970s:

> In those days the differences that are so important now, whether you are Hindu, Muslim or Sikh, weren't big differences. If people were Asian, you related to them, we had the same battles to fight. So, having a radio show in a way was one thing that every part of the community, everybody in the Asian community, felt that they could belong to. (Kamlesh Purohit 2015)

Purohit's recollection suggests that the BBC united disparate Asian groups into a coherent imagined listening community. The radio programme was aimed at all the Asian communities in Leicester, and the goals were to educate and integrate recent migrants into British life. The National Front movement in Leicester also had the effect of uniting people who arrived from Uganda or Kenya.

> You felt under attack there was a lot of National Front Activity, there was skin heads roaming the streets beating you up. You actually felt quite victimised and so having a radio show was something that gave us [Asian community] an opportunity to share experiences. (Purohit 2015)

Alia, a former senior manager, was hired when the BBC Asian Network was a regional station, she explained it was easier to visualise the listener in the early days of the station: "I knew the Asian community in Leicester, I kind of lived it." Although the BBC provided specific programme content on TV and local radio, Owen Bentley emphasised there was "no appetite for a national Asian station within the BBC. I think they saw Asian programming as essentially as part of the local radio scene." This changed in 2002, when the BBC Asian Network was re-launched and established as a national digital radio alongside 6 Music and 1Xtra. Director General Greg Dyke hoped that audiences who had been underserved would now have dedicated services. In 2017 the BBC merged the responsibility for programme management on both the BBC Asian Network and 1Xtra; this role was occupied by Mark Strippel who participated in this research. This changed in 2020 when the BBC reorganised. Born (2004) contends that the new digital services which included children's content through

Cbeebies and CBBC concentrated on making public service offer that was not available elsewhere. However, by 2002 a number of national and regional Asian had been established. A singular national service for Asian radio service was lacking, and at the time of writing, just a few commercial Asian stations have a national presence in the UK through DAB.

Although Greg Dyke re-branded the BBC Asian Network as a national station which began broadcasting on 28 October 2002, internally, organisational structures and programmes were not changed. The station continued to operate with staff working in three sites: London, Leicester, and Birmingham. The ownership of the station moved from Nations and Regions department which managed local radio at the time to Radio and Music which ran the other BBC radio stations. However, within the new management structure the BBC Asian Network was considered an anomaly and funding remained static. As such the content continued to target not only Asians aged under 35, but also first-, second-, and third-generation Asians and all communities whose origins were from the Indian subcontinent. In a book about the station, former news editor and Network Manager, Mike Curtis, described working at the station as a lonely experience, "we always felt we were on our own – challenging, different and complicated" (Curtis 2013).

In 2004 the Department for Culture, Media and Sport evaluated the impact of digital radio. Chaired by former Channel 4 and BBC executive, Tim Gardam, the report criticised the BBC Asian Network for having "unambitious" programme formats and no coherent target listener (Gardem 2004, p. 50). However, the report highlighted that the journalism from the station had "added value to UK Asian radio" (Gardem 2004, p. 5). In addition, it was questioned why the station was defined by the audience it served, whilst 1Xtra and Radio 1 were defined by the music offered on-air. Commercial Asian stations are also similarly defined by their target audience. It recommended that the station ought to be defined by content for two reasons: first, because the move would make the service distinctive in comparison to independent ethnic media and, second, because:

> The fragmenting nature of Britain's Asian community, as different groups settle into British society at different paces, will increasingly question the notion of a homogenous Asian community with a body of shared values and interests. This may undermine, in the longer term, the current defining criterion of the station. (Gardem 2004, p. 50)

Some of the challenges the station has faced post 2012 have been around creating a community of British Asian listeners. Chapters 7 and 8 scrutinise the notion of a coherent or homogenous British Asian community of listeners by also examining the changing British Asian identity in the UK and music. Sreberny (2005) has urged that ethnicity and diaspora is seen to be fluid because there is often an assumption that people "belong" to a single minority group and that the group operates within a single national public sphere. It is evident that a radio service aimed at a diverse audience fractured by class, faith, and language is forced to find ways to unite listeners, as opposed to focusing upon the issues that divide them. This is broadly achieved by broadcasting in English and by emphasising

> Britishness not Asian-ness, its Britishness. And that in a way is the definition of how the Asian network has totally changed over the course of its existence. But all of these things are real subtle shifts. This is about us being able to create a service that serves the need of a growing population at a time of massive technological and communication transformation not just for the BBC but for all of us and it's really quite hard. I think the secret is to get away from the walled garden, and to make it more porous. It's to make the Asian Network feel more like it's part of the warp and weft of life. Not a lovely well-kept secret that we can only open up at certain times of the day. (Former Controller, Bob Shennan 2015)

Following the critical DCMS report in 2004, Bob Shennan who was then Controller for 5 Live was also made responsible for the BBC Asian Network. Under his leadership a new audience engagement strategy was devised, and staff began to aggressively focus on listeners aged under 25 years of age. Non-Asian music was introduced to engage a younger listener and reflect their interests. Speaking in the interview in 2015 he reflected upon how the station has evolved over its existence and pointed out the common link for the listeners is in fact "Britishness" and not "Asian-ness" because all the listeners live a British Asian lifestyle.

The huge changes to the station sound resulted in the on-air sound becoming "edgy and trendy – achingly trendy" and "probably a bit too hip, the majority of the audience wanted a radio station a bit friendlier and warmer" (Husain Husaini, former head of Programmes and News). Listener figures dropped, and in 2010, the station was singled with 6 Music for closure as part of a cost-saving exercise. The spending cuts followed an unsuccessful negotiation between the BBC and the government to increase the licence fee in line with inflation, during the economic downturn. This forced the BBC to reduce spending by 20 per cent so that it could fulfil its programme commitments. The rationale to close the BBC Asian Network was based upon the cost per listener hour, which at 8.5 pence, was higher than the other national radio stations. There were some major flaws with the logic: the BBC Asian Network was compared to 5 Live and Radio 4 and not with other BBC language-specific radio services such as Radio Scotland, Radio Cymru, and Radio nan Gàidheal; both of these services cost significantly more than 8.5 pence per listener per hour to run. These language-specific services broadcast in non-English and were more comparable to the BBC Asian Network which in 2010 broadcast more three to four hours of South Asian language programmes daily.

The BBC had claimed the money saved, by closing services, including the BBC Asian Network, would be reinvested and a less expensive way to serve British Asian audiences would be found. The listening figures that followed the closure announcement in March 2010 measured audience consumption from March 2010 to 27 June 2010; they revealed the number of BBC Asian Network listeners had grown to 437,000 (RAJAR Q2 2018), see Fig. 2.1. The BBC Trust reversed the decision to close 6 Music within three months; a high-profile campaign to save the station was supported by celebrities. However, it took one year and a public consultation, before the BBC Asian Network was also saved from closure. The differences in how the two stations were dealt with illustrate the insignificance of the BBC Asian Network within the BBC hierarchy. A cheaper way to serve British Asian audiences was not found in the intervening twelve months, and therefore, the BBC Trust recommended that the BBC Asian Network be reprieved in 2011 and continue to broadcast with a smaller budget and half the staff.

In 2012, days ahead of the station's 10th birthday, a new schedule was unveiled showcasing longer shows, less presenters, and the consolidation of the staff into two bases Birmingham and New Broadcasting House in London for the news and key programmes such as Breakfast, phone-in, and Drive. The controllership was also changed; Bob Shennan took over again from Radio 1 Controller Andy Parfitt who retired. In 2015 a new audience strategy was rolled out to attract "digital natives," young people who traditionally do not listen to radio (see Chap. 7). The Radiocentre (a body representing the sector) expressed concerns that the BBC Asian Network was weighed down with an "overly ambitious remit which

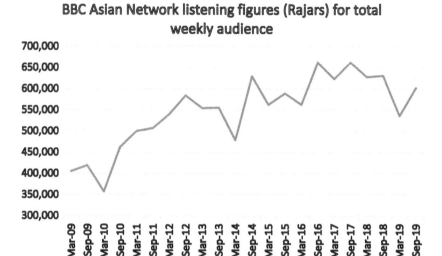

BBC Asian Network listening figures (Rajars) for total weekly audience

Fig. 2.1 RAJAR listening figures for the BBC Asian Network. Represents the total amount of people who tune into the station. A "listener" is counted as an adult aged 15+ who listens for at least five minutes

attempts to serve a broad diverse audience" (Radio Centre 2012, p. 8). The Radiocentre concluded by urging the BBC Trust to increase rather than reduce distinctive public service content such as the documentaries, drama, and language programmes arguing "the inherent danger is that the BBC will ultimately transform Asian Network into something akin to commercial offerings" (Radio Centre 2012, p. 11). This is a pertinent point the BBC Asian Network faces unique challenges operating as an ethnic-specific service within a public service broadcaster. The organisational structures, missions, and public goals thus influence how race, identity, and diversity are imagined and disseminated by staff. The rest of the chapters in this book will assess different aspects of the service to examine this in depth.

CONCLUSION

Whilst it is acknowledged that the BBC is a creative organisation established in the public interest and has become a cultural institution, its future is in doubt. The impact of Netflix which not only has branded itself as a diverse media organisation but also offers content that showcases sexuality and minority groups has placed further pressure on the BBC to up its game. It seems the BBC is trying to balance its historical roots as a national organisation that nurtures and supports democracy by enabling or promoting citizenship and social good and simultaneously trying to grow its audiences to better reflect diverse communities in order to justify its existence. The BBC is unable to claim relevance if audiences switch to alternative providers for stronger more robust reflections of other cultures. But the BBC is considered to be part of the status quo and is implicated in the manufacturing of problematic stereotypes of diversity on radio and television that can omit the lived inequalities as experienced by the working classes and minority communities.

REFERENCES

Ang, Ien. 1991. Desperately Seeking the Audience. London: Routledge

Bakir, Vian, and David M. Barlow. 2007. *Communication in the Age of Suspicion: Trust and the Media*. Basingstoke: Palgrave Macmillan.

BBC Trust. 2016. BBC Asian Network Service Licence 2016. BBC Trust. http://downloads.bbc.co.uk/bbctrust/assets/files/pdf/regulatory_framework/service_licences/radio/2016/asian_network_aug16.pdf. Accessed 13 Oct.

Bloch, Alice, and John Solomos, eds. 2010. *Race and Ethnicity in the 21st Century*. Basingstoke: Palgrave Macmillan.

Born, Georgina. 2004. *Uncertain Vision, Birt, Dyke and the Reinvention of the BBC*. London: Secker and Warburg.

Born, Georgina, and Tony Prosser. 2001. Culture and Consumerism: Citizenship, Public Service Broadcasting and the BBC's Fair-Trading Obligations. *The Modern Law Review* 64 (5): 657–687.

Bourdieu, Pierre. 1993. *The Field of Cultural Production: Essays on Art and Literature*. Cambridge: Polity Press.

Bruggeman, Michael, Sven Engesser, Florin Buchel, and Edda Humrecht. 2014. Hallin and Mancini Revisited: Four Empirical Types of Western Media Systems. *Journal of Communication* 64: 1037–1065.

Butsch, Richard. 2008. *The Citizen Audience, Crowds, Publics and Individuals*. New York: Routledge.

Campion, Mukti. 2005. *Look Who's Talking Cultural Diversity Public Service Broadcasting and the National Conversation*. Oxford: Nuffield college Oxford.

Christians, Clifford G., Theodore L. Glasser, Denis McQuail, Kaarle Nordenstreng, and Robert A. White, eds. 2009. *Normative Theories of the Media – Journalism in Democratic Societies*. Urbana and Chicago: University of Illinois Press.

Cottle, Simon. 2000. *Ethnic Minorities and The Media, Changing Cultural Boundaries.* Buckingham/Philadelphia: Open University Press.

Creeber, Glen. 2004. "Hideously White" British Television, Globalization, and National Identity. Television & New Media 5 (1): 27–39.

Curran, James, and Jean Seaton. 1997. *Power without Responsibility, the Press and Broadcasting in Britain.* 5th ed. London: Routledge.

Curtis, Mike. 2013. *Asian Auntie-Ji.* Troubador.

Dawes, Simon. 2017. *British Broadcasting and the Public-Private Dichotomy, Neoliberalism, Citizenship and the Public Sphere.* Switzerland: Palgrave Macmillan.

Department for Culture, Media and Sport. 2016. A BBC for the Future: A Broadcaster of Distinction. CM 9242. Government. https://www.gov.uk/government/uploads/system/uploads/attachment_data/file/524863/DCMS_A_BBC_for_the_future_linked_rev1.pdf

Freedman, Des. 2008. *The Politics of Media Policy.* Cambridge: Polity.

———. 2019. "Public Service" and the Journalism Crisis: Is the BBC the Answer? *Television and New Media* 20 (3): 203–218.

Freedman, Des, Trine Syvertsen, Vana Goblot, Mark Thompson, Jon Thoday, Amanda D. Lotz, Tess Alps, Patrick Barwise, Jennifer Holt, and Matthew Powers. 2018. *A Future for Public Service Television.* Cambridge: Goldsmiths, University London.

Gardem, Tim. 2004. Independent Review of the BBC's Digital Radio Services. http://news.bbc.co.uk/nol/shared/bsp/hi/pdfs/19_10_04_digital_radio.pdf. Accessed 13 Oct 2020.

Gunaratnam, Yasmin. 2003. *Researching 'race' and Ethnicity: Methods, Knowledge and Power.* London: Sage.

Hall, Stuart, Critcher Chas, Jefferson Tony, Clarke John, and Roberts Brian. 2013. *Policing the Crisis: Mugging, the State, and Law and Order.* 2nd, 35th Anniversary edition. Basingstoke: Palgrave Macmillan.

Hallin, Daniel C., and Paolo Mancini. 2004. *Comparing Media Systems: Three Models of Media and Politics.* Cambridge: Cambridge University Press.

Hesmondhalgh, David, and Anamik Saha. 2013. Race, Ethnicity, and Cultural Production. Popular Communication 11 (3): 179–195.

Ibrahim, Yasmin, and Anita Howarth. 2020. The Munchetty Controversy: Empire, Race and the BBC. *Gender, Work & Organization* 28 (1): 231–247.

Jigsaw Research. 2019. News Consumption in the UK. https://www.ofcom.org.uk/__data/assets/pdf_file/0027/157914/uk-news-consumption-2019-report.pdf. Accessed 13 Oct.

Kamlesh Purohit. 2015. Face to face interview, 17 March.

Lacey, Kate. 2018. Radio's Vernacular Modernism: The Schedule as Modernist Text. *Media History* 24 (2): 166–179.

Loviglio, Jason, and Michele Hilmes, eds. 2013. *Radio's New Wave Global Sound in the Digital Era*. New York/London: Routledge.

Lowe, Gregory Ferrell, and Fiona Martin, eds. 2013. *The Value of Public Service Media*. Göteborg: Nordicom.

Malik, S. 2008. 'Keeping It Real, the Politics of Channel 4 Multiculturalism. *Mainstreaming and Mandates* 49 (3): 343–353.

Malik, Sarita. 2013. "Creative Diversity": UK Public Service Broadcasting After Multiculturalism. *Popular Communication* 11 (3): 227–241.

Mayer, Vicki. 2011. *Below the Line Producers and Production Studies in New Television Economy*. Durham: Duke University Press.

Mills, Tom. 2016. *The BBC Myth of a Public Service*. London: Verso.

Morely, David, and Kuan-Hsing Chen. 1996. *Stuart Hall Critical Dialogues in Cultural Studies*. London: Routledge.

Moylan, Katie. 2013. *Broadcasting Diversity, Migrant Representation in Irish Radio*. Bristol: Intellect.

Ofcom. 2013. Ethnic Minority Groups and Communication Services. Research report.

———. 2019a. Review of BBC News and Current Affairs. https://www.ofcom.org.uk/__data/assets/pdf_file/0025/173734/bbc-news-review.pdf. Accessed 13 Oct 2020

———. 2019b. Media Nations: UK 2019. https://www.ofcom.org.uk/__data/assets/pdf_file/0019/160714/media-nations-2019-uk-report.pdf. Accessed 13 Oct 2020.

———. 2019c. Ofcom's Annual Report on the BBC. https://www.ofcom.org.uk/__data/assets/pdf_file/0026/173735/second-bbc-annual-report.pdf. Accessed 13 Oct 2020.

Parekh, Bhikhu. 2000. *The Future of Multi-Ethnic Britain*. London: Profile Books.

Pilkington, Harry. 1962. The Pilkington Report. CMND 1537. London.

Puttnam, David. 2016. A Future for Public Service Television: Content and Platforms in a Digital World. Goldsmith University. http://futureoftv.org.uk/wp-content/uploads/2016/06/FOTV-Report-Online-SP.pdf

Radio Centre. 2012. RadioCentre's Response to the BBC Trust's Service Licence Review of Asian Network. Radio Centre.

RAJAR Q2. 2018. retrieved from https://www.rajar.co.uk/listening/quarterly_listening.php

Randle, Keith. 2015. Class and Exclusion at Work: The Case of the UK Film and Television. In *The Routledge Companion to the Cultural Industries*, ed. Kate Oakley and Justin O'Connor. Abingdon: Routledge.

Saha, Anamik. 2018. *Race and the Cultural Industries*. Cambridge: Polity.

Savage, Philip, Mercedes Medina, and Gregory Ferrell Lowe, eds. 2019. *Universalism in Public Service Media*. Göteborg: Nordicom.

Scannell, Paddy. 1989. Public Service Broadcasting and Modern Public Life. *Media, Culture and Society* 11: 135–166.

Scannell, Paddy, and David Cardiff. 1991. *A Social History of British Broadcasting. Vol 1 1922–1939 Serving the Nation*. Oxford: Basil Blackwell.

Shohat, Ella, and Robert Stam. 2014. *Unthinking Eurocentrism Multiculturalism and the Media*. 2nd ed. Abingdon: Routledge.

Sreberny, Annabelle. 2005. Not Only, But Also': Mixedness and Media. *Journal of Ethnic and Migration Studies* 31 (3): 443–459.

Syvertsen, Trine. 1999. The Many Uses of the Public Service Concept. *Nordicom Review* 1 (99): 5–12.

———. 2004. Citizens, Audiences, Customers and Players a Conceptual Discussion of the Relationship between Broadcasters and Their Publics. *European Journal of Cultural Studies* 7 (3): 363–380.

Tambini, Damian, and Cowling, Jamie. 2004. *From Public Service Broadcasting to Public Service Communications*. London: Institute for Public Policy Research.

Titley, Gavan. 2014. After the End of Multiculturalism: Public Service Media and Integrationist Imaginaries for the Governance of Difference. *Global Media and Communication* 10 (3): 247–260.

Tracey, Michael. 1998. *The Decline and Fall of Public Service Broadcasting*. Oxford/New York: Oxford University Press.

van Dijk, Teun, and A. 1992. Discourse and the Denial of Racism. *Discourse and Society* 3 (1): 87–118.

Virdee, Satnam, and Brendan McGeever. 2018. Racism, Crisis, Brexit. *Ethnic and Racial Studies* 41 (10): 1802–1819.

Yu, S. Sherry. 2016. Ethnic Media as Communities of Practice: The Cultural and Institutional Identities. *Journalism* 11 (18): 1309–1326.

Yu, S. Sherry, and M.D. Matsaganis. 2019. *Ethnic Media in the Digital Age*. New York: Routledge.

CHAPTER 3

British Asian Audiences

INTRODUCTION

The previous chapter outlined how public service broadcasting has either neglected or marginalised ethnic audiences in terms of their on-air representation and in terms of their employment within the media. Collectively, the British Asian community form the largest minority ethnic group in the UK accounting for approximately 7.5 per cent of the population in 2011.[1] However, despite being a distinct minority group they are not homogenous. This chapter examines the notion of the collective British Asian audience and provides an historical overview of South Asian migration to the UK. The contribution to UK society in terms of culture, employment, and education by South Asians or British Asians has been widely acknowledged in academic research and by the media. This chapter does not seek to cover these areas and, instead, examines the unique contribution British Asians working in the BBC make to the media production and representation of these communities, specifically, within the context of the BBC Asian Network. In addition, there is examination of how the BBC has previously served these communities with specific television and radio output. The British Asian community is composed of a large second generation and a third generation, alongside a growing fourth and fifth generation

---

[1] https://www.ethnicity-facts-figures.service.gov.uk/uk-population-by-ethnicity/national-and-regional-populations/population-of-england-and-wales/latest

© The Author(s), under exclusive license to Springer Nature Switzerland AG 2021
G. Aujla-Sidhu, *The BBC Asian Network*,
https://doi.org/10.1007/978-3-030-65764-2_3

which means there is huge pool of talent able to participate in employment within the mainstream media. This presents media employers with
staff who possess specialist cultural knowledge alongside the ability to construct meaningful cultural representations of Asians.

ARE BRITISH ASIANS HOMOGENOUS?

Despite the established presence of the British Asian community in the
UK, there continues to be a debate on the most appropriate way to
describe this distinct group. Political legislation, the media, and educational organisations in the UK have tended to describe people who have
associations with Sri Lanka, India, Pakistan, and Bangladesh as being
"Asian," a term which seeks to homogenise the distinct nationalities,
faiths, and linguist differences among the groups. The term Asian also
ignores individuals who possess multiple heritage; in 2011, this group
comprised 2.2 per cent of the UK population. A number of studies of
diaspora have noted that these groups are not homogenous and that whilst
there is shared culture, there is also conflict and difference (Madianou
2005; Loomba 2015). Clark et al. (1990, p. 170) suggest that these
groups do "not exist as a concrete community. The group is dialectically
rather than absolutely defined" because people identify as Asian for specific purposes, for example, formal identity but dissolve into subgroups of
nationality, religion, or caste for other purposes. Although the term Asian
essentially erases people's national identity, when people in the UK are
required to identify their ethnic origins, the term Asian is used in conjunc-
tion with national identity such as Indian or Bangladeshi. The confusion
between ethnic and national identity is also replicated in the haphazard
manner in which institutions, including the media, tend to describe British
Asians with labels including BAME (Black, Asian, and minority ethnic),
Asian, British Asian, BME (Black minority ethnic), and South Asian. Kaur
and Kalra (in Sharma et al. 1996) have argued that British Asian is a
"poorly defined category" that "essentialises both terms, as well as hierar-
chising the former against the latter" (in Sharma et al. 1996, p. 219).

Ethnicity, nation, and race appear to be understood collectively because
they offer one means to categorise people. Ethnicity refers to someone's
background and culture and as such bestows admission to a social group,
foreign, or minority status (Fenton 1999, p. 3). Ethnicity is understood to
be socially constructed and attempts to label people usually based on skin
colour. The differences that exist between minority ethnic and majority

populations tend to be accentuated by society and the media, leading to sensationalist headlines or misrepresentation of communities, their links to unfamiliar cultures, languages, and the Global South. In contrast, the nation is often understood to collectively describe a group of people and it bestows a sense of belonging on the people who are deemed to belong to it and outsider status to those who are not seen to be part of the nation. The term culture is often used by the media as a "source of explanation" as opposed to describing relevant issues or factors that are pertinent to the story (Kruper 1999, p. 239). Consequently, the on-air portrayal of diverse cultures is often static due to the lack of knowledge on the part of the media producers, which, in turn, enables the naturalisation of norms such as arranged marriage, saris, and curry to define British Asians (Fortier 2000). In many ways, British Asians and other minority groups have by default emerged as an accidental audience for the BBC because they are UK citizens, and the BBC traditionally has imagined the audience as a public of citizens. Media histories of radio describe how the listening audience was perceived to be passive and receptive to content that would educate them. The listener was expected to engage actively in the act of listening because the BBC did not consider radio to be a background activity (Lewis and Booth 1989). Radio listeners are an imagined community constructed by programme makers who try to unite disparate communities together through similar experiences or views (Fitzgerald and Housley 2007). Some of the first and second generations of British Asians are united through the shared experience of migration to Britain. Public service broadcasting in the UK utilises the notion of the "nation" or the "national" to unite people from geographical regions and ethnic groups under a notion of shared values and normative behaviour. Sayyid (in Ali et al. 2006, p. 4) has argued that British Asians "share a sense of belonging to South Asia, a sense mediated by coloniality and marked by racialized subordination, and continually represented through the currency of Indological discourse." In other words, Sayyid believes the communities connect to each other because the process of moving from a colonised country to Britain meant they experienced racism, prejudice, and were paid less simply because they were immigrants from the Commonwealth. Some of the post-war South Asian migration to the UK was due in part to the huge upheaval of the partition of India which led to a huge movement of population in 1947, particularly in the Punjab region which was divided across two different countries, India and Pakistan. The immigrants found that in the UK, their educational qualifications were not valid, and their cultural or religious practices were considered anachronistic, hence the impact of colonialism and Eurocentrism meant they were seen to be inferior to the majority. In contemporary Britain, South Asians are often still seen and understood in the UK is specifically through post-colonial lens (Ali et al. 2006).

Large numbers of people also arrived from the Caribbean and Africa and were able to enter the country freely as British citizens. The so-called Windrush generation (Jamaica, Trinidad and Tobago, and Barbados) began arriving from 1948 to 1971, invited to the UK due to a labour shortage. Collectively, all immigrants faced racism and discrimination; many found it difficult to get accommodation and jobs. There was also a distinct lack of integration with the majority population because the new immigrants were not welcome. This appeared to be reflected in the political arena with successive governments seeking to restrict immigration, first through the imposition of 1971 Immigration Act which actively restricted entry to Britain because potential migrants had to provide evidence that their parents or grandparents had been born in Britain. Despite this, Britain was forced to accept a second wave of Asian migration in the 1970s following the expulsion of Asians from Uganda. The East African Asians were predominantly composed of Punjabi or Gujarati settlers who had originally left India at the start of the century to work in Africa. Later the 1981 Immigration Act further restricted movement of people. Brah (in Ali et al. 2006) has suggested the amendment of the bill was justified on the ground that the arranged marriage system practised by the Asian communities resulted in a continuous flow of immigration that the government wanted to stem.

Gandy (1998) has argued that the link between ethnic identity and the nation state has become salient because whilst countries allowed foreign nationals to labour in their industries, ethnic people were placed into hierarchical structures across Europe. Therefore, both the nation and ethnic identity are considered to be socially constructed, either imagined or invented, and thus, there are implications for the classification systems built around them. A similar argument is presented by Bates (2001) who outlines that contemporary identity is rooted in colonial hierarchies, where people were arranged into groups by the coloniser based on their faith. The colonial power then could maintain order by arbitrating between the groups. This is referred to as the policy of separate representation, and even after the end of colonisation in many countries, this feature was left in a number of constitutions (Bates 2001, p. 11).

Thus far, this chapter has only looked at the experience of migration to the UK. The 2011 Census revealed that 42 per cent of Asians were born in Britain.[2] This means that a sizeable proportion of subsequent generations of British Asians have been born and raised in the UK. Ramamurthy (in Price and Sabido 2015) defined second-generation British Asians as having either arriving in the UK as young children or were born in the UK. She suggests this group lacked a connection with their countries of origin because their "sense of belonging" to the UK is more "complex" and their "investment and interest in Britain was much greater"; hence, this group sought to carve out an identity or "make space within Britishness which they could occupy" (Ramamurthy, in Price and Sabido 2015, p. 191). The notion of making a space is important because non-white immigrants have never "blended in" because they remain visibly distinct. The different levels of interest and links that young British Asians have with South Asia including language differ from the first generation, who are now likely to be elderly. Campion (2005) has argued that because a number of minority ethnic people from various generations live in the UK, some have deeper connections than others to their heritage, and thus this community cannot be assumed to be homogeneous. Statistics from the 2011 census show that more than 43 per cent of the British Asian population is aged between 20 and 39 years of age with a considerable number of young adults aged between 18 and 24 years of age.[3] This suggests there exist sizeable groups of British Asian who have similar generational experiences in terms of language and assimilation into the UK. Bates (2001) has also noted that the identities of South Asians differ according to their faith and where they live; therefore, a Hindu in Leicester is different from a Hindu living in Durban South Africa, due to differences in their lived experiences of their countries. The population statistics reveal there is growing young ethnic audience that mainstream media can try to appeal to.

Ang (1991) has disputed the value of audience studies arguing that most of the research appears to passively accept the audience as being a single entity which ignores the socio-cultural and institutional contexts in which they are positioned. Some audiences are viewed in terms that are indicative of the institutional media viewpoint as opposed to an organic

[2] https://www.ethnicity-facts-figures. service.gov.uk/uk-population-by-ethnicity/demographics/people-born-outside-the-uk/latest
[3] https://www.ethnicity-facts-figures.service.gov.uk/uk-population-by-ethnicity/demographics/age-groups/latest#age-profile-by-ethnicity

representation of their group. Subsequently, the way in which the audience is viewed is either from above, from the outside, or from an institutional perspective. She argues that this reduces individuals to simply being numbers that belong to a specified income group, class, or ethnic group. However, by viewing ethnic groups as diaspora audiences recognises that their identities have been "transformed" through "relocation, cross cultural exchange and interaction" (Gillespie 1995, p. 7). Minority communities who have moved around the world possess a transnational culture because they maintain traditions, customs, and practices whilst simultaneously embracing new lifestyles and habits. Gillespie's (1995) ethnographic study focused on the Punjabi community in Southall, West London, and scrutinised how people watched British television and Bollywood films. She found television viewing enabled families to recreate cultural traditions. Therefore, minority communities do not necessarily develop an identity that is in opposition to mainstream society; instead, they tend to borrow and adapt aspects of the host nation, thus normalising a new cultural identity. As such, in Stuart Hall's words identity is "constantly in the process of change and transformation" (Hall and du Gay 1996, p. 4). Bates (2001, p. 11) has also noted that migrant communities across the world tend to display an "ease with which their identity is often integrated or otherwise transformed to meet the pressures of different circumstances." Parekh (2000) notes that post-migration communities are distinct cultural formations that are part of British society and not separate or distinct. Moreover, he stresses that the articulation of Asian identity by the communities does not remain static. Instead, as noted earlier identity adapts in response to experiences. Asians do not belong to a single group but vary in terms of nationality, religion, language, and class, and even within these groups, there are differences.

Questions have posed about what it means to be British and the national identity of Britain because immigration has profoundly changed the face of society. This question also poses difficulties for the BBC because it tries to showcase the British "nation" and its associated values through the media content. British identity is a "contested concept" because the term has different meanings (Condor et al. 2006, p. 126). Through interviews with members of minority communities, studies have examined the relevance of the term "English" and "British" in relation to people's identities. A study by McCrone (2002) revealed that unlike other minority groups, people of Indian background were more likely to consider themselves to be English; however, in practice, most people do not understand the difference between the terms. British and English have two different but interconnected meanings, and their meanings are subject to change due to changes in society and policies. Rupa Haq (in Sharma et al. 1996) has argued that the media largely presents Asians as people who are trapped or caught between two opposing cultures—modern and western and their faith, which is traditional. She explains these types of representations are not only reductive but also fail to understand the complexity of multiple identities. Sayyid (in Ali et al. 2006) has suggested the term Asian designates that a proportion or significant part of someone's identity is sign-posted in terms of South Asian heritage. Therefore, he believes that British Asians experience doubts or scepticism over their inclusion into British culture.

INTERGENERATIONAL CHANGE AND DIFFERENCES AMONG ASIAN AUDIENCES

Increasingly minority audiences have become significant to media organisations who recognise they can grow their audience figures and profits by targeting underserved or neglected groups. This is especially pertinent given that audience fragmentation is most pronounced among young audiences (Ofcom 2019). Minority communities tend to have a larger and younger demographic in contrast to the main population (Ballard 1990; Ofcom 2013). From the public service point of view, there is an obligation to serve all audiences and ensure that a wide range of voices and opinions are articulated in order to provide people with information so they can make their own decisions. Increasingly, the BBC has been forced to demonstrate this more clearly. An Ofcom review of representation and portrayal on the BBC recommended the reduction of labels, outlining "they are not helpful and can mask important details and differences" (Ofcom 2018, p. 5). However, for ease and familiarity, the media continue to use labels and stereotypes (see Chap. 6).

The previous discussion outlined problems with the concept of the homogenous audience this section examines why some negative stereotypes persist. Among the Asian groups, there are significant levels of social class differentiation (Ali et al. 2006). Despite the existence of an established bourgeoisie and a professional/entrepreneurial middle class, most of the Asian community are working class. A substantial proportion of Pakistani and Bangladeshi communities tend to work in blue collar roles and live in inner cities. Mcloughlin's (in Ali et al. 2006, p. 138) study of Muslims in Bradford describes them as an "economic underclass" among the Asian communities. His study notes that social divisions between Pakistani and Bangladeshi groups and Hindus and Sikhs are especially apparent in terms of class, education, and upward mobility. Ballard (1990, 2003) has tried to explain the different fortunes in the UK of the Mirpuri (Muslim) community and Sikhs specifically from Jalandhar, India. He found the economic differences that exist between the two groups who migrated to the UK at similar times is due in part to their different histories, political economies in South Asia, and social capital. He also suggests that Sikh women engaged in paid employment in larger numbers and far sooner than Mirpuri women. Employment statistics for 2018 reveal that members of the Pakistani and Bangladeshi community continue to have the lowest employment rate in the UK.[4]

The media more often than not depict Islam as being authoritarian, oppressive, or antiquated (Sian 2011). Whereas Sikhs and Hindus are portrayed and even praised for their integration, educational attainment, and role in the economy, this group appear more closely aligned with the majority middle class and many earn similar salaries to the majority population. As audience, they are understood by producers to be closer to the majority population. Sikhs are perceived to have integrated or assimilated and embraced notions of Britishness due to the community's roles in the UK life. However, Sian (2011) describes the Sikh communities' relationship with the West as being ambiguous because some Sikhs still maintain pride for their roles in the imperial rule in India. Therefore, she suggests that the process of decolonisation in this community is incomplete. Within the mainstream, there is an acceptance of Indian cultures due to the positive commodification of Bollywood (Malik 2002).

The contrast between the Indian, Pakistani, and Bangladeshi communities is essentially faith-based because since September 11, the media has been preoccupied with displaying the Muslim community within negative and restricted frames. The overt expression of the Islamic faith is seen to be "a threat to traditional British values" (Poole and John 2006, p. 22). The impact is that Muslim communities are excluded from the notion of being "British," a concept created and fed by political ideology and public service broadcasting. This results in an over-emphasis upon Islam within

[4] https://www.ethnicity-facts-figures.service.gov.uk/work-pay-and-benefits/employment/employment/latest

the news, whereby news stories about Muslims or Islam tend to be over-simplified or misrepresented. This is in part due to a focus upon difference and fear which propagates the political emphasis on assimilation. Furthermore, this situation primarily exists because there has been a lack of consideration of the power systems and how they operate within the media, with reference to class (Hesmondhalgh and Saha 2013).

As outlined earlier, the media understands and continues to showcase British Asian communities in terms prescribed by colonialism. Saeed in (in Brunt and Cere 2010) suggests it is precisely because British Asians are members of former colonised countries that they are forced to occupy a restricted space in society and their representation is influenced by the colonial experience. Therefore, greater attention needs to be paid to the impact post-colonialism has had on media practices (Brunt and Cere 2010). Problematically, the use of "post" is a misnomer because it signifies that these studies examine the period of time following the end of colonialism, but, in fact, they examine the entire period from the beginning of colonialism and the pervasive impact this history has had upon societies. Loomba (2015, p. 40) has defined colonialism as "the forcible takeover of land and economy and, in the case of European colonialism, a restructuring of non-capitalist economies in order to fuel European capitalism." In addition, European education and technology is regarded as being superior to Eastern education or beliefs. Post-colonial scholars have noted how the West is positioned as the centre of the world and the Eastern or Global South is simultaneously positioned as "other" and, consequently, as inferior. Former colonial countries are often presented as being static, traditional, or old fashioned. Gunaratnam (2003) has argued that researchers examining race and ethnicity have tended to rely upon findings and context that has been conducted within the context of colonialism as opposed to examining the impact colonialism has had on society's perceptions of inequality and racism. Post-colonial studies tend to be concentrated on literature and wider society; therefore, Shome (2016) has suggested its key contribution has been to unveil how Western or Eurocentric assumptions influence the production of knowledge in society. This includes the underlying assumption a developed media system is indicative of a democratic culture where power is dispersed and checked. Shohat and Stam (2014, p. 1) outline that Eurocentric thinking, ways of working, and structures are "so pervasive, that it often goes unnoticed" and is normalised.

As noted in Chap. 2 the media reflects the political debate on issues such as immigration, asylum, policing, education, and public housing stories which frame the migrant and minority communities as a "social problem" (Bloch and Solomos 2010). Sociology and cultural studies suggest that racial stereotyping is a consequence of the journalist's biases combined with economic and market pressures facing the media, which means that a comprehensive approach to representing minority audiences is undermined (Madianou, in Bloch and Solomos 2010). The problem is exacerbated further, by the fact that editorial roles in the media are often held by non-ethnic staff despite the existence of diversity initiatives to combat this. In addition, the prominent ideologies of professionalism and working practices within journalism also impact the representation of minority communities (Campion 2005). Public service broadcasting also depicts migrant cultures through "difference" or "otherness"' as judged by standards established by the West (Campion 2005; Moylan 2013; Shohat and Stam 2014). Said (1978), in his seminal work "*Orientalism*," presented the viewpoint that because European identity has historically been portrayed as "superior" to "all the non-European peoples and cultures," this has had an enduring impact on how they are understood. This view is supported by the cultural theorist Stuart Hall who has engaged with questions of race, hegemony, and society. Hall has outlined that the media frames ethnic difference through the parameters of "economic, political or ideological antagonisms" (1986, p. 23). Moreover, because the media is part of the structural and power elite in society, the message it articulates is supported and strengthened by the collaboration with other social institutions such as schools, cultural organisations, the family, church, and religion. This means the dominant view and perspective becomes normalised and natural. Hall notes that cultural difference is managed, regulated, and restricted and what is showcased is "a kind of carefully regulated segregated visibility" so that diverse cultures and experience are marginalised and permitted to exist on the fringes because Western democracies are tolerant (Morely and Chen 1996, p. 468). The point Hall makes about "segregated visibility" will be examined in Chap. 4 which concentrates on ethnic staff recruitment and their experiences of working within the BBC.

Campion interviewed more than 100 programme makers to try to understand the barriers to depicting diversity in media output. Her interviewees identified the news as a genre that establishes the agenda for other types of programmes such as documentaries and drama, but the participants acknowledged that the on-air portrayal of minority communities focused "excessively on their strangeness" (Campion 2005, p. 24).

Content that focused upon "bride burning and female circumcision, polygamy, and honour killings or stories of witchcraft and alleged ritual child abuse" were offered as examples of how minority communities are reduced to familiar stereotypes for consumption by mainstream audiences (Campion 2005, p. 28). Campion (2005) argued that unbalanced representation and misrepresentation of minorities within the media bolster racial stereotypes. Moreover, the incidental inclusion of visible ethnic minorities on screen may give the impression of greater diversity, but it often lacks the depth and substance to reflect the lived realities of minority groups. Interestingly, despite the emergence of multiple generations of the British Asian communities, who are considered to be integrated, Sian (2011) notes that Asians are still viewed as communities where religion is a central aspect of their identity and lifestyle.

Minority audiences have challenged the media to offer deeper and more meaningful representations and often complain if they are misrepresented in mainstream television. For example, the first series of *Citizen Khan*, a comedy about a British Muslim family written by a British Asian writer and comedian Adil Ray, drew over 200 complaints from viewers who claimed the comedy misrepresented Muslims because it featured a dated representation of British Asian life (BBC News 2012). The sitcom ran for five series between 2012 and 2016. Hundreds of viewers also objected to a number of storylines featuring a gay Muslim character in *Eastenders* in 2009–2012 (Love 2010). British Asian viewers find their limited representation on-air can be either negative or that their culture is misrepresented. Hesse (2000) and Sayyid (in Ali et al. 2006) acknowledge that whilst intergenerational change within minority communities is expected, the dominant representation of minorities within the media and society remains associated with cultures and practices from distant lands aboard. Subsequently, it is not surprising that minority audiences subscribe to satellite services to obtain programmes in other languages or about other cultures. Statistics from BARB[5] reveal that among British Asian audiences, channels featuring South Asian language content feature in the most watched channels (Ofcom 2018).

---

[5] The Broadcasters' Audience Research Board compiles audience measurement and television ratings in the UK.

EARLY PROGRAMMING FOR ASIAN COMMUNITIES

This chapter has outlined that younger generations of minority groups increase their acceptance within youth cultures, employment, and education through familiarity with the majority culture and thereby dilute their distinctive identity. In the early years of Asian programming, the BBC through regional radio and television programmes sought to provide South Asian communities with content in their mother tongue to support their settlement into Britain. There was an underlying aim to slowly conform the communities to British values and standards in line with the BBC's integrationist agenda that was evident in the 1970s and 1980s (Malik 2008). Ishani joined BBC Radio Leicester in the 1980s and worked on the early regional Asian programming before working for the national BBC Asian Network. She outlined how the contemporary BBC is no longer focused on the integration of British Asians

> When I got involved there was still the perception it was a service targeting the immigrant community. In 2012, the most significant shift was that it is accepted that the service targets the British Asian diaspora who are born and bred here [...] And that it is a significant and growing demographic, the emphasis in the early years was giving information because it was an immigrant community. (Former Manager, Ishani 2015)

The emphasis upon the British Asian listener has resulted in changes to the mode of address, programming, and music. The historical language programmes developed by the BBC were the first opportunities for Asian presenters and producers to find employment in British mainstream media. A number of these presenters either already possessed radio or television skills or were simply volunteers from the communities who had exceptional language skills. They were the early pioneers of "accented" production within a public service context (Naficy 2001). This type of production intrinsically incorporates characteristics of the transnational experience and addresses the diaspora in a relatable manner. It is interesting that the BBC through its Overseas Service (now the World Service) did broadcast to Asians in South Asia, but historically no programmes were produced for the Asian or Afro-Caribbean communities residing in Britain. In 1965 the Campaign Against Racial Discrimination called on the BBC to create content that included Britain's Black communities. Some of the notable television programmes to emerge were October 1965 *Apna Hi Ghar*

Samajhiye (Make Yourself at Home) and in 1968 *Nai Zindagi Naya Jeevan* (New Life). Make Yourself at Home was broadcast in a mix of Hindi, Urdu, and English and aimed to provide basic English lessons based on common activities newly arrived immigrants would need to complete. The magazine style format also included news, discussion, and Bollywood music. It was repeated on Radio 4 on Sunday mornings.

Malik (2002) has argued that although the specific Black and Asian programmes on the BBC were the consequence of debates around access and public service broadcasting in the 1970s, the BBC did not freely admit that the programmes were framed with assimilation in mind. However, the BBC did feel that the Asian community would benefit from language lessons and required advice and support to enable them to integrate. Malik (2002, p. 57) described the tone the BBC adopted as one that "favoured cultural co-existence" of British Asians and the majority population, and it quietly accepted "the inevitability of a racially-integrated system." David Hendy has examined a number of BBC archives as part of an oral history project which aims to document 100 hundred years of the BBC. He has argued that *Make Yourself at Home* and other minority programmes were purposely "ghettoised on the schedules" because they were broadcast at times when the BBC had fewer mainstream listeners (Hendy n.d.). This meant the immigrant audience was treated as being separate and distinct, but it also meant their specific programming was only available at unsociable or unpopular times of the day. The fact that the early programming on ITV and BBC situated minorities as immigrants began to become problematic in the 1970s and 1980s when increasing number of viewers/listeners were born in Britain. A notable change at the BBC was the renaming of the Immigrants Programme Unit to the Asian Programmes Unit in 1974.

Khamkar (2017) examined the emergence of Asian radio programming on commercial, community radio, and the BBC and notes that in the 1970s the conversation within the BBC was focused on serving Asian communities through local BBC Radio services because many of them scheduled programmes in South Asian languages such as Leicester, Sheffield, and Birmingham. She suggests that local radio offered a flexible and responsive structure; therefore, regions could choose to reflect key Asian festivals in one-off programmes as opposed to offering regular weekly or daily shows.

When commercial radio was initially launched, it was also mandated to provide content for immigrant communities and communities of interest under *The Sound Broadcasting Act* 1972. LBC (London Broadcasting Company) was among the first to come on air followed by Capital Radio, Radio Clyde, and BMRB (Birmingham). The notion of communities of interest made it possible for the introduction of radio services for clearly defined communities including minority ethnic as well as geographical. However, it was only through the introduction of Incremental Radio licences between 1989 and 1990 which permitted the introduction of additional stations in areas already served by an Independent Local Radio station that Asian radio emerged. Sunrise Radio first launched on an incremental radio contract to serve Southall, in West London. Prior to obtaining a licence, Sunrise had broadcast as Sina Radio via Cable since 1984. Sunrise is notable for being the first 24-hour Asian radio station in the UK and to this day continues to offer music, news, and entertainment from South Asia, broadcasting in English, Hindi, Urdu, and Punjabi. It has signed up to RAJAR and is a key competitor for the BBC Asian Network in 2018; it was the most listened radio station in the capital (RAJAR Q2, 2018).

The advantage of the co-existence of ethnic media alongside mainstream media is that it provides greater diversity within the public sphere through the inclusion of other voices and perspectives. Ethnic media explicitly acknowledges the history of migrant communities, their interests, and music or culture and, as a result, allows people to make space for their interests outside of the mainstream public sphere. However, two key discussions envelop ethnic media organisations—first, that mainstream media should also showcase minority voices and, second, that the existence of ethnic media contributes to audience fragmentation. Sreberny (2005) recognises the role that ethnic media play in enabling the self-representation of communities that challenges mainstream depictions of ethnic communities. This could be due to the fact that ownership of ethnic media tends to be independent and not part of large media conglomerates.

PRODUCTION AT THE BBC ASIAN NETWORK

There are differences within all minority communities due in part to age and socio-economic class. One of the significant findings to emerge from the study of production within the BBC is the divergence of perspectives between the older ethnic producers and the younger ethnic staff. The older staff, who are either first- or second-generation British Asian, outlined how they lacked the autonomy to promote and reflect a robust

British Asian identity and instead felt forced to showcase a fluid or ambiguous British Asian identity on the radio. They pose that the "standardised" version of British Asian identity emphasises notions of integration and in their words a "mainstream" perspective, to appeal specifically to young British Asian listeners and this excludes other listeners. The term integration is applied to people who adopt practices of the host nation and maintain some of their traditional culture. Whereas assimilation is understood to be a situation where minorities choose to dilute or relinquish their culture and adopt the dominant values and practices of society (Bloch and Solomos 2010), other indicators of assimilation include employment and contribution to the economy and society more widely. The older producers believe that the British Asian diaspora deserve a radio service that has a strong focus on promoting Asian culture, news from South Asia, and related music. The younger staff, primarily third-generation journalists and producers, are proficient using technology and can connect with young listeners through digital means. Former presenter Tommy Sandhu explained that the audience identify or relate to their heritage at different times of their lives:

> I think as people get older you become prouder of your Asian roots. I think having Indian, Pakistani, Gujarati, Kenyan roots is something to be proud of. Even if they are a generation or two generations ago. It enriches you; it gives you these values, that nobody else has and to have a radio station that reflects those values in a British world, will always be relevant as long as people are proud of those roots. (Former Presenter, Tommy Sandhu 2016)

Sandhu implies that the younger staff and listeners will in time value their heritage and bond to it in unique ways. This book proposes that representation of the British Asian audience offered by the BBC and the Asian Network is thus shaped and influenced by societal attitudes, BBC policies, the wider media ecology, and the lived experiences of ethnic staff. Matsaganis and Katz's (2014) study of ethnic producers in the USA found the size of the audience ethnic media serve influences not only the media content but also ethnic producers practices. Chapter 2 outlined that public service broadcasting is intrinsically associated with serving the public through the provision of information and entertainment for a range of taste and interests within society. The BBC Asian Network has adopted a "broad" approach to the notion of being "Asian" in terms of the music played, programme content, and the issues covered on-air, to appeal to all the groups that comprise the British Asian UK communities (Bangladeshi, Indian, Pakistani, and Sri Lankan). The former head of Programmes, Mark Strippel, explained why this approach was implemented:

> There is massive commonality between people of Punjabi origin, Gujarati origin, and Pakistani origin. Is there a commonality between those audiences and ties that bind? Yes, there are ties that bind in a cultural context in a faith approach and on discussions around race and immigration [...] there is a massive, shared experience whilst there are differences. (Former Head of Programmes, Mark Strippel 2015)

Strippel concentrates on the experiences and tastes British Asian listeners share as opposed to what divides them in order to create a cohesive community of listeners. This is an inclusive as opposed to exclusive approach, and it is optimistic. This is the tone promoted on-air that explicitly acknowledges that the "British Asian" experience is unique to those who belong to any of the groups within the label, and this unites them because it is a "tie." Unsurprisingly, most media organisations focus upon common themes or causes which are non-offensive to the audience in order to appeal widely. So, the producers work actively to unite listeners fractured by nationality, language, faith, and economic class. As a result, it can mean the BBC Asian Network does not examine some issues in great depth or detail. Malik (2013, p. 516) asserts that minority communities do not require a simplistic media reflection that showcase their life and the differences that exist between them and the mainstream population, but that crucially, the "representation constructs reality." In other words, the reflection should address the unique problems and challenges minority communities face collectively or within smaller groups. However, whilst the media recognise minority audiences have a right to "challenge and help shape the public and political culture of the society in which they live," the media has been unable to achieve this due to lack of knowledge among staff (Deveaux, cited in Christians et al. 2009, p. 174). Instead, programme makers rely upon familiar tropes and stereotypes to showcase minority audiences, meaning that news and programming across all the broadcasters have become "homogenous," "digestible and entertaining," leading to claims that broadcasting is "dumbing down" (Christians et al. 2009, p. 115). Success within broadcasting is measured specifically in terms of listening and viewing figures which means that the producers focus on creating material that is appealing for the majority tastes at the expense of minority interests. For example, former BBC Asian Network journalist, Danish *(not his real name)*, highlighted that the lack of specialist sports coverage for British Asian listeners was frustrating and that simply pushing the listener to 5 Live is not an adequate substitute.

> The management didn't understand our approach to covering cricket when it comes to India versus Pakistan or something like that. Those kinds of things are massive to our audience, and they are not covered in the same way across the BBC. (Former broadcast Journalist, Danish 2016)

Danish outlines here that mainstream BBC stations do not see the significance of the huge sports rivalry between British Asians who tend to support the national teams of their families. 5 Live naturally concentrates on the England Cricket team and their progress because the station is tasked with showcasing news and sport in the UK. In this manner, it is evident that smaller groups do not influence how media content is framed and made. Anish Shaikh, a programme producer, explained his pride in introducing the Shayri (poetry) Club to an evening programme on the BBC Asian Network which asked listeners to share their poems and allowed others to discuss.

> I'm quite proud of it and take pride in that that the majority of the people who are sharing this and commenting on this are young people. So even though their first language is English they still appreciate some of the Shayri poetry which is written in their mother tongue. (Producer, Anish Shaikh 2015)

This feature was subsequently removed in 2017 when the on-air schedule was modified. However, it is precisely because the BBC Asian Network is a public service radio station that staff are permitted to experiment with ideas that promotes and celebrate content produced in Urdu or Hindi. This type of content does not exist anywhere else. The former head of News, Kevin Silverton, also highlighted in his interview that the content produced by the station cannot be compared to any other BBC national output:

> There isn't anything like it in Britain, the debate we provoke and the stories we put out there, whether they be positive or negative, they add to the sum total to what the BBC is doing. Without it there would be a hole. (Kevin Silverton, former Head of News 2015)

This is a critical point; the histories of Black and Asian communities are often excluded in the classrooms in schools and Universities. Whilst older audiences may use the station as a platform to discuss and debate, younger audiences may listen to the BBC Asian Network to learn about their heritage. Sam (*not her real name*) was interviewed on Armistice Day in 2016; she remarked that the engagement with listeners on that particular day highlighted the educational role the BBC Asian Network has.

> The texts, emails and tweets that we've received today from the listeners said we've learnt more about the sub continental contribution to World War I and II through the Asian Network than we have through history lessons at school or through mainstream media. (Senior journalist, Sam 2016)

In 2020 there were calls to re-evaluate what histories are taught in schools in the wake of George Floyd's murder in the USA; however, the UK government rejected a review of the curriculum (Proctor 2020). Sam underlined in her interview that the public service mission consciously and unconsciously influences what stories and issues the station focuses upon:

> We are a broadcaster on the only real public service in this country and our job is basically to provide for those communities [...] So that's why we have to have a mix of news, current affairs, culture reflecting the arts even. We've supported a lot of really small theatre companies and people would never encounter the Asian Arts because it's not featured in their local newspapers. (Senior journalist Sam 2015)

The soft support provided by the BBC Asian Network means that events get promoted on-air. In 2016 the BBC ended its support of Asian Melas[6] in order to focus on its own concert and, consequently, some of the London events were postponed or cancelled. Although the BBC Asian Network provides no financial incentive to the organisers, the on-air publicity and the use of BBC talent as presenters on stages attract sponsors to run the events in the first place. The involvement in melas allows the BBC to reach out to new audiences in cities and regions where listener numbers are low.

The on-air talent is also chosen to showcase an equal balance as far as possible of the various Asian communities. This includes gender as well as

---

[6] Mela—usually a free event featuring music, dance acts, and cuisine from Pakistani, Bengali, Indian, and other South Asian cultures.

the representation of Muslims, Sikh, and Hindu presenters in acknowledgement that a number of Asian-specific community stations increasingly serve a single Asian community as opposed to trying to appeal to all British Asians, for example, Punjab Radio is for Punjabi speakers, Sanskar Radio appeals to Hindus, and Desi Radio for Punjabis. Gordon (2012) has argued that community radio stations challenge the power of the mainstream radio simply through their existence and how they operate. Furthermore, Gordon (2012) recognises community stations can provide a platform for listeners who feel they are inadequately served by other broadcasters. This means that smaller stations focused on one specific group in a defined geographical area can be responsive to their listeners in ways that commercial or PSB is unable because of their structures and frameworks. Moylan (2013) has outlined that community radio's strength lies in the fact that it encourages the listeners to take an active role in the production of programmes and content. The UK has a thriving ethnic media sector, and the key competitor to the BBC is Sunrise Radio. In 2019, Sunrise marked its 30th birthday, making it the longest running Asian radio station in the UK.

The increasing significance of the younger generations of British Asians and their increasing participation in media production roles has meant that the BBC and ethnic media are being forced to innovate as they respond to the evolving workforce and their audience. Although the majority of ethnic media organisations are founded by and targeted at first-generation migrants, they also recruit younger generations of their own communities who have diluted, hyphenated, and hybrid identities (Yu and Matsaganis 2019). These circumstances are replicated at the BBC Asian Network, and the disagreement over what age listener and the type of British Asian identity that should be articled on air influences the mode of address. Kamran *(not his real name)*, a former programme producer, found that some of the older members of staff have remained static in their ideas and creativity and are unable to cater for the target listener.

> I just think BBC Asian Network staff are not evolving. There's plenty who don't want to evolve, refuse to. This is the problem; this is coming from the producers and the teams so you can't move forward as a station if you are always living in Goodness Gracious Me era. (Former producer, Kamran 2015)

During his interview Kamran outlined his frustration that creativity is sidelined due to inertia or unwillingness among some of the staff to adapt their working practices to reflect the changing composition of the target audience and technology which has disrupted broadcast journalism. Kamran's view suggests there are differences in how programmes and presenters address the listener resulting in on-air content that is either unfocused or vague. Within programmes, stories and segments can move from material directed at first generation contrasted with music for a young listener. Or an open discussion about sex juxtaposed with a debate about faith.

CONCLUSION

The chapter illustrated some of the differences among the so-called homogenous British Asian audience and equally the existence of differences among the ethnic programme makers within the BBC. The British Asian community is now in its fourth and fifth generations, and increasingly members from these communities are playing prominent roles in employment, education, and society. Within the media, this is reflected in the growth of ethnic media workers across the sector. This chapter has shown the differences between how the older ethnic staff would like to serve the British Asian listener and the younger staff. The older staff describe some of the newer staff as being "integrated" and "assimilated." These terms were often used as within a negative context and are explored in depth in Chap. 4.

The chapter has also demonstrated that audience studies and the media tend to view the audience as a homogenous mass and ignore smaller groups. This also means the issues that are pertinent to small marginalised audiences are also overlooked and, therefore, do not become part of the public sphere. This means minority audiences turn to media in their own language accessing satellite service or language-specific community or commercial radio. Murdock (2005, p. 197) suggests that there is a significant contradiction with PSB because it tries to provide information in a balanced manner whilst also trying to construct the audience as a unified nation or imagined community. The underlying theme of the book is to look at how the BBC Asian Network is attempting to construct a cohesive British Asian listening community which is united on the shared notion of "Britishness" (Former Controller, Bob Shennan 2015). What is evident, however, is that audiences are distinct but strategies to cultivate audiences work to homogenise them. Chapter 5 details the different audience strategies that the BBC Asian Network has embarked upon to entice the preferred listener.

REFERENCES

Ali, Nasreen, Virinder S. Kalra, and S. Sayyid, eds. 2006. *A Postcolonial People, South Asians in Britain*. London: Hurst & Co.

Ang, Ien. 1991. *Desperately Seeking the Audience*. London/New York: Routledge.

Ballard, Roger. 1990. Migration and Kinship: The Differential Effect of Marriage Rules on the Processes of Punjabi Migration to Britain. In *South Asians Overseas Migration and Ethnicity*, ed. C. Clarke, C. Peach, and S. Vertovec, 219–249. Cambridge: Cambridge University Press.

———. 2003. The South Asian Presence in Britain and Its Transnational Connections. In *Culture and Economy in the Indian Diaspora*, ed. H. Singh and S. Vertovec. London: Routledge.

Bates, Crispin, ed. 2001. *Community, Empire and Migration*. Basingstoke: Palgrave.

BBC News. 2012. Muslim Sitcom Prompts Complaints. *BBC News*, 29 August 2012, sec. Entertainment & Arts. https://www.bbc.com/news/entertainment-arts-19395994. Accessed 14 Oct 2020.

Bloch, Alice, and John Solomos, eds. 2010. *Race and Ethnicity in the 21st Century*. Basingstoke: Palgrave Macmillan.

Brunt, Rosalind, and Rinella Cere. 2010. *Postcolonial Media Culture in Britain*. Basingstoke: Palgrave Macmillan.

Campion, Mukti. 2005. *Look Who's Talking Cultural Diversity Public Service Broadcasting and the National Conversation*. Oxford: Nuffield college Oxford.

Christians, Clifford, Theodore Glasser, Kaarle Nordenstreng, and Robert White, eds. 2009. *Normative Theories of the Media – Journalism in Democratic Societies*. Urbana and Chicago: University of Illinois Press.

Clarke, C., C. Peach, and S. Vertovec, eds. 1990. *South Asians Overseas Migration and Ethnicity*. Cambridge: Cambridge University Press.

Condor, Susan, Stephen Gibson, and Jackie Abell. 2006. English Identity and Ethnic Diversity in the Context of UK Constitutional Change. *Ethnicities* 6 (2): 123–158.

Fenton, Steve. 1999. *Ethnicity: Racism, Class and Culture*. Basingstoke: Palgrave Macmillan.

Fitzgerald, Richard, and William Housley. 2007. Talkback, Community and the Public Sphere. *Media International Australia* 122 (1): 150–163.

Fortier, Anne-Marie. 2000. *Migrant Belongings: Memory, Space, Identity*. Oxford: Berg Publishers.

Gandy, Oscar H. 1998. *Communication and Race*. New York/London: Hodder Arnold.

Gillespie, Marie. 1995. *Television, Ethnicity and Cultural Change*. London/New York: Routledge.

Gordon, Janey, ed. 2012. *Community Radio in the Twenty-First Century*. Bern, Oxford: Peter Lang.

Gunaratnam, Yasmin. 2003. *Researching 'race' and Ethnicity: Methods, Knowledge and Power.* London: Sage.

Hall, Stuart. 1986. Gramsci Relevance for the Study of Race and Ethnicity. *Journal of Communication Inquiry* 10 (2): 5–27.

Hall, Stuart, and Paul du Gay, eds. 1996. *Questions of Cultural Identity.* London: Sage Publications.

Hendy, David. n.d. One of Us? Make Yourself at Home In 1965, the BBC Launched Its First Programmes Specially for Immigrants. What Were They like? And Did They Deliver? BBC Website. https://www.bbc.com/historyofthebbc/100-voices/people-nation-empire/make-yourself-at-home

Hesmondhalgh, David, and Anamik Saha. 2013. Race, Ethnicity, and Cultural Production. *Popular Communication* 11 (3): 179–195.

Hesse, Barnor. 2000. *Unsettled Multiculturalisms: Diasporas, Entanglements, 'Transruptions'.* London/New York: Zed Books.

Khamkar, Gloria. 2017. The Evolution of British Asian Radio in England: 1960–2004' Bournemouth University. http://eprints.bournemouth.ac.uk/29335/.

Kruper, A. 1999. *Culture: The Anthropologists' Account.* Cambridge, MA: Harvard University Press.

Lewis, Peter M., and Jerry Booth. 1989. *The Invisible Medium Public, Commercial and Community Radio.* Basingstoke: Macmillan.

Loomba, Ania. 2015. *Colonialism/Postcolonialism.* 3rd ed. London/New York: Routledge.

Love, Ryan. 2010. BBC Defends "EastEnders" Qu'ran Treatment'. *Digital Spy*, 21 July 2010, sec. soaps. https://www.digitalspy.com/soaps/eastenders/a247881/bbc-defends-eastenders-quran-treatment/

Madianou, Mirca. 2005. Contested Communicative Spaces: Rethinking Identities, Boundaries and He Role of the Media Among Turkish Speakers in Greece. *Journal of Ethnic and Migration Studies* 31 (3): 521–541.

Malik, Sarita. 2002. *Representing Black Britain, Black and Asian Images on Television.* London: Sage.

———. 2008. Keeping It Real, the Politics of Channel 4 Multiculturalism, Mainstreaming and Mandates. *Screen* 49 (3): 343–353.

———. 2013. The Indian Family on UK Reality Television: Convivial Culture in Salient Context. *Television & New Media* 14 (6): 510–528.

Matsaganis, M.D., and V.S. Katz. 2014. How Ethnic Media Producers Constitute Their Communities of Practice: An Ecological Approach. *Journalism* 15 (7): 926–944.

McCrone, D. 2002. Who Do You Say You Are? *Ethnicities* 2: 301–320.

Morely, David, and Kuan-Hsing Chen. 1996. *Stuart Hall Critical Dialogues in Cultural Studies.* London: Routledge.

Moylan, Katie. 2013. *Broadcasting Diversity, Migrant Representation in Irish Radio*. Bristol: Intellect.

Murdock. Graham. 2005. Public Broadcasting and Democratic Culture: Consumers, Citizens and Communards in Wasko, Janet. Eds A Campion to Television. Oxford :Blackwell Publishing

Naficy, Hamid. 2001. *An Accented Cinema: Exilic and Diasporic Filmmaking*. Princeton/Oxford: Princeton University Press.

Ofcom. 2013. Ethnic Minority Groups and Communication Services. Research report.

———. 2018. Representation and Portray on BBC Television. https://www.ofcom.org.uk/__data/assets/pdf_file/0022/124078/report-bbc-representation-portrayal.pdf. Accessed 14 Oct 2020.

———. 2019. Review of BBC News and Current Affairs, 31. https://www.ofcom.org.uk/__data/assets/pdf_file/0025/173734/bbc-news-review.pdf. Accessed 14 Oct 2020.

Parekh, Bhikhu. 2000. *The Future of Multi-Ethnic Britain*. London: Profile Books.

Poole, Elizabeth, and Richardson E. John, eds. 2006. *Muslims and the News Media*. London: I B Tauris.

Price, Stuart, and Ruth S. Sabido, eds. 2015. *Contemporary Protest and the Legacy of Dissent*. London: Rowman and Littlefield.

Proctor, Kate. 2020. "Tone-Deaf" Ministers Reject BAME Review of English Curriculum. *The Guardian*, 30 July 2020, sec. Education. https://www.the-guardian.com/education/2020/jul/30/exclusive-tone-deaf-ministers-reject-bame-review-of-english-curriculum

RAJAR Q2. 2018. retrieved from https://www.rajar.co.uk/docs/2018_06/2018_Q2_Quarterly_Summary_Figures.pdf

Said, E. 1978. *Orientalism*. Harmondsworth: Penguin.

Sharma, S., John Hutnyk, and Ashwani Sharma. 1996. *Dis-Orienting Rhythms, The Politics of the New Asian Dance Music*. London: Zed Books.

Shohat, Ella, and Robert Stam. 2014. *Unthinking Eurocentrism Multiculturalism and the Media*. 2nd ed. Abingdon: Routledge.

Shome, Raka. 2016. When Postcolonial Studies Meets Media Studies. *Critical Studies in Media Communication* 33 (3): 245–263.

Sian, Katy P. 2011. "Forced" Conversions in the British Sikh Diaspora. *South Asian Popular Culture* 9 (2): 115–130.

Sreberny, Annabelle. 2005. Not Only, But Also': Mixedness and Media. *Journal of Ethnic and Migration Studies* 31 (3): 443–459.

Yu, S. Sherry, and M.D. Matsaganis. 2019. *Ethnic Media in the Digital Age*. New York: Routledge.

CHAPTER 4

Recruitment and Progression of Minority Ethnic Staff

INTRODUCTION

The BBC is not the UK leader in terms of having a diverse workforce, Channel 4 and ViacomCBS fare more strongly when it comes to recruiting minority ethnic staff (Ofcom 2020). However, Ofcom has singled out the radio sector in the UK for failing to reflect minority communities (Ofcom 2019a, 2020). In 2019 Ofcom radio broadcasters to set targets and delivery dates to assess their progress in this area. The BBC reports that approximately £7.3 million has been spent on entry-level schemes to specifically widen access to employment across the institution (BBC 2018a, p. 4). These schemes enable young people who have not attended university to apply for training alongside specific disability schemes. The principle aim of these schemes is to recruit Black, Asian, and Minority ethnic (BAME) staff or disabled staff by simplifying the barriers some communities face accessing the BBC. For example, the New Voices scheme has enabled people with no broadcast experience to participate in open auditions for BBC Local Radio to present 150 new evening shows (BBC 2019, p. 13). The BBC has also committed itself to narrowing the gender pay gap following the high-profile employment tribunal of journalist Samira Ahmed in 2019.

This chapter focuses on inequality in terms of ethnicity in recruitment and progression within the BBC. Therefore, there is an examination of recruitment practices, the barriers, and challenges BBC interviewees face.

© The Author(s), under exclusive license to Springer Nature Switzerland AG 2021
G. Aujla-Sidhu, *The BBC Asian Network*,
https://doi.org/10.1007/978-3-030-65764-2_4

The information used throughout the chapter was gathered through in-depth interviews with thirty members of BBC staff who held a range of roles within the organisation, from broadcast assistants, to editors, and the Controller. The staff perspectives are contrasted with employment statistics from the BBC and data from their focus groups. The material reveals that some differences exist in the terms of knowledge about the Asian communities, especially among the "integrated" employees. There was also a difference of opinions over whom the station should be targeting and how the content ought to be framed for the target listener. In addition, there is an examination of integration and assimilation from the point of view of ethnic journalists working at the BBC. The minority ethnic staff employed by the BBC Asian Network contribute to the BBC's reflection of UK society and they also educate and inform mainstream audiences about British Asians in keeping with their public service ethos.

Diversity and Inclusion Targets in the BBC

Director General of the BBC, Tim Davie, outlined when he was the Chief Executive Officer that whilst the BBC has made progress in tackling diversity "it's taking too long to see the change that we expect within our workforce" (BBC 2018a, p. 1). Whilst some departments within the BBC have small numbers of ethnic minority workers, at the BBC Asian Network, the journalists recruited are primarily from British Asian backgrounds. They are a mix of first- and second-generation British Asian journalists who joined the station when it was a regional service and the latter group, who are younger, educated to degree and postgraduate levels, born and raised in the UK, and belong to third and sometimes fourth generation of British Asians. The interviews revealed differences of opinions between the multiple generations of British Asian employees leading to disagreement within the team over working practices, strategies to engage the desired listener, and skillset. It emerged in the interviews that younger staff who are third or fourth generation of British Asian are likely to be middle class, assimilated, and westernised (these concepts are examined in detail later in this chapter). In contrast, first- and second-generation British Asians may have been born abroad, often speak a South Asian language, and are likely to have learned journalism skills on the job or from broadcasting experience abroad, notably Africa. Husain Husaini, who worked at the station as the former head of Programmes and head of News, described how he recruited:

We had a mixed staff they came from different backgrounds and they tend to know different parts of the audience and some people had no connection with the audience. You can have some of those in the mix but not too many, there always had to be people who had some understandings of the communities. (Former head of Programmes, Husain Husaini 2015)

What became evident in the research is that although British Asians are born in the UK, they are also knowledgeable about the different Asian cultures and have diasporic connections with the Global South through links across the world with family and friends. Therefore, the diaspora operates within "transnational spaces" because they are part of the British community meaning they situate themselves in the British Asian community, identify with Britain, and maintain a globalised identity (Moylan 2013, p. 8). In essence, this inherent transcultural knowledge and wisdom informs their media practices and the content created for the Asian Network is best described as "accented radio" (Moylan 2013, 2018). The concept is borrowed from Naficy (2001) who described the process of film making where migrants speak to their community as an "accented mode of production." Katie Moylan (2018) argues that it is important to examine and categorise programmes that are produced by and for minority groups as "accented radio" as opposed to "ethnic media" because the latter can reinforce hierarchies of difference. In other words that ethnic audiences can be considered inferior or less important in comparison to mainstream audiences. Moylan (2018) also argues that if minority programming on community radio is understood in the framework of accented radio, this enables the study of identity, mode of address, and the articulation of the prevalent social political norms. Moylan (2018) focused explicitly upon community radio, however, the BBC as a public service provider is required to not only serve all communities but also to showcase that it is achieving its diversity targets for staff recruitment and on-screen representation. The BBC Asian Network operates as an ethnic service within the public service broadcaster, meaning that it has a unique opportunity to articulate minority concerns and perspectives to wider mainstream audiences. Riaan (*not his real name*), a producer at the station, explained that in addition to core journalism skills, ethnic staff offer the BBC bonus skills.

The Asian network is broadcasting to a marginalised audience, or an audience that isn't served elsewhere by the BBC. I think as ethnic producers we are uniquely skilled to do that, we have the same skills as producers across the BBC, but we have that extra bit of knowledge about our audience and so every time we put together a programme, I think that instinctive knowledge of our audience comes to the forefront. (Producer, Riaan 2015)

Riaan describes the knowledge and awareness of diverse cultures as being instinctive. He implies that ethnic journalists offer the BBC a unique perspective which can be language skills, specialist knowledge of Bollywood or Asian music alongside cultural awareness. The BBC has been harnessing the extra skills minority ethnic staff possess by recruiting them into roles across regional radio and television newsrooms. Kaylon *(not his real name)* has worked for both BBC Asian Network and BBC's regional television.

Even though I am not Muslim, I am more aware of how things work in a Mosque. You have got those contacts and you are a bit more comfortable. I think it's important that the BBC is serving the diversity of the country and it recognises that hiring people from different backgrounds is perhaps a better way of getting the contacts. (Former Journalist, Kaylon 2016)

Kaylon believes that minority staff can foster trust and build relationships with diverse audiences easily. This is beneficial because the BBC is mandated to serve all audiences. Sam (*not her real name*), a senior journalist at the station, explained she is able to make connections with potential contributors on sensitive issues because she is able to communicate in South Asian languages: "Even though they were scared to say anything, they are willing to talk to me simply because I use their language. They all spoke Gujarati and I speak Gujarati." Sam also observed that the press now routinely sends ethnic journalists to cover terror-related news, "they dispatch their Asian journalists even though they may not necessarily be on that beat." This indicates that it is not just a BBC policy to use minority journalists for some stories. Safia (*not her real name*) a reporter believes it is imperative that ethnic reporters are given greater opportunities to cover diverse stories because it is not logical to "send somebody out who doesn't understand" Asian languages or issues. Moreover, she highlighted that traditionally specialisms or beats exist within the sector such as politics or business, and thus, it is essential that race-related issues are covered by journalists who can speak and understand a South Asian language.

I think anybody who works there should know the language, at least one of the languages [...] I can understand certain cultural sensitivities, which my white counterparts might not, and they might just look editorial balance and say we will have that, and it balances itself out. But being a member of the Asian community, being Muslim, I know the sensitivities, so I think it is important to have that. The Asian Network understands the cultural sensitivities and I feel it is a big tick. (Reporter, Safia 2015)

Safia suggests that new journalists need to be member of the minority communities to fully understand the issues Asian communities face, those who lack lived experiences may not sufficiently examine issues with the clarity or depth they deserve. She also recognised that most media organisations see the benefit of accessing communities through language, "I can say certain words and it can connect me with somebody whereas if an English reporter goes into that community, they won't have that connection. There will be a distance." Kaylon also highlighted that his ethnicity enabled him to obtain interviews with members of diverse communities in contrast to his non-minority colleagues:

They had more challenging experiences when they were at Bury Park, Luton. A really predominately Pakistani Muslim part of Luton, and for varied reasons, perhaps found that the shutters came up. I found it a lot easier. There was less suspicion perhaps. (Former Journalist, Kaylon 2016)

Kaylon noted that because mainstream media find it difficult to engage minority communities they can inadvertently be side-lined. He believes his gender and ethnic background have been helpful to connect with ethnic communities. Sam underlined that she is supported by editors who have cultural awareness to investigate specialist ethnic stories:

I think I'm able to do the type of stories that wouldn't necessarily get supported elsewhere or there would be no scope for me to do the type of stories that I uncover. Why would you pose the questions if you didn't have prior knowledge of that area, for example, know how British Asians were using fertility treatment, to develop a potential story? (Senior Journalist, Sam 2015)

Sam acknowledges that some of the content featured on the Asian Network is unique to the station and perhaps would not be encouraged or understood in other departments because editorial staff may lack South Asian knowledge to support staff endeavours.

Internally the BBC has been trying to accelerate the recruitment of minority staff across the organisation and to address the perception that it is institutionally white. However, despite its success in attracting diverse staff to the organisation, the numbers of minority staff who leave the BBC is also high (BBC 2018b). Ahmed (2012, p. 33) points out that diversity initiatives that specifically focus on the inclusion of people of colour or disability also reveal "the whiteness of what is already in place" because inclusion targets reveal the absence or failure of diversity. Whilst 14 per cent of the BBC's workforce is classified as minority ethnic employees, in line with the national representation of minority groups in the UK most Black, Asian, and Minority ethnic (BAME) staff are predominantly employed in either the professional service or the World Service Group. The professional service division encompasses the business services of the BBC, legal and corporate finance roles, procurement, commercial rights, and business affairs. The World Service includes production roles, where the primary function is to broadcast material in other languages to various parts of the world. The numbers of BAME staff working in creative areas or programme making remain low, especially in BBC local radio and regional television newsrooms which are in diverse cities such as Birmingham, Manchester, and Leicester (BBC 2018b, p. 5). Nadine (*not her real name*), a senior manager in the BBC, emphasised that schemes to recruit minority staff ought to be measured through the "retainment of staff, and whether that staff is retained within the BBC, and I think that's still a work in progress." The strategy to recruit minority ethnic reporters has two benefits: the number of minority staff across the BBC continues to grow and in turn the on-air reflection is improved. However, it is simplistic to expect that minority ethnic staff desire to specifically report or produce content only about and for minority groups because this elides the employees' interests or specialist skills and tacitly allows an employee's ethnic identity to remain salient through the ethnocentrism of the workplace (Husband 2005). Interestingly, non-ethnic staff find that their ethnicity is effectively invisible and subsequently not discussed. Minority ethnic staff working in mainstream media can find fusing their ethnic identity with their media roles difficult, due to the way the race is framed in terms of immigration, asylum seekers, and difference. Husband (2005) argues that mainstream media actively seek ethnic staff to address their deficiencies in reporting and to fulfil diversity targets. However, he suggests that the "class and educational profile of young people from many minority ethnic communities effectively inhibits their entry into the media industries, irrespective of active or indirect discrimination" (Husband 2005, p. 469). He suggests the media can hide behind the guise of "professional standards" within journalism which demands an emotional detachment from the audience and from the issue, or story, itself in order to create objective and impartial news content. The implication is that ethnic staff are less able to detach themselves from their communities or heritage, and this poses a risk to the so-called professional standards of journalism. Radio broadcasters have not been required to collate data on the socio-economic class of their employees. However, the Diversity in Television report in 2019 found that media employees who work in television were twice as likely to have attended private school compared to the working age population more generally (Ofcom 2019b). The intersectionality of race and class is especially relevant to the study of recruitment and career progression of minority staff in media roles.

Matsaganis and Katz (2014) have examined how ethnic media producers in Los Angeles negotiate and develop their professional identity through their interaction with mainstream media and the communities they serve. They found that the producer's identity is influenced and shaped by managerial ideologies, newsroom norms, routines, and institutional imperatives, and crucially, managerial ideologies conflict with established production routines. They also found that the amount of power an editor or publisher has is determined by the organisational structure as opposed to managerial norms.

Mya (*not her real name*), a reporter argued in her interview that the pace of change will progress only occur when "you have Black and Asian people actually in senior positions" where decisions are made—"that's when you are going to see a real difference." However, she also highlighted that minority staff who occupy senior roles tend to reflect the status quo.

These people often come from private education backgrounds. They have been to Oxford and Cambridge, so you got people very similar to people who represent the hierarchy within the BBC coming from very similar upper-class backgrounds. (Reporter, Mya 2015)

Many organisations face this conundrum because there is a tendency to recruit people based on shared values and beliefs. Mya outlines that there is a difference of opinion and understanding between the journalists at the lower end of the pay scale and the senior roles—even when minority ethnic staff are placed into them—with the implication being that they lack an understanding of the audiences the BBC seeks to serve. This point emerged in other interviews; one interviewee emphasised it was problematic that the management of the BBC Asian Network had at periods of time been devolved to non-ethnic staff.

In 2020 the Controller of Pop is Lorna Clarke (she oversees Radio 1, 2, 1Xtra, Asian Network, and 6 Music). Head of BBC Asian Network is Ahmed Hussain, and he is supported by the head of News, Arif Ansari, and editor, Khaliq Meer (Commissioning and Programmes). This is a diverse team, notably Clarke, Ansari, and Hussain are from minority ethnic backgrounds. However, when the interviews took place in 2015–2016, the team was led by former Controller, Bob Shennan (now BBC Group Managing Director), Mark Strippel, head of Programmes, and head of News, Kevin Silverton. "I just don't think they are ethnic enough" (Kamran, former producer, 2015). Kamran *(not his real name)* pointed out that it is imperative senior staff have specialist knowledge pertaining to Asian culture, music, and religious festivals: "We still get people who say, 'What is Eid?' Can you explain that to me?" In Kamran's opinion, senior staff working at Radio 2 and 1Xtra are superior in terms of skills:

> The knowledge that they have of their genre of music is incredible. They inspire you; they push you and tell you that's not right. So, you want that bit of guidance. But the knowledge is lacking at the BBC Asian Network. (Former Producer, Kamran 2015)

This is revealing insight into the internal culture at a radio station historically accused by DCMS of having lower editorial standards (Gardem 2004, p. 47). Kamran believes production staff are not supported in their roles which he attributes directly with the ethnicity of managers. Kamlesh Purohit expressed a similar viewpoint:

> It is part of the BBC's remit to develop talent from within the Asian community. For me, the BBC hasn't succeeded in developing talent from within the Asian community into senior managers. If the BBC can't have senior Asian managers on an Asian output – what chances are there of having senior management on the rest of the output? (Former Asian Network Senior Journalist, Kamlesh Purohit 2015)

Across BBC Radio only 9 per cent of staff from minority ethnic backgrounds (Ofcom 2019, p. 8). Purohit's interview took place in 2015 a period when key management roles were not occupied by minority ethnic members of staff. Purohit was also not convinced that minority ethnic staff receive the support they require to progress through the appraisal process, development opportunities, or in-house training to move into more senior roles. Across the BBC 11.5 per cent of staff employed in leadership roles across the BBC are from BAME (Black, Asian, and Minority ethnic) backgrounds (BBC Annual Report 2018–19, p. 259). To combat barriers to progression, the BBC has recommended that shortlists for senior roles should include at least one BAME candidate. Hence, internally there is a stronger drive to ensure that interview panels are diverse and that managers better support BAME staff, by identifying career development opportunities. In addition, accountability targets will be set for managers pertaining to diversity and inclusion (BBC 2018b, p. 8). Whilst these strategies place the responsibility upon senior leaders to be supportive and held to account, they do not appear to give any tangible mechanism for non-management staff to support diversity and inclusion strategies. Sara Ahmed (2012) argues such recommendations contribute to professionalisation of diversity because it is imperative all employers visibly showcase their recruitment figures or positive images of their organisation. When visibly ethnic staff are recruited by organisations there is an underlying demand upon them to conform to institutional norms, for example, "to share in it or have a share of it, requires not only that one inhabits its buildings but that one follows its lines" (Ahmed 2012, p. 39). This means that any employee who is unable to follow the ethos of an employer is unlikely to succeed, but the internal culture remains unchanged and the duty to conform is placed firmly upon the employee. Saha (2018) also presents a similar view, recommending that diversity has been commodified in the cultural industries to generate financial reward or gain for the employers. Both these perspectives suggest the challenge is not simply recruiting minority employees but retaining employees, which involves changing cultures.

The diversity and equal opportunities study by Ofcom acknowledges that whilst radio needs to improve the recruitment of minority ethnic employees, BBC radio leads the way in confronting the issue with focussed initiatives (Ofcom 2019a, p. 20). There are some weaknesses with how media organisations report figures to Ofcom, the regulator has recognised that how the data is collated and reported needs to be re-examined to establish where representation of specific groups in the workforce is lacking. One significant shortcoming of the diversity assessment by Ofcom is that freelance staff are excluded, yet they account for one-third of the total workforce in radio production. Data on race, gender, or disability is not collected on freelance journalists by the broadcasters.

GETTING INTO THE BBC

Media work is described as precarious; it is difficult to break into and tough to progress to senior levels (Hesmondhalgh 2019). One significant view is that the creative industries favour employees from wealthy backgrounds and the middle classes because they are more able to freelance or work for free whilst relying upon another source of income to get their foot in the door (Hesmondhalgh and Baker 2011). Potential employees who possess the relevant work experience, a degree, or postgraduate qualification find there are limited numbers of permanent or fixed-term contracts and freelance which means they effectively work on zero-hour contracts. The hours are long and because the supply of workers exceeds the demand, salaries remain depressed. They also note that women aged in their late thirties and mid-forties are less visible in some roles due to the long hours these careers may demand.

> I feel as though there are barriers to Asian people coming into our industry. I feel as though Asian people have to work a lot harder to prove their skills and demonstrate what they can do. (Producer, Riaan 2015)

One reason Riaan perceives there are barriers is because there appears to be an underlying requirement for ethnic journalists to prove themselves, their experience, and professional credentials when they pitch story ideas for the wider BBC (see Chap. 6). Riaan's perspective is interesting given that the BBC is working to widen access to the institution and to remove perceived barriers to improve career progression. The BBC's own research into the internal culture within the organisation found that ethnic minority employees feel that "opportunities are lacking for BAME staff development and progression. Some believe this is the result of favouritism conscious bias" (BBC 2018a, p. 7). What also emerged is the lack of understanding internally of other cultures and that many non-ethnic staff perceived mainstream content featuring some diversity as having fully addressed and meeting the diversity and inclusion agenda.

In contrast, Alia (*not her real name*), a former senior manager, offered a different perspective, arguing the key problem with the recruitment system is that new ethnic journalists lack cultural knowledge about the British Asian communities, despite coming from those backgrounds.

> There are people working at the Asian Network who do not know the Asian community because they haven't lived in it. They probably live in a very westernised household then moved on to university and then got into their job. (Former senior manager, Alia 2015)

The term "westernised" is used to describe British Asian households where a South Asian language may not be spoken regularly or where some cultural and religious traditions are no longer adhered to. Unlike some of the other BBC employees, who emphasised the extra specialist knowledge and benefits they bring to the BBC, Alia is concerned that people are hired who lack specialist knowledge. Furthermore, she explained that the lack of knowledge about Bollywood movies is often treated as an office joke in the newsroom. Owen Bentley, former editor of BBC Radio Leicester concurred with Alia; he recommended in his interview that there is value in hiring presenters who have lived experiences and knowledge of their listeners; "if you have a hinterland behind you of a much broader experience than a narrow journalism degree you are probably going to be much better in the presentation stakes." Kamran, a former producer who had some involvement in recruitment also recognised that the lack of knowledge among some workers was an issue.

> I would employ anybody who has got passion over the skill because you can teach skills, but you can't teach passion. But I guess it is easier to hire somebody who knows how to use all the facilities because then there is less training involved and it means you can get them in doing stuff quicker. You could be the best producer at Radio 1 but that doesn't mean you can knock out a Bollywood show, or the breakfast show. They [the management] are not seeing that. There are people out there who would die to work at Asian Network, their knowledge of music, film, different genres of music, independent music bhangra, Asian urban stuff is immense, but they are not going to get a chance at the Asian Network. This includes presenters as well, because they don't know the BBC way. (Former producer, Kamran 2016)

It is implied that specialist cultural knowledge of Asian arts is secondary to specialist journalism skills for some roles. It is possible that the broadcaster places an emphasis upon journalism and digital skills because they are transferable to other roles in the BBC, and thereby, cultural knowledge is less significant. Mark Strippel, former head of Programmes, explained new employees do need to:

> Demonstrate the cultural awareness is there and the judgement calls they would need to make on a regular basis. That's really important and the broader experience. You would never appoint someone for the Asian Network just on the basis of ethnicity you need a broad range of skills. (Former Head of Programmes, Mark Strippel 2015)

The obligation to have the relevant skills and experience for media careers is placed upon the potential employees. Ursell (2000) has noted that experienced directors, camera, and lighting specialists are able to command good salaries but at the lower or entry-level roles, newcomers and those with less experience tend to work for very little or nothing. Most graduates feel compelled to intern for free to learn about production processes or gain newsroom experience in the hope that the contacts they make and skills achieved will help start their careers.

Internships and work experience have become been normalised in the creative sector and this has a dire impact upon the class composition of employees because only those with wealth can afford to labour for free (Randle 2015). Hesmondhalgh (2017, 2019) has also noted that people working in production roles in the media tend to be from higher or middle-class backgrounds, and this results in the poor representation of working-class life and interests. Hesmondhalgh (2017) has labelled this as "class asymmetry explanation," in other words, media staff have inherently different interests, experiences, and values to the working class who are also part of the audience (in Deery and Press 2017, p. 24). It is an argument supported by O'Brien et al. (2016); they examined the composition of the creative industries by drawing on the 2014 British Labour Force and revealed there is a significant under-representation of working-class people. One explanation offered is that the working conditions are "poor" due to a high number of short-term contract roles, an emphasis upon freelance work, and low or no salary (O'Brien et al. 2016, p. 117). Whilst diversity targets tackle issues such as under-representation of gender or disability, Randle (2015) has argued that there is no legislative imperative to tackle class disadvantage, and moreover, it is less obvious how this can be addressed.

The issue of class arose in several interviews, due in part because the BBC Asian Network successfully appeals to working-class British Asian listeners in contrast to other parts of the BBC (Eustace 2016). Other BBC radio stations find it difficult to attract working-class listeners. Mark Strippel was proud of this achievement but explained it is difficult to reflect the listeners.

> We have much more flow of staff than we used to with more interns coming in. I see a broad range of people from across society. The truth is as well; the Asian audience is quite working class focused in many ways. But it's not just working class there's middle class. One of the key factors around Asian audiences is that there has always been a real focus on higher education, it sits in the centre of the family. I see our staff group and it changes and shifts ethnically and geographically across the country. (Mark Strippel 2015)

Strippel broadly believes the staff are reflective of the listener. It is perhaps impossible for any media organisation to be entirely reflective of all the groups that comprise the audience. The Asian community is broadly described as working class (Bennett et al. 2009). However, Brah (in Ali et al. 2006) and others have demonstrated that class differentiation does exist among south Asian groups (see Chap. 3). Although there is an established bourgeoisie and a professional/entrepreneurial middle class, the majority of British Asians remain within the working-class group. Pakistani and Bangladeshi communities tend to be employed in blue collar roles and continue to live in inner cities (Ali et al. 2006). This influences who applies to work within the cultural sector. (O'Brien et al. 2016) suggest that only people who share similar backgrounds, tastes, and experiences to the interviewing panel are successful in gaining entry, and this maintains the dominance of middle-class and male employees. The Bourdieusian approach to class is distinctive because it creates a separation between high (elite or establishment) culture and so-called popular culture. Cultural capital is embedded into societal structures enabling the educated middle classes to appreciate the arts. Owen Bentley, former editor of Radio Leicester, highlighted that when the soap Silver Street was launched on the Asian Network in 2004, it was evident that British Asian listening habits differed to Radio 4 listeners.

> It was set up in Birmingham and very good people were recruited to run it and write for it. But it never took off. That has a lot do with listening habits

if you never been used to a soap opera you don't then get into it on radio especially when there was huge competition from commercial Asian TV networks. But one thing I noticed as an outsider to the Asian community was that the people, they had recruited were basically not in touch with the working-class Asian community at all. They were all Asian graduates, very much of the London literary scene. The soap never really ever managed to get down to an average Asian family in Birmingham or Leeds or whatever. (Owen Bentley 2015)

Bentley recognises the value of appointing writers who have a range of lived experiences. He did recognise that Asian listeners had not previously been exposed to a radio soap, he also acknowledges the failure could be attributed to the story lines that failed to connect with the core BBC Asian Network listener. Bela *(not her real name)*, on the other hand, emphasised that

We [the staff] come from families who are our listeners who don't have a Higher Education. So, we're still very connected to the community. I've got members of my family who haven't been to University and because we have such large families you can still pinpoint a working-class family, they're not all professionals. So, I feel like we are better at reflecting class than other radio stations. (Producer, Bela 2015)

Although the preferred or ideal employee for the station is required to have a range of skills, there is a broad consensus that prospective candidates ought to have an insight into the lived experience of the British Asian lifestyle, so that they are able to bond and relate to the listeners. A minority of the staff found it problematic that new members of staff do not feel compelled to engage or learn about Asian culture or music as part of their role. Other interviewees believe the senior broadcast journalists and editors ought to have a stronger knowledge of British Asian communities and preferably also be British Asian.

Westernised, Mainstream, Integrated, and Assimilated

The qualitative interviews also offered an insight into how BBC producers envisage their listeners and understand their fellow colleagues. It is important to emphasise that identity was only discussed within the context of being a BBC employee and the audience, and not necessarily in terms of the participants' personal life. Key phrases such as "westernised," integration, assimilated, and mainstream were used to describe fourth and fifth generations of British Asians living in the UK. The terminology "integrated" or "assimilated" mirrors official legislation on race and immigration. Assimilation is understood to be a situation where minorities choose to dilute or relinquish their culture and adopt the culture and practices of society (Bloch and Solomos 2010, p. 187). Meaning, minorities adopt the practices of the new host nation, for example, embracing British clothing over traditional costume, or speaking English instead of their mother tongue. Integration, on the other hand, entails the maintenance of some cultural practices along with a contribution to society. Sikhs, for example, are depicted by both the government and media as integrated, and this is showcased as a positive attribute because integration is considered to be a catalyst for cohesion (Sian 2011). Official indicators of integration include employment, education, and contribution to society. Heath et al. (in Blochs and Solomos 2010) suggests that most minority communities adopt the "integration strategy" and thus preserve a strong and positive affiliation with their ethnic heritage and a relationship to the wider British society. The prevailing contemporary political discourse presented in the media is the need, on the part of immigrants, to integrate into British society, with an onus on them to conform to perceived British norms and values.

Britain is associated with the term "multiculturalism." The term is linked with the acceptance and celebration of diverse cultures, religions, and ethnicities and promotes the concept of unity and an ambition to collectively build a common life. However, it has been critiqued as being "slippery and fluid" because multiculturalism can be associated or understood in many ways and in different contexts (Lentin and Titley 2011, p. 2). Uberoi and Modood (2013) recommend that multiculturalism should be understood in three distinct ways: as simply diverse citizens, as an ideology to create an inclusive environment and to reduce fear of immigration. Whilst anti-discrimination measures naturally affect the identity of a nation, it does not mean the nation's character or a person's sense of their identity becomes "wholly different" because identity is inevitably conditioned by the history of the society. However, ideology can be utilised to create a vision which re-imagines the nation (Uberoi and Modood 2013, p. 132). Fortier (2008) holds a similar viewpoint that multiculturalism is a societal construct which is informed by historical events and views and is used by media and politicians to advocate a vision of social cohesion.

She explains that ethnicity is primarily understood in British politics to signify difference from British culture with an underlying expectation that this can be exchanged for citizenship. However, it is suggested that multiculturalism as a concept or idea is now absent in politics, and therefore, the media try to depict diversity within the context of mainstream media programmes (Saha 2018; Malik 2013).

Multiculturalism was very rarely discussed by the interviewees to describe British Asian culture or lifestyle; instead, "mainstream" was used to express the listener, media content, or employees. Kamlesh Purohit believes that the concept of "mainstream" has created a gap between the staff and the listeners.

> A number of the journalists and producers who work at the Asian Network are people born in this country and they are mainstream in their outlook. They are not necessarily watching Bollywood movies and intimately in touch with Asian culture. Whereas the audiences are very different, particularly the older audiences. (Kamlesh Purohit 2015)

Purohit is concerned about difference of lifestyles, views, and practices that exist between the staff hired and the audience, especially the older listeners. He is aware that the British Asian identity is evolving and hence describes young British Asians as being mainstream in terms of their identity and lifestyle. His concern is that staff recruited from this base are not able to understand the issues that impact the British Asian community. Bob Shennan, the former Controller of the Asian Network, underlined why it is important the station adapts in response to the changing needs of the listeners:

> A lot of people who come from an Asian background have no relationship with it [The BBC Asian Network] at all, don't want one, they want to live in a totally mainstream world. I think what we are trying to do is to make an Asian Network that feels like a mainstream service but has some kind of clear sort of delineation that makes people feel comfortable in a kind of multifaceted life that they lead every day. (Former Controller, Bob Shennan 2015)

Shennan's core concern is that the on-air content must evolve with the listener and that the station accepts the different nuances of people's lives. Alia, a former senior manager, outlined in her interview that listeners are "losing their 'Asian-ness', they are becoming more westernised and more integrated, so they don't rely heavily on the Asian culture and identity." This gives the impression whilst she accepts changes within the young demographic of British Asians, she is also worried about the future of the station. She described how the mix of staff work together.

> We have Asian people working here who do not consume Asian entertainment, who cannot speak an Asian language, who probably have Asian food once a month. We've also got people who are totally engrossed in that Asian world and probably watch a Bollywood movie twice a week. We've got a variety and somehow, you've got to find a balance. (Former Senior Member of Staff, Alia 2015)

It is implied that the balance has not been struck and it is ambiguous if it can indeed be found. There is not a huge difference between the notions mainstream and westernised, both describe people who have a hybrid identity that utilises aspects of both cultures to the individual's advantage. The deeper issue that Alia exposes is that the differences pertaining to cultural knowledge or capital between the different generations of Asian staff cause divisions. The older staff appear to want to focus on the needs of the heritage or older listener, whilst the younger staff, third- and fourth-generation British Asians, who may not consume Asian music or *Bollywood* regularly are able to chase the young listener as directed by the BBC but lack knowledge about the underlying issues affecting the listeners.

Identity is complex. It is considered to be a mixture of a person's cultural and ethnic heritage (e.g. their faith, language, or tradition), their nationality if relevant, and the values of the country they live in. Dey et al. (2017) found there are both differences and similarities with how British-born Asians and first-generation migrants adopt acculturation strategies. They outline that British-born South Asians are more attached to British culture due in part to their schooling and upbringing and thus find it easier to integrate with the mainstream population. They advocate understanding dual identity and differences in assimilation through the context of a quadripartite approach that considers consonance, context, convenience, and constraint. Their study found that people not only maintain some cultural practices but also embrace British values based on their compatibility with their new lives and that people adopt different behaviours depending on the situation or context they are in, for example, some British Asians celebrate both Christmas and Diwali. Bela, a producer, also had concerns about the gap between the BBC staff and the British Asian community in general.

> Where are the people who go and watch every Shahrukh Khan movie? I don't meet these people when I am out. I meet these people in the BBC office and I'll meet these people when we go and do an event. But will we [the station] be relevant in the future is a bit of a worrying question. I feel like we're so integrated but then there are other Asian communities who feel less integrated than they did i.e. the Muslim community. They probably feel quite isolated. (Producer, Bella 2015)

Bella also recognises that not all British Asians share the same tastes in music and the arts. She is worried that this makes her and the BBC out of touch with the average listener. What is evident is that she feels pressured to reach out to all British Asians. Although the remit does not specify this, there does appear to be unwritten convention that suggests British Asians ought to be compelled to engage with the BBC Asian Network.

Within the framework of this study, it was interesting to see how the interviewees conceptualised the listener. Some of the older staff seemed to apply a nation framework, in this instance the nation is understood to be South Asia and then the terminology "westernised," "integrated," and "assimilated," was used to "other" members who do not conform to the interviewee's preconceived notion of Asian identity. In other words, they sought to examine the degree to which other British Asian employees share in the dominant cultural behaviours of Asian lifestyle or habitus (Bourdieu 2010). Kamlesh Purohit also questioned the purpose of the station targeting younger Asians listeners:

> Apart from a bit of Bollywood I think most Asian youngsters are quite white in their interests, they follow mainstream music they watch Hollywood movies and follow football and sport. I am not sure if an Asian Network is really suitable for them. If you are a producer you think about targeting the younger audience, I am not sure how much that younger audience needs an Asian Network. (Kamlesh Purohit 2015)

The reference to "white" can be considered contentious because Purohit appears to suggest that it is regrettable that people are rejecting Asian music, arts, and culture in favour of Hollywood and football. It was assumed by most of the interviewees that the audience is connected to British Asian music, their culture or faith, and *Bollywood* and that they are also interested in British TV and music. Purohit points out that the young British Asian listener has a lower need for an ethnic-specific service. Both Purohit and Alia appear to view British Asians as belonging to two distinct groups, one that still is deeply connected to their culture and the other who are Asian in terms of their ethnic background only. Alia explained that some British-born Asians are unable to:

> Relate to us [the station] they can't relate to the music, they can't relate to the language, and if you talk about Amitabh Bachan or whoever they never seen a film of theirs. They're Asian in race, but they have no links with the Asian Network. (Former senior manager, Alia 2015)

Alia's perspective does not take into account variations or nuances to a person's identity and how it is informed by the legacy of their personal family history, religion, and culture and ignores how Britons including British Asians enact British norms, values, and heritage. In contrast, producer Riaan offered a nuanced viewpoint on the listener:

> Although they are British, they also have other parts which makes them who they are [...] so a British Asian girl who is 25 years old, although she watches EastEnders and consumes Rhianna and mainstream pop music, she also has an appetite for Bollywood because that is part of her culture. There is no harm in us nourishing that bit of culture. (Producer, Riaan 2015)

Riaan recognises that the listener is British first and foremost and he does not feel threatened by this. He accepts that being Asian is simply one aspect of the listener's identity and the station's role is to nurture Asian culture and maintain it for those listeners who are interested in it. Riaan's approach recognises that British Asians occupy a space in the UK that is unique, and he recognises that identity is complex and that not all British Asians identify exclusively with a so-called homeland or culture because it has become diluted.

The BBC has adopted a similar stance; it encourages a mainstream or integrated dissemination of young British Asian identity in line with the internal culture that exists within the organisation. This version of British Asian identity is also carefully curated, diluted, modified, and marketed at both British Asian and white British audiences (Burdsey 2004, p. 759). Consequently, this works to marginalise the experiences of working-class British Asian listener, despite the recognition by the former head of

Programme, Mark Strippel, that the British Asian listeners "quite working class-focused in many ways."

APPEALING TO LISTENERS

Media research has paid limited attention to the role of the radio producer. There are of course exceptions including Bonini and Monclus (2015) and Moylan (2013). A number of scholars have set out there is a link between the media producer's views and identity and the content created for broadcast because this process can be described as interpretive information or knowledge (Hesmondhalgh and Baker 2011; Mayer 2011). This means the type of content reflected on-air has an impact on how majority audiences perceive and understand minority ethnic groups.

> When I first took on the job the journalism the Asian Network could do and was doing just wasn't seen or heard or written anywhere else. My personal history had always been in creating journalism for audiences which are not necessarily the mainstream core. (Kevin Silverton 2015)

In his role as head of News, Kevin Silverton attempted to amplify British Asian news stories across the BBC by sharing the journalism so that majority audiences were also offered opportunities to hear/see complex diverse coverage. Media research has highlighted that minority voices are not given prominence within the media, and as such, their problems and views are not adequately reflected. Ethnic media is able to articulate their viewers and listeners voices to promote a sense of community and strengthen people's cultural and ethnic identities (Yu and Matsaganis 2019). One advantage of ethnic media is that listeners can discuss their concerns in their mother tongue and find relevant information and join a community of listeners. The Asian Network is an ethnic specialist service within an established public service institution, and this enables the BBC to showcase rich and meaningful creative original journalism:

> There aren't that many places in [BBC] radio news that you can be creative with your work. They have established styles, ie Radio 4 has a very distinctive style. Whereas the BBC Asian Network has more freedom. Also, the thing about BBC Asian Network was it was almost like a gem that hadn't been discovered in the BBC. It was something that kind of occasionally you

heard about but actually the content deserves much more of an airing across the BBC and in the country. (Former head of news, Kevin Silverton 2016)

Since 2012, The BBC Asian Network has been positioned as a centre of expertise upon British Asian audiences in the BBC. Other departments across the institution are encouraged to utilise the specialist knowledge of the staff in order to include authentic diverse content on their programmes. The station has faced particular challenges due in part to its incremental emergence from local radio specialist programming into a national digital radio station. Historically, both the employees at the station and the programme content were marginalised and considered inferior by other parts of the BBC. Mike Curtis was hired as the station's first news editor in 1996; in a book about the radio station he described working there as a lonely experience because "we always felt we were on our own – challenging, different and complicated" (Curtis 2014). The former Controller, Bob Shennan, highlighted how this has changed:

> A lot of our journalists now regularly appear on major BBC news outlets from the News Channel, to the Today Programme, to the BBC World Service, with their stories in a way it never happened 10 years ago. So, the BBC Asian Network influence gets beyond the radio station and that is part of our strategy to be less niche and less of a ghetto and more of a sort of source of content for the rest of the BBC. (Former Controller, Bob Shennan 2015)

The references to "niche" and "ghetto" acknowledge the history of the BBC Asian Network within the BBC, but the use of this terminology also reveals that the station is still peripheral despite the positioning by the management. Shennan is happy that ethnic journalists are successfully sharing their diverse stories across the BBC and thus contributing to the overall strategy of growing the brand and influence of the station. So far, this chapter has focused upon producers and journalists, but often these employees are invisible to the listener because listeners identify and bond with the station through the presenters. The presenters are the voices and faces of radio. Lacey (in Loviglio and Hilmes 2013) has suggested historically listeners were viewed as passive but in the digital era it is evident, they actively select what they want to listen to from podcasts, traditional radio, listen again options, and streaming services such as Spotify. Therefore, the role of the presenter to entice the intended audience to the output has become especially important.

> I think Noreen appeals to everyone because she has a cracking sense of humour. One thing Noreen's brilliant at is if there's nothing else going on, she will just have the mic and her, and she'll just make a brilliant show, because she's so good at interacting with the audience, and she's not afraid of what they are trying to say. (Producer, Joy 2015)

Noreen Khan, the afternoon presenter, was also one of the first presenters at the BBC Asian Network to strongly engage with social media through her YouTube Channel. Her "Khandaan" feature, launched in 2012 to around 2015, actively invited listeners to join her extended radio family, described by Noreen as being "an exclusive club." Raychaudhuri (2018) has noted that in this manner Khan was able to construct a community of listeners. Khan credits her success in engaging female listeners and increasing her programme's audience to social media:

> I think it just happened quite naturally and the listeners just grew and grew. I have the biggest Facebook account and I've got the biggest following on Twitter and I'm the most followed on Instagram. (Presenter, Noreen Khan 2015)

Khan also works as a stand-up female comedian and models designer Asian couture; this allows her to connect and interact with British Asian communities in several ways. Raychaudhuri (2018, p. 169) also singles out Noreen Khan and Harpz Kaur as two presenters on the Asian Network who use "diasporic nostalgia" and "make the case that the culture of diasporic immigrants is central to British national identity." In other words, both female presenters draw upon their listeners' interests, cultures, and histories, to articulate on-air a unique vision of British Asian identity which has naturally incorporated the histories of the diaspora. Similarly, Dipps Bhamrah, presenter of the Punjabi show on the station, is also a *Bhangra* artist and a DJ. He also outlined how he combines knowledge from all of his roles to engage with listeners on-air:

> I think the DJing side is important. If I am out DJing I am constantly with people, constantly performing going up and down the country that allows me to get a snapshot of what it is people want. (Presenter, Dipps Bhamrah 2015)

Bhamrah measures the success of new *Bhangra* at clubs or private functions and uses the knowledge to select music for his specialist community programme to curate a community through sound.

CONCLUSION

This chapter has tried to offer an insight into recruitment at the BBC and tried to look at progression or the lack of it and the knowledge needed to work at the BBC Asian Network as a producer. It is unclear if potential journalists must have specialist cultural knowledge alongside journalism and broadcasting skills or if British Asian knowledge is secondary. This can result in staff being hired who lack knowledge about the Asian communities, Asian music, or *Bollywood* and yet work on an ethnic-specific service because they have the relevant skillset. However, to remain a centre of expertise on British Asian communities the station requires staff who understand the differences and the similarities of the Asian communities. As noted by Dey et al. (2017) British Asian find meaning and identity in their concomitant interaction with their ethnic heritage, their nationality, and country of residence. This forces the BBC and the BBC Asian Network to continuously adapt to remain relevant. However, as this chapter has discussed increasingly the ethnic journalists hired into roles are considered to be "mainstream" or integrated in their unique outlook and this leaves some older staff to grapple with how to serve the listener who is now also becoming more mainstream and work colleagues who they do not understand. Also, it seems clear that minority ethnic staff are hired specifically to improve or enhance the articulation of race on-air, but they face challenges in enacting change and improving representations within the organisation.

REFERENCES

Ahmed, Sara. 2012. *On Being Included*. Durham/London: Duke University Press.
Ali, Nasreen, Virinder S. Kalra, and S. Sayyid, eds. 2006. *A Postcolonial People, South Asians in Britain*. London: Hurst & Co.
Alia. 2015 (anonymised). Face to face interview, 16 June.
BBC. 2018a. Reflecting the Socio-Economic Diversity of the UK within the BBC Workforce. A Report on Career Progression and Culture at the BBC. http://downloads.bbc.co.uk/mediacentre/socio-economic-diversity.pdf. Accessed on 14 Oct 2020.

———. 2018b. Reflecting the Ethnic Diversity of the UK within the BBC Workforce. A Report on Career Progression and Culture for BAME Staff at the BBC. http://downloads.bbc.co.uk/mediacentre/bame-career-progression-and-culture-report.pdf. Accessed 14 Oct 2020.

———. 2019. BBC Group Annual Report and Accounts 2018/19. https://downloads.bbc.co.uk/aboutthebbc/reports/annualreport/2018-19.pdf. Accessed 14 Oct.

Bela. 2015 (anonymised). Face to face interview, 9 November.

Bennett, Tony, Mike Savage, Elizabeth Silva, Alan Warde, Modesto Gayo-Cal, and David Wright. 2009. *Culture, Class, Distinction*. Abingdon: Routledge.

Bloch, Alice, and John Solomos, eds. 2010. *Race and Ethnicity in the 21st Century*. Basingstoke: Palgrave Macmillan.

Bob Shennan. 2015. Face to face interview, 11 November.

Bonini, Tiziano, and Belen Monclus, eds. 2015. *Radio Audiences and Participation in the Age of Network Society*. Abingdon: Routledge.

Bourdieu, Pierre. 2010. *Distinction: A Social Critique of the Judgement of Taste*. Abingdon: Routledge.

Burdsey, Daniel. 2004. "One of the Lads"? Dual Ethnicity and Assimilated Ethnicities in the Careers of British Asian Professional Footballers. *Ethnic and Racial Studies* 27 (5): 757–779.

Deery, June, and Andrea Press, eds. 2017. *Media and Class, TV Film and Digital Culture*. New York/London: Routledge.

Dey, Bidit Lal, John M.T. Balmer, Ameet Pandit, Mike Saren, and Ben Binsardi. 2017. A Quadripartite Approach to Analysing Young British South Asian Adults' Dual Cultural Identity. *Journal of Marketing Management* 33 (9–10): 789–816.

Dipps Bhamra. 2015. Face to face interview, 14 December.

Eustace, Mathew. 2016. BBC Asian Network Live Listening Performance Q1 2016 (6 Month Weight). BBC Marketing and Audiences. http://downloads.bbc.co.uk/commissioning/site/asian-network-indie-rajar-summary-q1-2016.pdf. Accessed 14 Oct 2020.

Fortier, Anne-Marie. 2008. Multicultural Horizons, Diversity and the Limits of the Civil Nation. Abingdon: Routledge.

Gardem, Tim. 2004. Independent Review of the BBC's Digital Radio Services. http://news.bbc.co.uk/nol/shared/bsp/hi/pdfs/19_10_04_digital_radio.pdf.

Hesmondhalgh, D. 2017. The Media's Failure to Represent the Working Class: Explanations from Media Production and Beyond in Deery, June. and Press, Andrea (eds) Media and Class, TV Film and Digital Culture. New York: Routledge.

Hesmondhalgh, David. 2019. *The Cultural Industries*. 4th ed. London: Sage.

Hesmondhalgh, David, and Sarah Baker. 2011. *Creative Labour, Media Work in Three Cultural Industries*. London/New Yok: Routledge.

Husain, Husaini. 2015. Skype Interview, 8 October.

Husband, Charles. 2005. Minority Ethnic Media as Communities of Practice: Professionalism and Identity Politics in Interaction. *Journal of Ethnic & Migration Studies* 31 (3): 461–479.

Joy. 2015 (anonymised). Face to face interview, 14 December.

Kamlesh Purohit. 2015. Face to face interview, 17 March.

Kaylon. 2016 (anonymised). Skype Interview, 2 March.

Kevin Silverton. 2015. Face to face interview, 15 June.

Lentin, Alana, and Gavan Titley. 2011. *The Crises of Multiculturalism: Racism in a Neoliberal Age*. London/New York: Zed Books.

Loviglio, Jason, and Michele Hilmes, eds. 2013. *Radio's New Wave Global Sound in the Digital Era*. New York/London: Routledge.

Malik, Sarita. 2013. "Creative Diversity": UK Public Service Broadcasting After Multiculturalism. *Popular Communication* 11 (3): 227–241.

Mark Strippel. 2015. Face to face interview, 15 June.

Matsaganis, M.D., and V.S. Katz. 2014. How Ethnic Media Producers Constitute Their Communities of Practice: An Ecological Approach. *Journalism* 15 (7): 926–944.

Mayer, Vicki. 2011. *Below the Line Producers and Production Studies in New Television Economy*. Durham: Duke University Press.

Mike Curtis. 2014. Face to face interview, 1 December.

Moylan, Katie. 2013. *Broadcasting Diversity, Migrant Representation in Irish Radio*. Bristol: Intellect.

———. 2018. Accented Radio: Articulations of British Caribbean Experience and Identity in UK Community Radio. *Global Media and Communication* 14 (3): 283–299.

Mya. 2015 (anonymised). Skype Interview, 10 July.

Naficy, Hamid. 2001. *An Accented Cinema: Exilic and Diasporic Filmmaking*. Princeton/Oxford: Princeton University Press.

Noreen Khan. 2015. Face to face interview, 29 June.

O'Brien, Dave, Daniel Laurison, Andrew Miles, and Sam Friedman. 2016. Are the Creative Industries Meritocratic? An Analysis of the 2014 British Labour Force Survey. *Cultural Trends* 25 (2): 116–131.

Ofcom. 2019a. Diversity and Equal Opportunities in Radio Monitoring Report on the UK Radio Industry. https://www.ofcom.org.uk/__data/assets/pdf_file/0022/159421/diversity-in-radio-2019-report.pdf. Accessed 25 Nov 2020.

———. 2019b. Diversity and Equal Opportunities in Television, Monitoring Report on the UK Based Broadcasting Industry. https://www.ofcom.org.uk/__data/assets/pdf_file/0028/166807/Diversity-in-TV-2019.pdf. Accessed 25 Nov 2020.

———. 2020. Diversity and Equal Opportunities in Television and Radio. 2019/20 retrieved from https://www.ofcom.org.uk/__data/assets/pdf_

file/0022/207229/2019-20-report-diversity-equal-opportunities-tv-and-radio.pdf.

Owen Bentley. 2015. Face to face interview, 20th January.

Randle, Keith. 2015. Class and Exclusion at Work: The Case of the UK Film and Television. In *The Routledge Companion to the Cultural Industries*, ed. Kate Oakley and Justin O'Connor. Abingdon: Routledge.

Raychaudhuri, A. 2018. *Homemaking: Radical Nostalgia and the Construction of a South Asian Diaspora*, Critical Perspectives on Theory, Culture and Politics. London/New York: Rowman & Littlefield International.

Riaan. 2015 (anonymised). Face to face interview, 14 September.

Safia. 2015 (anonymised). Face to face interview, 15 June.

Saha, Anamik. 2018. *Race and the Cultural Industries*. Cambridge: Polity.

Sam. 2015 (anonymised). Face to face interview, 11 November.

Sian, Katy P. 2011. "Forced" Conversions in the British Sikh Diaspora. *South Asian Popular Culture* 9 (2): 115–130.

Uberoi, Varun, and Tariq Modood. 2013. Has Multiculturalism in Britain Retreated? *Soundings* 53: 129–142.

Ursell, Gillian. 2000. Turning a Way of Life into a Business: An Account and Critique of the Transformation of British Television from Public Service to Commercial Enterprise. *Critical Perspectives on Accounting* 11 (6): 741–764.

Yu, Sherry. and Matsaganis, Matthew. 2019. Ethnic Media in the Digital Age. New York: Routledge.

CHAPTER 5

Audience Strategies at the BBC Asian Network

One of the principal reasons the BBC launched a national digital radio station specifically for British Asian listeners in 2002 was to combat the chronic under-representation of minority audiences and challenge racialised stereotypes. This chapter studies the BBC Asian Network remit and examines three different audience strategies enacted by the BBC, to entice the intended audience to the output. The listener figures have fluctuated over the past 18 years, with a low point in 2009 that led to the proposed closure of the service in 2010 (see Fig. 5.1). Uniquely the British Asian community are the only minority community in the UK who have a dedicated station on a public service broadcaster. Australia's Special Broadcasting Service (SBS) has broadly similar aims but has a hybrid-funded model, which means approximately 80 per cent of funding is from the Australian Government. The aim of SBS is to provide multilingual and multicultural radio and television for ethnic communities. In Britain, British Asians are also served by a range of commercial and community ethnic media, including community and commercial radio and satellite TV services. It is not possible to study one radio service for a distinct community without understanding how that the service fits into the ecology of the BBC and the wider UK radio sector. Throughout the book there is an underlying consideration on how operating as an ethnic service within the parameters of the BBC influences the manner in which BBC

© The Author(s), under exclusive license to Springer Nature Switzerland AG 2021
G. Aujla-Sidhu, *The BBC Asian Network*,
https://doi.org/10.1007/978-3-030-65764-2_5

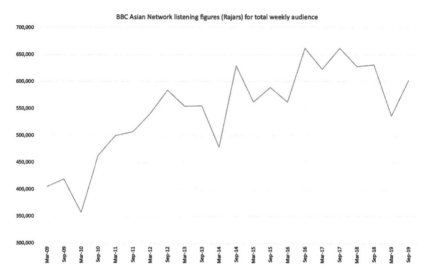

BBC Asian Network listening figures (Rajars) for total weekly audience

Fig. 5.1   BBC Asian Network listening figures (RAJARs) for total weekly audience

Asian Network staff envisage, understand, and address the listeners. The previous chapter outlined that among the BBC staff differences are evident in their mode of address for listeners due to intergenerational change.

THE SERVICE LICENCE

The station is mandated to have a strong focus on news and current affairs, to produce high-quality, original, and challenging programmes. The service licence describes the target listener as British Asian aged up to 35 years of age because there has been an institutional drive to attract younger listeners to the BBC Asian Network and Radio 1. The station broadcasts primarily in English for the main content with some programming presented in a hybrid of South Asian language (usually Urdu or Hindi) mixed with English. There is a rare fifty-fifty division of music and speech, making the BBC Asian Network unique in comparison to the BBC's other national radio stations. Furthermore, no other BBC station is defined by the audience it serves, for example, explicit Asian programming for British Asian audiences. A report by the Department for Culture, Media and Sport (DCMS) in 2004 assessed the BBC's digital radio stations and criticised the BBC for adopting this approach, questioning how homogenous the Asian communities really are? (see Chap. 2). Some of interviewees discussed the pressure they feel to attract all British Asians:

> I sometimes get a little bit frustrated because I feel like we are trying to attract those listeners but if someone is saying to you blatantly, I couldn't care less that I'm Asian what do you do? I've got my own family members who aren't even interested in listening even though I work here. That's not even attracting them. They're listening to KISS; they are listening to their own music. They are basically saying don't come after me, but I sometimes feel that we are pushing ourselves to get that audience. (Producer, Bela 2015)

Bela has made visible a contradiction between the station's goals and actions. On the one hand, the BBC promotes a mainstream vision of British Asian identity that implicitly accepts that listeners are likely to be integrated to attract young listeners, but on the other hand, there is also an expectation that listeners have some interest in Bollywood and their heritage. Some British Asians choose to listen to the BBC Asian Network simply due to their ethnic background and cultural interests, whilst other people do not relate to, or identify deeply, with this aspect of their background. Former Controller Bob Shennan explained they try to be appealing.

> It's not for everyone and it's not for everyone who is Asian. A lot of people who come from an Asian background have no relationship with it at all, don't want one. They want to live in a totally mainstream world. I think what we're trying to do is to make an Asian Network that feels like a mainstream service. That makes people feel comfortable in their kind of multi-faceted life that they lead every day we want a multi-faceted station. (Former Controller, Bob Shennan 2015)

In August 2016 the service licence was refreshed in a strategic move to concentrate specifically upon younger digital audiences. There remains an emphasis upon news and current affairs combined with "debate entertainment and culture relevant for a modern British Asian audience" (BBC Trust 2016, p. 2). There is also a stipulation that the "listeners should be encouraged to explore a broad range of subjects, to share their experiences, and to be offered regular opportunities to engage in debate" (BBC Trust 2016, p. 3). This type of format is highly managed, meaning the listener's voice can be manipulated by producers "to create an impression of participation" (Pinseler in Bonini and Monclus 2015, p. 69). Radio stations are compelled to showcase a coherent community of listeners to attract further listeners. Crucially because the views and voices of the listeners are used as programme "material," this means that their views are only expressed in response to a question framed by the producer. The *raison d'être* for the existence of the BBC Asian Network is to enable the voice of minority citizens to be heard in the public sphere; however, Pinseler makes a valid point that this type of discussion is managed and directed by the station. The views and perspectives uttered on the Asian Network debate programme are shared with other BBC stations to showcase the so-called Asian perspective on a national news story, a move that implicitly marks the journalism as being ethnic (Bowman 2010).

The remit also stipulates that the content ought to recognise the "diversity of the British Asian population in terms of geography, interests, ethnicity, and religion" (BBC Trust 2016, p. 4). This means that the BBC recognises that the lived experiences of British Asians differ according to the region or city they reside in, their class, and culture. However, the station and its staff are pushed to showcase a cohesive homogenous community of Asian listeners. Ethnic minorities tend to be concentrated within the working class (Bennett et al. 2009), and correspondingly a large proportion of the BBC Asian Network listeners are also working class (Watson 2016). However, operating as a national station and reflecting all British Asians pose some challenges:

> Because we are a national station, we are always trying to broaden stories. For example, something is happening in Leicester we try and widen it, see if we can look at other communities. Physically we can't do that, we just don't have the resources to get 10 examples from across the country like BBC 5 Live would do. So, we need to make the language and the scripting as broad as possible. But have faith in the idea that Asian communities especially the past few generations are actually interlinked and connected. (Former Senior Manager, Alia 2015)

A lack of reporters in a range of cities and regions, for example, Scotland, means that staff try to generalise. This poses a huge challenge to producers who are tasked with trying to reflect the range and depth of Asian communities in the UK because they lack the necessary insight into how communities differ due to regional locations. The BBC as an organisation places huge value on building relationships with contributors in the regions, but this is harder at the BBC Asian Network:

Locally there is that sense that it's your patch and because you are often dealing with the same people you are able to build up those stronger contacts and stronger relationships. At the Asian Network, working nationally and with the nature of that job you are out of the office less. I mean, unless you were out reporting in Leicester getting voxes and whatever else a lot of it was dealing with phone interviews or taking national packages. (Former Journalist, Kaylon 2016)

The desk bound journalist is a new phenomenon in journalism due to technological changes which make it easier to perform the journalistic tasks but offers less opportunities for reporters to connect and develop relationships with the audience because they often cannot meet them in person.

One of the station's key duties is to offer a platform for new and established British Asian talent in order to meet objectives pertaining to stimulating creative and cultural excellence in the remit. Thus, the BBC Asian Network promotes British Asian music through initiatives such as BBC Introducing stages at Asian Music Melas, The *Bhangra* Project, and the Future Sounds projects. New and emerging artists are often discovered and championed by the station. The music played on-air is a mix of *Bollywood*, *Bhangra*, and UK chart music. There are some further conditions; at least 30 per cent of music should be from UK artists, this is translated as being "British Asian" artists. This requirement is in keeping with other BBC radio stations that emphasise British artists in their playlists. Radio 1, for example, has to play 40 per cent of British music. A further 30 per cent is defined as new music which has been released within the last two months. The definition of "new music" has become contentious because downloads and streaming have overtaken physical music sales. Ofcom recommended in 2018 that on Radio 1 and 2 a music track should be considered "new music" for a period of twelve months from first release or six weeks from the date the track first enters the Top 20 of the UK Official Singles Chart (Ofcom 2018). A final 10 per cent of music must be South Asian, this does not include mainstream *Bollywood* music, instead genres such as Pakistani pop, Bangladeshi, Sri Lankan, and regional/classical music, alongside Qawwali and Ghazal music genres are emphasised.

The station is often stereotyped as only playing *Bhangra* or *Bollywood*, whereas the remit demands a wide range of music genres are made available. However, among the staff there are differences of opinion about the genres of music.

We are moving towards, a much more British Asian sound and as far as I'm concerned that's a BBC thing. It is almost like a BBC trust thing where we've got to show that we are supporting British Asian music to keep getting our money and remain a station on the BBC. I am not entirely sure if putting such strictures on a playlist is the best thing for the growth of listeners. (Presenter, Bobby Friction 2016)

The music quotas are imposed upon the station. Therefore, the staff, including the presenters, have limited input into the music played in their shows. Some of the interviewees worried that the wrong music is being played on-air—with many wanting to emphasise *Bollywood* far more (see Chap. 8). Historically, radio was considered to be a "tastemaker," but this role has diminished with the advent of streaming services such as Spotify that allow the listener to pick and choose music. Hendy (2000, p. 743) has argued that "radio remains a central force for shaping music tastes," and in the digital age, radio still attracts listeners and people are listening to the radio for longer (Ofcom 2017, p. 97). There are, however, age differences, younger people are tuning in less and older people are on average listening for longer.

The station playlist is considered by radio studies scholars to be a musical "gatekeeper" because it works to restrict the range of music played (Negus 1993). Gallego (in Bonini and Monclus 2015) has contended that listeners are also highly managed by the music played because playlist tends to be limited. Those who want to seek out new music can do so through music streaming services which has impacted radio's gatekeeper and tastemaker role. Wall and Dubber (2009, p. 36) recommend that music streaming is understood as "reshaping (rather than replicating or replacing) traditional radio broadcasting." Radio's role in digital age has become fragmented, mobile and, interestingly, the manner in which people listen has become more personal (Lacey 2013 in Loviglio and Hilmes). According to Lacey (2013) listening is a learned art, people adapted to having a wireless in their home and to accept personalised content from the BBC (a formal institution).

The service licence plays an important role in steering the BBC Asian Network and keeping it distinct from commercial Asian radio stations. The former head of Programmes Mark Strippel explained that the objectives set out in the remit work to "preserve our distinctiveness against the commercial Asian sector." The BBC must justify the existence of the station and demonstrate how the Asian Network fills a gap in the market that commercial Asian stations cannot or are unable to fulfil. The news journalism and the new music aspects are especially significant. As a consequence, Strippel explained the news and music combined with the civic functions the station facilitates means "we [Asian Network] are seen as good value for money. We are also delivering on an important core mission for the BBC" (Strippel 2015).

The BBC Asian Network, unlike its competitors, also has to conform to the normative structures and working practises within the BBC. However, radio stations are not shaped and influenced purely in terms of organisational structures, but they are also shaped by the people who work there.

> There was a lot of varied opinions about what the station should be doing. On individual news stories there were often a lot of disagreements about what we should be doing. There were often disagreements about the music played. There were often disagreements about the mix of programmes, there were disagreements about the language programming. Everybody had an opinion about the Asian Network and that was always part of the challenge. Staff felt very personally about the station. We all do, whatever radio station we are working/broadcasting for we tend to get very fond of it. (Former Head of news and programmes, Husain, Husaini 2015)

The employees feel a sense of proprietorship of the station and also are empowered to offer their opinions. This came across in the research interviews for the study as well. It is also likely that minority ethnic staff feel a sense of ownership and pride in their ability to serve Asian communities. However, they also objected to some of top-down management imperatives. For example, the interview material demonstrated a lack of consensus on the music policies, the target listener, and the news agenda. The disagreements appear to be due to intergenerational differences as opposed to people simply disagreeing with policies. The core target listener caused the most divergence of opinion with a number of staff opposing the emphasis upon the young British Asian demographic. The rest of this chapter examines three audience strategies employed by the BBC to increase the listening figures: young, friend of the family, and digital native.

AUDIENCE STRATEGIES: 2006 YOUNG

Charles Husband's work has focused upon the political economy of minority ethnic media and participation of minority ethnic staff in the media industries. Downing and Husband (2005) suggest ethnic media are important because they place minorities centre stage of media content.

They also recognise ethnic media organisations are often characterised by the intended target audience, hence a British Asian audience for Asian programming. Minority communities are far smaller than mainstream audiences but are also fractured due to differences of age, intergenerational changes, gender, and class; therefore, ethnic media are forced to often serve their audience in a broad manner (Husband 2005, p. 463). The BBC Asian Network since its inception as a national digital radio station in 2002 has also embraced this approach, by presenting in English but offering some specific South Asian Language programmes to cater specific communities. Equally, the Asian Network is also defined by the audience it serves. The Asian Network is forced to find ways to unite listeners, as opposed to focusing upon the issues that divide them. This is broadly achieved by broadcasting in English and by emphasising shared cultures, particularly with reference to entertainment. Several commercial Asian radio stations such as Sunrise and Sabras radio have enacted similar strategies successfully because almost half the funding that commercial ethnic stations receive was through on-air advertising or sponsorship by companies who want to get their message to a particular demographic (Ofcom 2017, p. 115).

Prior to 2006 the BBC Asian Network's audience strategy was described by DCMS as an attempt to be "all things to all Asians" (Gardem 2004, p. 50). Focus groups held with listeners in 2004 found a lack of clarity over whom the station was intended for. The review recommended the introduction of adventurous music playlists and ambitious news and current affairs content. The distinctiveness of the service was questioned, especially because during this period commercial Asian radio stations were broadcasting similar programmes and music to the BBC, and equally, they defined their radio station by the intended audience. The report suggested that the BBC ought to define distinctiveness based upon content. In response, the BBC appointed Bob Shennan, Controller of BBC 5 Live, to take over responsibility of the BBC Asian Network. The BBC also made a one-million-pound investment to recruit a new management tier, assistant editors, to improve editorial standards. Mike Curtis was News Editor at the time and explained the staff were receptive to change "there was a general feeling that network radio was actually really behind us we can go on and get thousands more listeners." He emphasised that generally the staff felt the station and its content was misunderstood by the BBC.

We did documentaries about racism within the Asian communities, we had interviews with Asian people complaining about immigration, which certain people in the BBC didn't understand at all. They just saw the word Asian, the one stop-shop for everybody and that was it. It was down to us to actually reflect this back to the BBC and say this is actually this is a bit more complicated than you think it is and that certainly got us into trouble at the top of the BBC. (Former news editor, Mike Curtis 2014)

Curtis appears to suggest that the station and the staff were historically unsupported by the wider BBC. He explained it was left to the editors and managing director at the station to work out how to be fair and balanced in respect of the various Asian communities they served. He believes this contributed to the image problem that has plagued the BBC Asian Network within the organisation. Some of the content was considered to be substandard, "local radio would look down a bit on the Asian Network and its reporters without actually looking at what was being actually broadcast and the sort of stories people were digging out" (Mike Curtis 2014). Within the BBC local radio has always been subordinate to national radio and television (Lewis and Booth 1989, p. 89).

Under Shennan's leadership the station aggressively changed its sound and presentation by emphasising British Asians aged 15–25 years of age at the expense of the older listeners. Media research revealed that Pakistani, Indian, and Bangladeshi households are on average larger and younger, compared to the general population (Ofcom 2013, p. 14, 15). Shennan explained the change in strategy was primarily age focused, "we were going to move from effectively a first generation and second-generation network to a second and third generation. It was based on the trends in the audience and those trends have just got more and more accelerated and extreme." This approach meant some of the "older" presenters were dropped from the on-air schedule and the breakfast programme adopted a 5 Live format, meaning a stronger emphasis on news and current affairs blended with music. The music policies were also refreshed, and for the first time in its history, music from the UK Top 40 was played alongside *Bollywood* and *Bhangra*. A daily news programme was introduced, alongside a soap, *Silver Street*, to allow the BBC to capitalise on the success of *The Archers* on Radio 4. Former head of Programmes, Husain Husaini, underlined the strategy was an attempt to "reposition" in the light of criticism from the DCMS. However, the new format ultimately led to a reduction of listeners:

> It caused a problem because there was a heritage audience on the medium
> wave in Leicester and Birmingham who absolutely loved the Asian Network
> and wanted it to be in their lives, so there was a kind of tension relationship.
> (Former Head of Programmes, Husain Husaini 2015)

The changes resulted in a disjointed schedule that attempted to combine
aspects of BBC 5 Live and Radio 4 into one schedule mixed with Asian
music and content. Unsurprisingly it was not popular with the listeners. At
its lowest point in 2009, just 360,000 listeners were tuning in each week
(RAJAR Q4 2009, see Fig. 5.1). In contrast, Sunrise Radio reached
483,000 listeners in the same period. Kavya (*not her real name*) a former
senior manager underlined that the staff lacked a sense of direction.

> We had a cultural identity crisis. If you asked 6 people what does the Asian
> Network stand for? You would get 6 different answers. We weren't sure of
> our strategy, our vision, our direction, we were creating programmes believ-
> ing we knew what the audience wanted but we didn't really listen to what
> they wanted. We weren't in the spaces and places that they were. There was
> almost a cavalier approach to how we made our programmes, with passion
> of course, but I think 2012 was actually the chance to rip it up and start
> again. (Former senior manager, Kavya 2015)

A lack of direction and a lack of connection to the listeners seem evident
here. It is notable that when the Asian Network became a national BBC
station the governance structures remained static. The internal management was unchanged, and the station continued to broadcast from three
cities: Birmingham, Leicester, and London. A new national audience strategy was not enacted and hence staff continued to cater for first-, second-,
and third-generation British Asians collectively. Therefore, it is unsurprising that Shennan sought to implement a distinctive approach to serving
the British Asian communities whilst also trying to tackle the weaknesses
of the radio station prior to 2004. However, the on-air sound became
extremely "edgy and trendy – achingly trendy" and "probably a bit too
hip, the majority of the audience wanted a radio station a bit friendlier and
warmer" (Former Head of Programmes and News, Husain Husaini 2015).
Listener figures initially rose before declining over 2008. It was during this
period that the controllership of the station moved to the former Radio 1
and 1Xtra Controller, Andy Parfitt. Reflecting on the strategy Mike
Curtis said:

I think it was a bit of a BBC exercise in that we have a got a new way of managing it all, we've got some money, let's be dynamic and have a big re-launch with this exciting new line-up. But it didn't work. (former news edi-tor, Mike Curtis 2014)

Friend of the Family and the Proposed Closure

Under Parfitt's leadership, a new strategy was launched, "friend of the family." The strategy sought to recognise that several age groups and generations listened to the station at different times of the day and each had unique needs. The BBC Asian Network drew on lessons Radio 1 had learnt when it underwent a major transformation in the late 1990s.

> Andy went and spoke one to one with a lot of staff. A lot of anguish came out about the way the station was being run, blaming particularly the assis-tant editors for the way they managed their own particular areas. The whole point of the changes was the make the station sound like one radio station, but it sounded like a number of different radio stations. There was a general unhappiness which was reflecting by the fact that the audience figures were dropping despite all the money chucked at it. (Former News Editor, Mike Curtis 2014)

Under Parfitt leadership, staff were forced to construct a cohesive and distinct radio station before focusing on creating a community of listeners. The new editorial strategy reached out to a core group of listeners who were offered a revitalised daytime programme offer, whilst the evenings and weekends were designed to appeal to younger or older listeners.

> The average Asian household was five rather than two. So, two things came about: one was to say, "we'll do something that feels like it's at the heart of that family" and "let's do something that reflects all those relationships in what we're doing". I thought that was successful in pulling us all together. (Former Head of Programmes and News, Husain Husaini 2015)

The breakfast and drive programmes embraced a family-centric approach to widely appeal to everyone: grandparents, middle aged, and teenagers. There is a sense from the interview material that staff were strongly steered and directed to focus upon the intended listener. Radio studies research has documented that normative BBC music policies have resulted in genres being selected that have wide appeal for daytime programmes, whilst specialist music tends to be confined to the evenings to attract niche groups (Wall and Dubber 2009). The "friend of the family" strategy appears to be an extension of this policy but with specific reference to programme and speech content on the BBC Asian Network. This strategy is best described as "safe" because the station tried to appeal to all British Asians in order to maintain listener figures. There were some objections but Husaini recounted that "I think everyone got on board because it felt to me that the strategy reflected the people who worked at the station and their lives." The Former head of News, Silverton, emphasised it was a logical strategy "you always try and aim for what you think is the core audience. I suppose that was someone who fell into the middle of our target age range, so 25ish. Most of the time its people who have ordinary British Asian Experience."

The impact of the strategy was limited because on 2 March 2010, approximately one year into the "friend of the family," the Director General Mark Thomson announced the proposed closure of the BBC Asian Network, BBC 6 Music, and teen services Blast and Switch, as part of a cost-cutting exercise. The move came after an unsuccessful negotiation between the BBC and the government to increase the licence fee in line with inflation. The BBC was forced to reduce spending by 20 per cent in order to deliver its programme commitments. The BBC explained that it cost 8.5 pence per listener per hour to run the BBC Asian Network, a figure far higher than the other national radio stations. There were some major flaws with the rationale: the BBC Asian Network was compared to 5 Live and Radio 4, and not to BBC language-specific radio services such as Radio Scotland, Radio Cymru, and Radio nan Gàidheal, whose operational costs were significantly higher than 8.5 pence per listener per hour. These language-specific services broadcast in non-English and were directly comparable to the BBC Asian Network, which at the time broadcast more than twenty hours per week in South Asian languages and played foreign language music. Reflecting on the closure, Mike Curtis said it was a difficult time:

> The audience was dropping and the fact some 8 million a year was being thrown at the Asian Network and it wasn't working. The senior executives aided by advisors saw something had to be done here. It was just the top line, but it was the wrong decision. They should have taken into consideration that we had changed the strategy and we needed time to make it work. It shone the spotlight on us internally and the cost was one of things that

changed the strategy in an attempt to bring it down. It was embarrassing and we knew we were in for a fight to survive. (Former News Editor, Mike Curtis 2014)

The proposed closure reconfirmed to many Asian Network employees that the station and thus the staff were still inferior to other BBC services. The staff once again felt isolated and unsupported by the BBC and they were worried about their future career prospects. The station management undertook a series of negotiations to preserve some type of Asian radio programming within the BBC. Ishani (*not her real name*) outlined in her interview there appeared to be an expectation that British Asian listeners should only listen to the BBC Asian Network:

> I am sure they [the BBC] did understand but it took them a while to accept that it's about having a choice of listening. A British Asian at the younger end of the spectrum could be listening to 1xtra, Asian Network, 5 Live depending on what they wanted to hear on certain moments in time. This the accepted norm for the white diaspora, but it took them a while to get their head around that Asians consume radio in the same way, they don't just permanently keep their dial on the Asian Network. (Former manager, Ishani 2015)

Ishani's insight connects to Bela's comment in Chap. 4 that she feels pressured to entice Asian listeners to the output even though the Asian aspect of their identity is not prevalent, and thus, they do have an interest in the related culture. The notion that the British Asian audience is not dissimilar to the majority population emerged in a number of the interviews, although a minority did argue that the British Asian audience are different or have distinct media habits. Ishani has highlighted that the core challenge in trying to serve British Asian audiences through a single service means it is forced to try and offer everyone something. The fluctuating listening figures over the course of the station's existence can be attributed to the lack of clear editorial strategy and defining the station by the audience as opposed to the content. A sense of isolation among some of the ethnic staff became apparent during the interview process, largely the journalists and presenters felt unable to draw on support from the wider institution.

> The argument went along the lines of that BBC Asian Network brings in no unique users to the BBC, or very few and so it doesn't actually increase the overall BBC audience. But the reality is that no service does, no service

within the BBC only appeals to one group of people. Everyone watches BBC 1 or 2 at some point in their lives, so it was kind of an unfair test. There was a more sophisticated analysis which showed that although the station wasn't bringing new people to the BBC it was extending the amount of time, they spent with the BBC quite significantly. Your average Asian Network listener used the BBC very sparingly, they would spend a lot of time watching satellite TV, they may have watched Eastenders or Match of the Day. But the Asian Network produced hours and hours of listening for that group of people. (Former head of programmes, Husain Husaini 2015)

The BBC has always focused on serving all audiences simply because the licence fee is universal and the organisation at least in theory is not restricted by commercial imperatives. However, in reality, due to the structural changes implemented in the BBC in the 1990s the broadcaster is required to engage with economic goals and efficiencies as opposed to simply social or political welfare missions. Since 2016 this has becoming more pressing as it appears the BBC will be forced to switch to a subscription model in the near future. Jakubowitcz (2007) has recommended that public service media needs to re-define their role and activities in order to remain relevant whilst reflecting "multi-ethnic and multicultural societies, without unduly accentuating differences or 'ghettosing' different social and ethnic groups by locking them into 'walled gardens' of programme services, dedicated solely to them" (De Bens and Cees 2007, p. 128).

The BBC had claimed the money saved, by closing services, including the BBC Asian Network, would be reinvested into the BBC. It was imperative that a new and less expensive way to serve British Asian audiences was found. The listening figures that followed the closure announcement in March 2010 measured audience consumption from the end of March 2010 to 27 June 2010 and revealed the number of BBC Asian Network listeners had grown to 437,000 (RAJAR Q2 2010), see Fig. 5.1. 6 Music listeners also grew and exceeded one million, due in part to the publicity generated over their proposed closures. The BBC Trust took three months to reverse the decision to close 6 Music, claiming the existence of the station encouraged audiences to embrace digital radio; however, it took another year and a public consultation before the BBC Asian Network was saved from closure. The differences in how the two stations were dealt with illustrates the low value and insignificance of the Asian Network within the BBC hierarchy.

The save Asian Network campaign was more muted and less able to catch the attention of the broad section of the audience. Whereas 6 Music has a broader appeal. But I think in a way it does say something about the potency and the heft of 6 Music and actually frankly the Asian Network has always suffered from not having a very loud voice inside or outside the BBC. (Former Controller, Bob Shannon 2015)

The Asian Network campaign relied upon the voices of British Asian artists who had benefitted from the platform, for example, Jay Sean, but these artists themselves are marginalised within the music industry (see Chap. 8). An alternative and less expensive way to serve British Asian audiences was not found, and therefore, the BBC Trust recommended in 2011 that the BBC Asian Network be reprieved but operate with a smaller budget and half the number of staff. A review of the station in 2012 found that it made a "strong contribution to delivering the BBC's public purposes" via the station's news, British Asian music, and coverage of live cultural events. It concluded that these aspects make it "highly distinctive within the UK's Asian radio market" (BBC Trust 2012). Following the reprieve, the station was restructured, the Leicester office was closed, and staff moved to Broadcasting House in London with some programming remaining in Birmingham. Conversely at the same time within the BBC, a substantial proportion of 5 Live, Radio 4, BBC Breakfast, and Children's television were forced to re-locate to Salford as part of the BBC's efforts to better reflect the regions of the UK.

Post 2012 and Digital Native 2016

In 2012 a new on-air schedule was unveiled to mark the BBC Asian Network's 10th Birthday. The "friend of the family" strategy remained in the background. There was a clear imperative to staff to focus on reflecting young British Asians, their interests, and musical tastes to signal that the station would henceforth focus on British-born Asians and not first-generation Asians.

This is a service which targets British Asian diaspora who are born and bred here. They live here. The myth of returning has disappeared completely. And it is a significant and growing demographic, something which needs to be paid attention to. (Former manager, Ishani 2015)

A number of high-profile presenters left, and a number of staff were made redundant. The remaining employees were responsible for producing longer shows; twenty hours of news and current affairs content per week, special documentaries, and ten live music events per year. Radiocentre (a body representing the sector) responded to the changes and set out their concerns about an "overly ambitious remit which attempts to serve a broad diverse audience" (Radio Centre 2012, p. 8). This has been a key weakness of the station that, since its inception, it has tried to serve all British Asians and is the only media that "encompass[es] a large range of music, culture, language, news, documentaries and current affairs that cover British Asian culture from an accessible perspective" (Radio Centre 2012, p. 8). This is a pertinent point—no other Asian radio service attempts to provide this level of content.

After operating for ten years in three cities, the station was consolidated into two bases: Birmingham and New Broadcasting House in London for the news and key programmes such as Breakfast, phone-in, and Drive. A new presenter line-up was unveiled with a mix of old and new presenters joining the roster. The Controllership of the station switched hands once again from Andy Parfitt (Controller of Radio 1 and 1Xtra), who retired, back to Bob Shennan. A stronger emphasis was placed on digital content and social media in recognition that radio has increasingly become a visual and a web experience (Loviglio and Hilmes 2013). A number of key changes were also instigated among the news team to make the journalism even more influential and distinctive. Despite the job reductions across the station, BBC news funded specific "impact reporter" roles with the intention that original journalism sourced by the Asian Network impact reporters could be shared easily, and widely, across the BBC. The language programmes were also transformed, previously they had sought to serve specific linguist communities. New younger presenters were recruited to present in a hybrid of English and a South Asian language; "the biggest radical change I suppose is how we transformed Sundays. How we broadcast language programmes is not through one linear platform it is through sprawling networks and through social media" (former manager, Kavya 2015). The changes in terms of music, news, and presentation resulted in an upward trajectory in terms of listener figures, forcing the BBC's key competitor, Sunrise Radio, into second place (see Fig. 5.1).

Kevin Silverton outlined that post 2012 the station management sought to demonstrate that the Asian Network is "bigger" than Asian music and entertainment. "We are adding more to the BBC. That seems to be the major part of the argument: the comedy, news, the debates. That's got to be beneficial to the BBC" (Former Head of News, Kevin Silverton 2015). Strippel explained the decision to reverse the proposed closure permitted the management team to change the Asian Network, "we refined what we were doing and had a much clearer focus. I think the audience felt that coherence."

However, the young demographic remained elusive despite the growth in listener figures. Shennan underlined that capturing the young age group is difficult for all media "I don't think it is particularly a public service challenge, I think it's a challenge for radio brands to connect with what is effectively a younger audience." Minority communities tend to have a younger demographic compared to the main population (Ballard 1990; Wilson and Gutierrez 1995; Ofcom 2013). This group is considered to be both significant and profitable, from the perspective of commercial media. From the public service point of view, there is an obligation to serve all audiences, ensure that a wide range of voices and opinions are articulated, to provide people with information so that they can make their own decisions. Increasingly, the BBC has been forced to demonstrate this more clearly. Shennan emphasised that the audience strategy had to evolve:

> I think the whole of the BBC has been brilliant at catering for a quite well-off white licence fee paying public for years. But the nature of the population shifts and is more complicated and we need to be an organisation able to meet the needs of that audience otherwise that universality and the licence fee if definitely under threat. (Former Controller, Bob Shannon 2015)

A BBC Trust review of the BBC Asian Network in 2015 urged the station to offer a stronger online presence in order to improve engagement (BBC Service Review 2015, p. 65).

Accordingly, the station has concentrated on young people who do not listen to radio but engage with social media. The digital native strategy focuses on British Asians aged between 15 and 25, living primarily in London, where a large proportion of the available British Asian listenership reside. This was described by Shennan as "another version of that [2006] strategy, but carefully. Ten years on, the Asian population of the UK is an incredibly young population." Some of the staff do not support the changes; programme producer, Anish Shaikh, outlined his worries about the continuous change to music, schedules, and feeling "pressured" to serve a large and disparate audience:

> I think we are pulled in every single direction. You've got to appeal to the young, you've got to appeal to the old, you've got to appeal to the traditional, you've got to appeal to the middle aged. I think that the pressure can prove fatal for the Asian Network. (Producer, Anish Shaikh 2015)

Shaikh's role is to create programmes that appeal to a wide range of British Asian listeners. He explained he finds this aspect of the role challenging. Neeta (*not her real name*), a language programme producer, explained that the digital strategy has enabled her programmes to be more "daring." She described that replacing the presenter with someone who is younger as opposed to first- or second-generation Asian means they can connect with the younger audience.

> It's a massive deal. There is an understanding of everyday life and culture and the kind of things that we do, recognising that we don't do things that the older generation does and being able to get their head around what it means to be British Asian. (Language producer, Neeta 2015)

The changes to the presenters have meant that the BBC is able to try and reflect the lifestyle of British Asians as opposed to the values or traditions held by the first generations of the communities. Shaikh perhaps naturally feels a deeper connection to older listeners and finds the demands placed on him as a producer creates a pressured environment. For the digital strategy to be a success it is imperative that BBC Asian Network staff have a strong understanding of how "Asian communities have implemented social media and social networks into their lives." Sam, a senior journalist, was not entirely convinced everyone understood how best to engage via social media.

> We've got to think about how people are going to access us via the internet, via apps. They've got to choose to want to come to us and, unless we are reflecting their world, they're not going to be a part of it. (Senior Journalist, Sam 2015)

The social media policies at the station have not always been right; Sam noted there was an emphasis on Twitter for a long time when, in fact, the listeners were elsewhere.

> A lot of people don't listen to the output via the radio, but they will engage via social media, so the way that people are approaching the Asian Network

is changing and I think we just need to keep ahead of the game. So being in the places that they're in beforehand or signpost it very early on. (Senior Journalist, Sam 2015)

Sam did not believe journalists can simply follow popular social media platforms because this means the broadcaster is always one step behind. Instead, she recognised it is important that the station and its presenters lead and establish themselves on social media platforms as they appear to find new listeners. The limited understanding of digital platforms could be a generational issue whereby non-digital natives are forced to engage with platforms inhabited by young people and find it challenging. Other staff such as Bela believe the station has been innovative compared to other BBC teams, "they are probably a little bit behind us in terms of what we are doing because their audiences aren't as young." 5 Live or Radio 4 may not be as creative in their methods due to the age difference in their listeners and the content they emphasise. Mithra *(not her real name)* a journalist explained she has adapted her journalism practice to incorporate digital journalism skills and social media to showcase her work. She highlighted that everyone working at the station is aware that the BBC Asian Network like other stations is operating "in the digital age and a lot of listeners are accessing the Asian Network through their tablets, smart phones and listening back, and that's where the market is." Strippel explained that he found social media interaction illuminating and informative alongside RAJAR listening figures.

Does it count if someone views our content on iPlayer? Yes, it does. It is engagement with the Asian Network. They are watching content that's linked to radio and it's linked to our core values. So, it's really important. I am more than comfortable with that, and Radio 1 and other networks approach it with the same way. (Former Head of Programmes, Mark Strippel 2015)

ENGAGING THE LISTENER

There was no consensus among the thirty BBC interviews over which strategy or target listener is preferred. What is demonstrated in this chapter is the huge shift in the station's content and tone as it has adapted in the radio market to appeal to its intended listener. The wider BBC may not intricately understand this diverse audience, but it appears to be trying to.

The Asian Network has moved around so much. First, we were based in the English Regions, then we were under Audio and Music and then we moved to Bob Shennan and then Andy Parfit then back to Bob Shennan. People did try and understand, and they showed a lot of commitment, but to what extent their understanding got under the skin of what the station is about? I won't say it was non-existent, I think it depended on individuals and also it depended on what we were trying to do. (Former Senior Manager, Ishani 2015)

One advantage of the change in leadership at the station is that different parts of the BBC have strategically influenced how the station has developed. Among the interviewees, there was some trepidation about the digital native strategy.

When you are out and about and in your social time people will give opinions. I personally find that the youngsters that I come across don't know about the BBC Asian Network, they are not really interested, and the older ones are not happy with it. (Former Senior Manager, Alia 2015)

The views that Alia (*not her real name*) has heard socially are perhaps the consequence of the friend of the family strategy that tried to serve the multiple generations of the family. Listener figures only reveal a partial picture because they are based on retrospective listening diaries. Since 1992, they have been compiled by asking 130,000 respondents to complete a one-week diary listing all the stations the respondent has listened to in quarter-hour time blocks for RAJAR.[1] Approximately 340 radio stations are signed up to the service making it the largest audience research survey in the UK. Each station has to pay for the option to join the service; consequently, a number of independent and community stations cannot gather listener figures due to the cost. It is a disputed method due to the retrospective nature of the data. Moreover, ethnic and niche media argue that minority respondents are under-represented in the survey (Starkey 2004, p. 9). In 2020, Avtar Lit, founder of Sunrise Radio, launched the Asian Radio Audience Measuring body to measure British Asians listening to Asian radio but also to capture British Asians listening to mainstream stations. Newer digital reporting tools allow different networks to assess

---

[1] RAJAR stands for Radio Joint Audience Research and is the official body in charge of measuring radio audiences in the UK. It is jointly owned by the BBC and the Radiocentre on behalf of the commercial sector.

the number of clicks a story or content have generated, but in radio and television, RAJAR and BARB figures are still used to calculate the number of listeners.

Internal BBC research has demonstrated that the BBC Asian Network's reach is highest in the West Midlands. Increasingly the staff are directed to focus upon listeners in London, where a greater number of British Asians are concentrated (see Watson 2016). But mainstream stations such as Radio 2 and Radio 4 have the largest listener share in London, and non-BBC, Capital Radio has the largest audience share (RAJAR Q4 2019). Chapter 4 highlighted issues regarding the skillset and knowledge of new producers hired at the station and this could be significant in the divide that exists between some staff and the listeners. Kamran outlined it is especially problematic that some producers take the attitude that the station is simply "steppingstone" for a career elsewhere in the BBC.

> I think you can probably count on one hand the number of people who actually should be working at the Asian Network. Who are dedicated, who know the scene and actually want to move it on. Anyone can produce a show, but you would expect someone on a Bollywood show to have Bollywood knowledge. (Former Producer, Kamran 2015)

People who are often involved in community radio are likely to be volunteers, and in commercial Asian radio, people may not necessarily be "professional" journalists by Western standards, but they have knowledge or language specialisms to serve their communities.

> People who work at Asian commercial stations are by and large people who have an interest in the Asian community, so they are passionate about radio they are not professional broadcasters or professional journalists, but they do a fantastic job because they have a knowledge of the community and they have a real passion for the content of the what they put out. (Kamlesh Purohit 2015)

Both Kamran and Kamlesh have emphasised that employees need to have passion and knowledge to create engaging content. Kamlesh implies that people who opt to work in either community or commercial stations demonstrate more passion for their communities and knowledge and are thus able to secure listeners.

Conclusion

This chapter has offered an overview of the different audience strategies enacted at the station from the point of view of the BBC employees. Since the launch of the digital radio stations, 6 Music has emerged as the most listened to BBC digital station with almost 2.5 million listeners. BBC Radio 4 Extra now reaches 2.2 million (RAJAR Q4 2019) and 1Xtra has a strong reach with Black, Asian, and minority ethnic listeners reaching over a million listeners.

The BBC Asian Network is still trying to construct a cohesive audience to serve. It promotes a broad vision of "British Asian" identity and culture in an attempt to appeal to third- and fourth-generation British Asians, who may not feel a deep connection to their heritage. In contrast, independent and commercial Asian radio and television services showcase a version of identity that is closely aligned to South Asia through the language and tone. This makes the BBC Asian Network distinct from the competition because commercial services tend to focus on first and second generations (there are some specific services, such as BritAsia TV, aimed at young British Asians). Ethnic media services continue to remain marginalised within the broader media ecology, whilst the BBC Asian Network is offered on a public service platform and, in theory, is accessible to all audiences. Despite efforts across the management of the BBC to grow the BBC Asian Network audience, the interviews reveal that staff have grappled with how best to serve these listeners.

References

Alia. 2015 (anonymised). Face to face interview, 16 June.
Anish Shaikh. 2015. Face to face interview, 9 December.
Ballard, Roger. 1990. Migration and Kinship: The Differential Effect of Marriage Rules on the Processes of Punjabi Migration to Britain. In *South Asians Overseas Migration and Ethnicity*, ed. C. Clarke, C. Peach, and S. Vertovec, 219–249. Cambridge: Cambridge University Press.
BBC Trust. 2012. BBC Asian Network Service Licence Review 2012. http://downloads.bbc.co.uk/bbctrust/assets/files/pdf/regulatory_framework/service_licences/radio/2012/asian_network_may12.pdf. Accessed 15 Oct 2020.
———. 2015. BBC Trust Service Review 2015. BBC Trust. http://downloads.bbc.co.uk/bbctrust/assets/files/pdf/our_work/music_radio/music_radio.pdf. Accessed 15 Oct 2020.

————. 2016. BBC Asian Network Service Licence 2016. BBC Trust. http://downloads.bbc.co.uk/bbctrust/assets/files/pdf/regulatory_framework/service_licences/radio/2016/asian_network_aug16.pdf. Accessed 15 Oct 2020.

Bela. 2015 (anonymised). Face to face interview, 9 November.

Bennett, Tony, Mike Savage, Elizabeth Silva, Alan Warde, Modesto Gayo-Cal, and David Wright. 2009. *Culture, Class, Distinction.* Abingdon: Routledge.

Bob Shennan. 2015. Face to face interview, 11 November.

Bobby Friction. 2016. Skype Interview, 9 February.

Bonini, Tiziano, and Belen Monclus, eds. 2015. *Radio Audiences and Participation in the Age of Network Society.* Abingdon: Routledge.

Bowman, Paul, ed. 2010. The Rey Chow Reader. NEW YORK: Columbia University Press,

De Bens, Els, and Hamelink J. Cees, eds. 2007. *Media Between Culture and Commercialisation.* Bristol: Intellect.

Downing, John, and Charles Husband. 2005. *Representing 'Race' Racisms, Ethnicities and Media.* London: Sage Publications.

Gardem, Tim. 2004. Independent Review of the BBC's Digital Radio Services. http://news.bbc.co.uk/nol/shared/bsp/hi/pdfs/19_10_04_digital_radio.pdf

Hendy, David. 2000. Pop Music Radio in the Public Service: BBC Radio 1 and Music in the 1990s. *Media, Culture & Society* 22 (6): 743–761.

Husband, Charles. 2005. Minority Ethnic Media as Communities of Practice: Professionalism and Identity Politics in Interaction. *Journal of Ethnic & Migration Studies* 31 (3): 461–479.

Husain Hussaini. 2015. Skype Interview, 8 October.

Ishani. 2015 (anonymised), 9 September.

Kamlesh Purohit. 2015. Face to face interview, 17 March.

Kamran. 2015 (anonymised). Face to face interview, 11 November.

Kavya. 2015 (anonymised). Face to face interview, 25 March.

Kaylon. 2016 (anonymised). Skype Interview, 2 March.

Kevin Silverton. 2015. Face to face interview, 15 June.

Lewis, Peter M., and Jerry Booth. 1989. *The Invisible Medium Public, Commercial and Community Radio.* Basingstoke: Macmillan.

Loviglio, Jason, and Michele Hilmes, eds. 2013. *Radio's New Wave Global Sound in the Digital Era.* New York/London: Routledge.

Mark Strippel. 2015. Face to face interview, 15 June.

Mike Curtis. 2014. Face to face interview, 1 December.

Neeta. 2015 (anonymised). Skype Interview, 15 May.

Negus, Keith. 1993. Plugging and Programming: Pop Radio and Record Promotion in Britain and the United States. *Popular Music* 12 (1): 57–68.

Ofcom. 2013. Ethnic Minority Groups and Communication Services. Research Report.

————. 2017. The Communications Market: Digital Radio Report. Ofcom's Eighth Annual Digital Progress Report. Research Report. Ofcom. https://www.ofcom.org.uk/__data/assets/pdf_file/0014/108311/Digital-Radio-Report-2017.pdf

————. 2018. Definition of New Music on Radio 1 and Radio 2. Variation to Ofcom's Operating Licence for the BBC's UK Public Services. Ofcom.

RAJAR Q4. 2009 retrieved from https://www.rajar.co.uk/docs/2009_12/2009_Q4_Quarterly_Summary_Figures.pdf

RAJAR Q2. 2010 https://www.rajar.co.uk/docs/2010_06/2010_Q2_Quarterly_Summary_Figures.pdf

Radio Centre. 2012. RadioCentre's Response to the BBC Trust's Service Licence Review of Asian Network. Radio Centre.

Sam. 2015 (anonymised). Face to face interview, 11 November.

Starkey, Guy. 2004. Estimating Audiences: Sampling in Television and Radio Audience Research. *Cultural Trends* 13 (1): 3–25.

Wall, Tim, and Andrew Dubber. 2009. Specialist Music, Public Service and the BBC in the Internet Age. *The Radio Journal: International Studies in Broadcast and Audio Media* 7 (1): 27–47.

Watson, Tamara. 2016. Asian Network Live Listening Performance. Rajar Q4 2016 (6 Month Weight). BBC Marketing and Audiences. http://downloads.bbc.co.uk/commissioning/site/asian-network-rajar-summary-q4-2016.pdf. Accessed 15 Oct 2020.

Wilson, Clint C., and Felix Gutierrez. 1995. *Race, Multiculturalism, and The Media*. 2nd ed. Thousand Oaks: Sage.

CHAPTER 6

Diverse Journalism

How can public service journalism be embedded within diversity and offer non-mainstream viewpoints? What impact do the organisational structures of the BBC have on how race, ethnicity, and identity are imagined and recreated by the BBC Asian Network? This chapter sets out the argument that because race understood as a "political construct" the media, including the BBC, reflects the government's stance on race, by showcasing content that implicitly demands minority communities integrate and are loyal (Gunaratnam 2003). In addition to the political impact upon the BBC, the broadcaster is also restrained and governed by external economic aims and relatedly managerialist principles. More widely societal attitudes to public service broadcasting also influence the scope of the BBC.

This chapter examines the BBC's normative working practices by focusing on the gatekeeping process within the context of news and current affairs content that features race or diversity. There is also a consideration of how news conventions restrict the amount of coverage Sri Lankan and Indian communities received by the BBC, and the chapter explores the idea if negative stereotyped content about Muslim communities is disseminated because it is likely to appeal to majority audiences. The chapter contends that gatekeeping systems across the BBC encourage the reproduction of difference even though the organisation is focused on improving the quality and quantity of content about minority audiences. Combined with drive to recruit diverse employees this contradiction is problematic.

© The Author(s), under exclusive license to Springer Nature Switzerland AG 2021
G. Aujla-Sidhu, *The BBC Asian Network*,
https://doi.org/10.1007/978-3-030-65764-2_6

BBC ASIAN NETWORK NEWS

In-depth interviews with BBC production staff offered an opportunity to gain an insight into the production process within the institution and enabled an examination of the impact the internal culture has upon working methods. Therefore, the manner in which BBC staff experience the institution enables researchers to offer a deeper and granular description of working practices in public service broadcasting (PSB). Throughout this book, the BBC is described as an institution, due to the significant role it plays in British society. It is widely accepted the BBC is the leading public service broadcaster in the world (Born 2004; Curran and Seaton 1997; Tracey 1998). Sociological research into institutions or "new institutionalism" considers how organisations become instituted over time, for example why some acquire the stability or the reputation the BBC has (Nee 1998). Ahmed (2012) has recommended that institutionalism is best understood through the examination of work norms and conventions which are habitual or ordinary and thus normalised. Often these actions may not be named or made explicit, especially to new staff, because they are not formally written down or communicated, because they tend to be a reflection of the organisational and cultural norms as opposed to a reflection of the needs or desires of the audience (Harcup and O'Neill 2016). Ahmed (2012, p. 26) notes in her study of diversity in higher education that the habits of institutions are often revealed only when a person fails to conform or breaks an unwritten rule. Therefore, this chapter recognises that whilst diversity has been made an explicit institutional goal, it causes ambivalence among the organisation's gatekeepers when ethnic staff foreground their journalistic work within diversity.

All the BBC interviewees agreed that the radio station has a key role to play in enabling and amplifying the voice of British Asian communities. Senior reporter, Safia (*not her real name*), explained that the role of BBC Asian Network is to "give people a voice." Specifically, the radio station is a platform for ethnic communities to discuss their concerns and issues because historically they have been absent from mainstream news, in part, because journalism practices endorse the "official" or voice of authority, for example the Police or politicians over ordinary people (Bourdieu 1993; Cottle 2000; Hall et al. 2013; Hesmondhalgh and Saha 2013). Bourdieu

(1993) has argued that journalism like other forms of cultural production is heteronomous, and consequently, the content created is not due to conscious agreements between producers and the audience. Instead, the content is a homology of external forces (including, economic, political, and societal) and that the producers themselves are also influenced by the fierce competition that exists between themselves, and this is placed ahead of the needs of the viewer or listener (Bourdieu 1993, p. 54). Moreover, Bourdieu (1998, p. 2) has outlined that journalists are able to impose "a very particular vision" upon the audience, and crucially this vision tends to be based upon the journalist's interests and existing knowledge. Thus, eliding the needs, desires, and issues that affect ordinary people and minority communities in order to advance the interests of mainstream media organisation that reflect hegemonic views in society. Former head of News, Kevin Silverton, explained that in order to showcase marginalised voices and viewpoints, it is imperative that minority ethnic journalists are recruited so that their insider knowledge and cultural expertise and "their understanding of the issues is heard" by mainstream audiences and politicians. This approach firmly places the burden of improving the representation of minorities on new minority ethnic employees. Chapter 2 described how younger generations of British Asians born in Britain are knowledgeable about the different Asian cultures because they operate in "transnational spaces": although they live in Britain, they have connections through family and friends with the Global South and the rest of the world (Moylan 2013, p. 8). Thus, third- and fourth-generation British Asians have globalised knowledge, and because they are part of the British community, they are able to locate themselves in the British Asian community or their specific community, identify with Britain, and maintain a globalised identity. This practice results in "accented" production (Moylan 2013). However, if accented production is available only on the BBC Asian Network, an ethnic service, equally consumed by a predominantly ethnic listenership, there is a danger that these voices are not heard by the wider society. Yu (in Yu and Matsaganis 2019) have outlined that if ethnic media lack a meaningful connection to the wider media ecology, it means that they simply facilitate speaking on behalf of the minority, but there is no reciprocal listening on the part of the majority population.

The BBC Asian Network established a newsroom to create news content that offers and displays the British Asian perspective and voice in the news output. The content created by the station is shared with the news service within the BBC and with other BBC departments. The former

Controller Bob Shennan explained BBC Asian Network journalists contribute to enhancing the broadcaster's coverage of minority communities. However, due to the changes in the news agenda in the UK, Kevin Silverton, the former news editor, acknowledged there is a stronger awareness among programme editors about the need to showcase minority communities in their programming: "our difficulty now is that a story which historically only we did, is that actually lots of other people are doing it as well." Increasingly new journalists hired to work at the station come from Asian backgrounds, ordinarily educated to degree or postgraduate level and have been born and raised in the UK, and are likely to be third- or fourth-generation British Asian. They work alongside a mix of first- and second-generation British Asian journalists who joined the station when it became a national digital radio station or when it was a regional service. Danish (*not his real name*) a broadcast journalist explained that the journalists try to make their stories, interviews, and programmes distinct from the rest of the BBC:

> We're giving an Asian point of view on a specific story, so we make sure we get their names in there. We make sure it is quite obvious that they're Asian because they might not sound Asian on-air. (Broadcast Journalist, Danish 2016)

Danish suggests that the journalists are careful to emphasise the interviewees' connection to Asian culture to highlight the uniqueness of the story, its value, and authenticity. This also has the effect of marking the journalism as "ethnic," Chow (in Bowman 2010) suggest that this is a method of "differentiation" that whilst it tries to showcase diversity it also naturally frames the content as "other" Chow (Bowman 2010, p. 35). Mithra (*not her real name*) a former journalist explained she has been directed to seek out young people to interview "they *(editors)* don't like people who are too old they will always try and get you to interview their grandchildren rather than the subject because they feel that age range isn't relevant." This also reveals that the editors pursue the younger demographic at all costs. Moreover, Mithra explained she believed the people she interviews are representative of the listeners. However, this is questionable, as only specific age groups are approached for a contribution in the first place.

The remit stipulates that the BBC Asian Network should make "a very important contribution" to sustaining citizenship and civil society through an emphasis upon current affairs presented accessibly for the target listener (BBC Trust 2016, p. 3). The news content thus encompasses national stories: politics; economics; health; education; International news stories from South Asia, but also USA (United States); and in addition, any relevant unique content, for example religion, culture, and entertainment, that is important to the target listener. Husain Husaini worked as the head of News between 2006 and 2009:

> In news there was an issue about how newsworthy different cultures are. Islam and Muslim communities are quite newsworthy and the Sikh community are actually quite newsworthy. I am not sure what we would do if we sought to do positive cultural things about different communities. There was definitely an aim to be representative of the audience, we sent reporters to different places, trips to cities where we had no coverage. (Former Head of Programmes, Husain Husaini 2015)

There are issues over how a radio station can proportionally balance the amount of coverage the various Asian communities receive. This has become increasingly problematic following September 11 because the Muslim community has been propelled into mainstream news, often in negative contexts. Consequently, there are days and weeks when the Muslim community may receive heightened coverage in the Asian Network debate programme and news due to international or national events that happen to involve members of this community. The staff are aware that other communities feel marginalised or negatively depicted. For example, the Sikh community have frequently complained about the Asian Network's portrayal of their faith and culture. There have been complaints against former phone-in presenter Nihal and Bobby Friction, Drive presenter (and incidentally, a member of the Sikh community). BBC staff are also keenly aware that Muslim listeners dislike the negative connotations about their faith and culture that are broadcast by the BBC. Kevin Silverton, who took over from Husain Husaini as news editor from 2009 to 2016, pointed out that because the BBC Asian Network seeks to serve a diverse and disparate audience it is challenging to cover them equally:

> I have never been a believer in specifically saying I need you to find me a Hindu story, or a Sikh story, or a Muslim story, or a Sri Lankan story, or a Bangladeshi story. I am very much a believer that you only put news on the radio if it is worthwhile news and if you have enough contacts in those communities or if you have enough people scouring the right places for stories

in those communities then they should come to the surface. The only danger with that is some of the communities don't surface as much as others. So, the Hindu community are not terribly active about pushing up their community or the things that they are feeling passionate about. (Former News Editor, Kevin Silverton 2015)

Silverton acknowledges that inevitably some communities do not get adequate airtime in news bulletins or the debate discussions. He highlights the Hindu community is likely to miss out on coverage. The Asian Network journalists also have some challenges in generating original unique news angles on the Muslim community due, in part, to the fact that content about terror and Islam is a key element of the mainstream global news agenda (Gerhards and Mike Schafer 2014). Subsequently, Silverton admitted the BBC Asian Network is forced to cover Islam-related stories with the mainstream framing simply, because other mainstream news organisations are promoting this agenda. However, he recognised there is strong drive within the BBC to incorporate diverse content and that some programmes will include material about, for example, Ramadan because they have some "worth." This suggests that journalism that covers diverse issues is considered interesting and potentially worthy but that historically it was not.

I like to think part of the reason is to do with the Asian Network, we have become better at telling people our stories reaching out and pushing out. (Former News Editor, Kevin Silverton 2015)

The Asian Network newsroom was moved to London in 2013 to sit alongside the BBC's other national radio stations. This has physically enabled collaboration with other teams and naturally the promotion of the BBC Asian Network agenda. Alia *(not her real name)* outlined that the journalism crafted by the minority journalists is distinctive and relatable for the Asian listener through the language and phrasing used in the pieces:

We can paint pictures that people identify with, so if I'm in one part of Leicester standing outside Belgrave road and there are 3 big vans selling 3 boxes of mangoes for 10 quid and my listeners buy them, they know exactly what I am talking about. Its targeted it's not patronising its relatable its identifiable. (Former senior manager, Alia 2015)

Here, Alia underlines the connection between the language used by the journalists in their scripts, the tone they take, and how they situate the content to make stories both accessible and applicable for the listener. Media content that speaks to the audience and harnesses their language or voice to convey their culture, accent, or perspective is likely to encourage people to listen, and this allows the station to build trust with audiences. The interviewees acknowledged that whilst mainstream media tries report on the minority communities, their stories can lack authenticity and, moreover, that it can be perceived to be patronising by the audience. Nadine *(not her real name)*, a former senior member of staff, argued: "I strongly, passionately believe that unless you are from that background you will not understand the story or do it in an authentic way." It is argued that the recruitment of diverse employees positively influences the news production process because they naturally bring their identities and frame of reference to the newsroom (Yu and Matsaganis 2019, p. 5). Alia underlined that journalists must be "confident" and "know their stories inside out" and "the communities inside out because you are representing the Asian community." Although this sounds obvious, Alia makes a critical point that, for ethnic media to survive serving small audiences, building trust through good journalistic practices of fact checking and non-misrepresentation of communities increases and retains the listener. However, Matsaganis and Katz (2014, p. 937) have argued that very close ties with the community can "shape the identity of the ethnic media organisation and its journalists in forceful ways." In other words, if the community is unhappy with their representation, they will complain and even protest. Kaylon (*not his real name*) explained the Asian Network listeners are empowered to articulate their views and give feedback, but he felt this was not the case in the BBC regional news departments:

> On the phone-in you receive instant reaction through text, tweets whatever else. Maybe because the Asian Network audience is younger than a local TV audience. When I produced lead regional TV stories, I actually missed the involvement with the audience because we weren't asking people to tweet or text. So actually, the Asian Network is good at connecting with its audience. (Former journalist, Kaylon 2016)

The previous chapter studied the digital native editorial strategy enacted from 2016 to engage with young people who do not traditionally listen to radio, through visual means on social media. Kamran (*not his real name*) a producer emphasised that "radio has become visualised" and that for the station to remain relevant the programmes must engage with listeners via social media. However, whilst this strategy does enable the BBC Asian Network brand to extend its presence, Danish noted when he interacted with potential listeners many were not aware of the station, "they just don't realise there is an Asian Network. They think we are from some sort of BBC World Service or this thing called BBC Asia as they paraphrase it." Moreover, he highlighted on occasions contributors were unaware the station has a dedicated news programme, which suggests that stronger promotion of the station's content is required.

It was only when the Asian Network was threatened with closure that the value and worth of the original journalism produced by the employees was taken more seriously internally and externally. Producer, Joy *(not her real name)*, emphasised that:

> The paradox is that if we didn't have the Asian Network we would have far less in the BBC about Asian cultures. So, the Asian Network is a kind of cultural centre of excellence and knowledge that needs to be shared. (Producer, Joy 2015)

Joy's perspective echoes Shennan's viewpoint that the BBC Asian Network plays a significant role in enhancing diverse content across the BBC. Due to economic pressures the various BBC departments are forced to collaborate and pool their resources to create public service content. This has also meant that Asian Network employees have opportunities to push and share their journalism on other BBC programmes:

> There's less money in the BBC but greater collaboration and partnership. Things are much more genre based rather than station specific, there's a greater need to work together. In news for every good idea there is a discussion about where else it can work. For example, the Khaliafat documentary was followed up with a discussion with 7 contributors from different Muslim sects in a round table which was filmed for YouTube. That was complementary to the documentary which went out on Newsnight, Today etc. (Former senior manager, Kavya 2015)

Whilst this is a positive example of how pooling resources works well, the rest of this chapter examines the challenges that ethnic staff working at the Asian Network face when their work centres diversity as the key purpose of their journalism. Therefore, the rest of this chapter explores from the perspective of minority staff why the station remains marginalised within the BBC, and it examines why Muslim-related content is noticed and shared across the BBC.

GATEKEEPING: BRITISH ASIAN COMMUNITIES VERSUS ISLAMIC STORIES

In theory, ethnic media workers with their specialist knowledge ought to have the editorial freedom to produce media content that offers an alternative or unique insight into the lived experiences of ethnic audiences. However, because BBC minority staff operate within the umbrella of the BBC, this means their ideas must pass the standards set centrally within the organisation. Meaning, some unique stories which prominently feature smaller diverse groups can be ignored by BBC commissioners and editors who are more interested in content that will have a wide appeal among the general audience. The emphasis within any media organisation is to gain viewers or listeners, which enables the organisations to profit from their media content. However, Hesmondhalgh and Baker (2011) point out that economic imperatives in programme making conflict with cultural and creative goals. For example, documentaries are a genre considered to be unlikely to generate money and thus are aired as a public service commitment on part of the broadcasters. Thus Banks (2007) has argued that cultural workers are forced to contend with institutional power structures and financial frameworks, and may be forced to compromise their creative standards because the former imperatives are important. It is a perspective supported by Hesmondhalgh and Baker (2011), who found media workers compromise their standards to create material that attracts the largest possible audience. This resonates with the interview material gathered for this study. Ethnic journalists working at the BBC Asian Network are required to get their original stories onto several BBC platforms; those who are successful are likely to be praised or promoted to work on other prestigious programmes or departments across the BBC. Therefore, there is underlying pressure upon staff, because the management encourage the sharing of journalism to demonstrate the pivotal role the station plays in reflecting minority audiences for the BBC, but on the other hand, a journalist's performance is measured against the quantity of their shared original work. Sam (*not her real name*), a senior journalist, explained the expectation to share stories has created a very pressured working environment:

> It's not simply saying "I've got this story; does anyone want it?" They have to trust your judgment about a story. They have to trust that your packages are going to sound right on their output because often you're not offering bespoke packages, you're having to tailor your work for a mass market. (Senior journalist, Sam 2015)

What Sam has implied is that editorial strength of the story is not the only reason a journalist would be commissioned. Instead, the journalist making the pitch is also assessed by the commissioners. For example, have they covered other stories for the outlet they are pitching to? Do they have the same tone or style as the intended programme? The "sound" of the journalist means that commissioners determine if the journalist's presentation style complements their output. This is replicated in television, whereby how a journalist appears on-screen, and more controversially their age, can determine what programmes they work on. What is demonstrated here is that in addition to journalistic skills, employees need a range of other soft skills in order to pitch their knowledge and specialism to non-ethnic commissioners and senior staff. Therefore, the notion of trust is central: if the commissioner is unaware or has no previous knowledge of the journalist, it is possible the story will not be commissioned. If the journalist is known, they are also evaluated on their previous work before they can be given the opportunity of producing another story. Therefore, if a journalist has made a mistake previously, this potentially limits the chances of the new pitch being commissioned.

Several staff outlined in their interviews that content relating to Islam is more likely to be selected by other BBC programmes. Kamlesh Purohit worked as a planning editor at Asian Network until 2014. His role involved promoting content from the Asian Network and collaborating with other planning editors to enhance their programme. The aim of the role was to maximise the impact of BBC Asian Network content across the organisation. However, he found it challenging:

> I found I could talk about a story that I thought was really important, but if it didn't fall in the remit of what they wanted it would fail. The moment I mentioned the word Muslim, or radicalisation, or forced marriage they loved the story, no matter how many times it had been done. That for me

was the frustration. One of my roles should not be just to provide those stories for the rest of the BBC but to educate the BBC. (Kamlesh Purohit 2015)

This perspective was echoed by some of the other interviewees: Safia (*not her real name*), a reporter, outlined that although she tends to pitch a range of British Asian ideas those involving the Muslim communities were more successful because "there is a lot of appetite in the BBC for Muslim stories." Former journalist Kaylon *(not his real name)* highlighted "there's a bit of talk at the Asian Network that when there's a Hindu story its harder to get that done." Former senior manager Alia suggested that content about Muslims is preferred by the wider BBC because it is familiar:

Forced marriages are a stereotype, honour killings, terrorism, Islam, Muslim, those stories you don't need to get people's attention, their ears will pipe up because people feel comfortable with those because they have already done them before. If you go to them with another story you have to be a very convincing salesman. I don't think its institutional, sometimes it's just the people in those positions. (Former senior member of staff, Alia 2015)

Alia has underlined two significant issues: first, those stories that are familiar, that is Islam and terrorism, are selected over unknown groups because the commissioners are aware this type of content can appeal to a larger audience. This means that new and untested ideas and innovative formats are considered too risky, and commissioners favour sticking with tried and tested content, even though public service broadcasters are expected to innovate. Second, the ethnic staff who are successful in getting commissioned are competent and able to navigate institutional norms, standards, and meet external expectations, for example societal and political.

Chow in (Bowman 2010) has argued that the use of stereotypes which she describes as being a generalisation restricts creativity and originality, whilst conflating aspects of identity which are likely to be incorrect in the first place. Safia acknowledged that "the negative stories sell more, if you put jihadism or Jihadi brides or radicalisation and Muslim in the same sentence, automatically it's like light bulbs go and they want it." Saha (2018) has argued that production studies of news have often failed to ground themselves adequately in social theory to explain why some patterns of discrimination and marginalisation occur in the newsroom. Production studies tend to focus on how organisations are structured and operate, and concentrate less on studying how power is dispersed among these organisations. Saha (2018) has also outlined that issues pertaining to diversity, professional codes, and practices are inherently racialised and conflict with the commercial, political, and social goals of media organisations. There is pressure on the BBC to both be a commercial success whilst simultaneously show its national and cultural relevance at a period of time when diasporic communities are less reliant upon PSB. As a result, the BBC has been forced to re-evaluate how it serves minority communities.

Historically these communities were served by specific departments with specialised programmes. However, as Malik (2002, 2013) has outlined, Channel 4 and the BBC have sought to appeal to minorities within broad mainstream programmes in the past decade. Therefore, although the BBC Asian Network is a specific service for a group of communities, the same approach is implemented whereby the content also seeks to offer a broad version of Asian identity. The articulation of a broad and integrated British Asian identity on-air has caused anxiety among staff at the station (see Chap. 5). This version of identity has been referred to as a marketized version of diversity which works to mask social inequalities (Malik 2013). Saha (2018) also presents a similar argument, specifically that because race and diversity are considered to be problematic, the BBC has moved from a paternalistic and accommodating stance to a position that emphasises integration and social cohesion. In practice this means there is an emphasis upon "how diversity can contribute to innovation, efficiency and competition on the new knowledge economy" (Saha 2018, p. 109). Therefore, in his view, "gatekeepers" or commissioners maintain working practices that appear to be "common business sense" and select ideas that they believe are popular in winning audiences over, which, in turn, leads to the dominant negative or stereotyped framing on stories about race being selected (Saha 2018, p. 135). Mithra explained she gets frustrated because "it's hard to convince other editors what the story is because they *don't get* [emphasised] South Asian stories. Or they don't understand the value of the stories." This appears to be the crux of the issue; commissioners can stifle originality simply, due to a lack of knowledge or awareness of the diverse needs among the audiences. The former head of News acknowledged that difference of opinion over the worthiness of stories continues to be an issue within the organisation:

> Sometimes what you think is a strong story isn't always their [BBC] idea of a strong story. I find now that most things we approach people with are seen

as something worth doing. Sometimes it is about finding the outlet the story suits the best, because they all have different agendas and style. If you offer a quirky Asian story people love to grab onto that. (Former Head of News, Kevin Silverton 2015)

Although Silverton recognises the positives of the collaboration process, he alludes that some genres are more successful. The pressure to find the right BBC department falls on the journalist making the pitch. He does seem to imply that the BBC is trying to broaden its mindset to include diverse content. In contrast, Sam outlined that successful pitches need to have some mainstream audience appeal:

I think a good journalist at the Asian network will think about what the mainstream audience would think about the issue. Often the stories that get interest from the rest of mainstream radio and on TV are those that have some sort of impact on the mainstream or host community. So, there's got to be a current within the story that's running through the rest of the media. (Senior Journalist, Sam 2015)

The onus is on the journalist to spell the tangible link to mainstream current affairs or audience. Mya (*not her real name*) also offered a similar rationale; she said it is imperative that minority journalists pitch ideas that connect or engage with non-ethnic listeners:

I think the audience has to be at the heart of the stories because we are providing a service for both our Asian Listeners and our non-Asian listeners. So, I think the stories have to really strike a chord not just with the Asian audience but the mainstream communities. (Reporter, Mya 2015)

This suggests that although the staff seek to serve young British Asian listeners with distinctive entertainment, music, and current affairs to appeal to their dual identities and heritage, some stories on the Asian Network are created for the mainstream community and happened to feature British Asians. This contradicts the remit that BBC has set for the station. Sam suggests that the issues they tackle should have some resonance, meaning, or appeal for mainstream audiences for the pitch to be successful. This means that terrorism or stories that examine the host nation's anxieties or concerns about minority communities are likely to be selected. Mya appears to believe as a BBC employee she ought to try and reach all audiences—a core BBC mission. These observations connect with Malik's (2013) argument that diversity has been reconfigured to be understood as creative diversity, and essentially what is depicted is a cleansed or "marketized version of diversity" (Malik 2013, p. 325). This means that the content does not tackle genuine issues faced by the minority communities. Both Malik (2013) and Saha (2018) suggest that a diluted or ambiguous version of creative diversity is being presented by the media which offers false images of community cohesion, multiculturalism, and integration because deep underlying issues and inequitable outcomes are not visible. Alia proposed in her interview that the commissioners need to improve their knowledge of diverse cultures: "They need to widen their horizons and acknowledge that there is a wider audience out there" (former senior manager, Alia 2015). Alia has proposed that the BBC needs to accept parts of the audiences hold viewpoints that contradict or differ from the hegemonic stance presented by mainstream media. She implies that the BBC is focused upon the general mainstream audience at the expense of minority audiences. The issue is further compounded by the concerns some staff outlined in Chap. 4, that new ethnic employees lack cultural knowledge about the Asian communities and consequently create news stories or programmes which focus on difference or negative aspects of the communities.

The BBC held a series of focus groups with staff in 2018 specifically scrutinising diversity and disability within the institution. They also conducted a survey to understand their employees' socio-economic backgrounds. Within the focus groups some staff highlighted their ideas are unable to flourish within the BBC due to how different editors apply their version of "creative freedom." All programmes and stations have their own in-house style and agenda which journalists must adhere to in terms of the type of content selected, overall tone, the scripting, contributors featured, the framing, and their presentation style. Editors largely dictate the agenda of their individual programme. Hesmondhalgh and Baker (2011) describe journalists as being a hybrid creative worker because although they coexist in the cultural industries, they do not possess aesthetic autonomy, which is associated with artistic creative workers, and instead, they have a type autonomy that aligns with professional workers. Hesmondhalgh and Baker's study of creative work concludes that creative autonomy has been eroded due to commercial imperatives. The BBC acknowledged that there is a need for cultural awareness training for team managers in addition to internal unconscious bias training programme. The BBC has recommended that when team managers apply for promotion, they should supply evidence of their contribution to championing diversity and inclusion within their department. This suggests, therefore, that there is greater pressure on programmes makers to highlight diversity.

Within the BBC, the commissioning of content from external production companies for programmes is a formal procedure intended to maintain the public service broadcaster's values of quality, impartiality, and balance. The BBC has a detailed set of codes and rules referred to as the producer guidelines, which rationalise working practices for all producers, reporters, and presenters, and in 2020 they imposed diversity conditions upon radio and television productions. ITV and Channel 4 have their own versions of these rules. June Sarpong, BBC's director of Creative Diversity, has outlined that the BBC wants to achieve "creativity that thrives because of diversity of thought, delivers innovation, enhances performance and content that reaches the widest audience possible" (BBC Media Centre 2020). However, the informal internal commissioning system that exists between departments and programmes often features (inexperienced) producers who are seeking to fill space in their programmes. In addition, stories that are successfully channelled to other BBC programmes are not crafted into multiple versions, that is, one for Newsnight and one version of Asian Network. Due to economic constraints the version of the story that is crafted collaboratively is framed by other BBC staff, so a uniquely British Asian angle may be reduced and diluted to make the story appeal or more easily understood by mainstream audiences. There are two problems here: the Asian audience are more likely to disagree with the framing and language of a story pitched at a mainstream audience and may feel compelled to switch to alternative diasporic services, which are aimed exclusively at them. Second, minority ethnic staff are forced to structure the content according to the desires of other BBC staff in order to broadcast their work; if they do not conform this can have a detrimental impact on their career prospects. Sam suggested that ethnic journalists do face problems in getting promoted and proposed the "reputation" of the station "isn't necessarily where it should be at even though we've got all those connections, and I think we've got to work harder at trying to develop that reputation." Former member of staff Kamlesh Purohit concurred with Sam explaining he has worked in the BBC for more than 20 years and yet "people see you as somebody who is Asian rather than somebody who is a good broadcaster." Purohit now occupies a senior leadership role in local radio, but he feels this perception has hindered his career within the BBC. Purohit also pointed out that although minority journalists are encouraged to bring to the fore their expertise, this could be further utilised:

> The reporters are very good journalists at the BBC Asian Network and very hard working. They are able to bring stories to the wider BBC with their backgrounds, with their knowledge they are in some ways helping to avoid the stereotypes and break down barriers and give a platform for stories that would never get an airing otherwise. I think it has fallen short of what it can achieve. I think the phenomenal potential that the Asian Network had, and still has, could be further exploited. (Purohit 2015)

As explored in Chap. 5 the producer's personal experience, their education, their socio-economic class, and ethnicity intersects, and is bought into the newsroom and, hence, influences the ideas they have, and the news stories they create and through this the contribution they make to the public sphere. The public sphere as defined by Habermas is an influential theoretical framework within media and communication studies, and within its parameters is the place where journalism has the potential to improve the quality of public life alongside informing citizens. This does not always occur as ethnic staff outlined; they feel they are constrained in their working practices due to gatekeeping and internal power systems.

Sport is one area where the BBC Asian Network must cooperate with other departments such as BBC 5 Live, because "the only way the BBC Asian Network can cover these sorts of big tournaments is to collaborate" (Danish, journalist, 2016). However, Danish (*not his real name*) also pointed out this method has some principal flaws: the 5 Live framing and focus in cricket are on the England team:

> Perhaps the management didn't understand what we did with regards to cricket was very Asian specific when it comes to India versus Pakistan or something like that. Those kinds of things are massive to our audience, and they are not covered in the same way across the BBC, so it is frustrating at times, that we can't cover certain things in the way we would like to. (Journalist, Danish 2016)

The competitive cricket rivalry between Indian and Pakistan is not prominent in the wider BBC because they focus on the England team's successes or failures as opposed to Bangladesh, India, and Pakistan. Collaboration is fruitful when both sides mutually gain from the process, but when there is a lack of awareness of the listeners' needs for one output, this adversely impacts their listening experience. Ang (1991) has highlighted that although the BBC strives to include and showcase diversity, the professionalisation of production codes can mean that producers place "editorial judgement over audience tastes or demand" (Ang 1991, p. 115). Born (2004) outlined that the BBC's tendency to attract "journalists from elite social and educational backgrounds" cements views that "news and current affairs is an intellectual elite within the BBC" (Born 2004, p. 379):

> Unfortunately, there are people with pre-formed ideas and pre-conceived kind of thoughts about what are the important stories for their output and not what is important for the Asian audience. So, the BBC cannot complain that not enough Asian people watch the BBC output or listen to BBC radio. It's no surprise if most of the Asian families I know will watch Zee TV or Sony TV and watch all the soaps and the dramas and NDTV for their news when actually they should as licence fee payers be getting those services from the BBC. The BBC has to provide something for those audiences otherwise people aren't going to tune in. Where you are making Asian news for a non-Asian audience for me that is the difficulty in the structure for the Asian Network. (Kamlesh Purohit 2015)

Purohit opposes the idea of producing Asia-specific media content for mainstream audiences. His views contrast with Mya and Sam, who earlier noted there is a need for their work to have some mainstream appeal. June Sarpong, director of Creative Diversity, acknowledged that "we [BBC] understand our responsibility to share stories and experiences of all of communities that make up the rich and diverse fabric of the United Kingdom" (BBC 2020, p. 3). Moreover, it is through the "diversity of experiences and perspectives" that the BBC can deliver on this (BBC Media Centre 2020, p. 4). The discussion so far has highlighted that ethnic staff feel less supported and perceive their skills are judged by other BBC staff. This may not apply in the same way for non-ethnic staff, and there is a suggestion that the skillset of a BBC Asian Network journalist, or simply an ethnic journalist, is seen as being different from other journalists. Clearly, if a story is delivered across a range of BBC platforms it will reach a larger audience, but the insights from staff reveal that this move impacts the creative freedom of the journalist, because the originality of the idea can be diluted to make it appealing. June Sarpong adds to the foreword of the progress report on the Diversity Commissioning code of practice that if the BBC and its partners do not act on diversity imperatives that "ultimately, this can lead to losing market share through failing to connect with an increasingly diverse audience" (BBC 2020, p. 3). In other words, the BBC is focused on engaging with audiences due to the pressures the institution faces to justify its existence and role in broadcasting.

REPORTING THE MUSLIM COMMUNITIES

This chapter has noted that there is a disproportional emphasis upon stories about Muslims and Islam across the media. The increasingly sensationalist narrative that is articulated contributes to a racialised discourse on national identity and belonging and was evident in the Brexit Referendum in 2016 in the UK (Virdee and McGeever 2018). Despite the objections from Muslim viewers and listener, Nadine pointed out for journalists to "hold people to account" it is impossible to "ignore" Islamic stories. She believes that journalists are compelled to cover the Muslim communities, positively and negatively simply because it is their duty. Mya agreed with this argument and described the need to report on sensitive issues even when she is aware it upsets the listeners:

> What happened in Bradford and Dewsbury where the mothers took their children to Syria that is a massive news story. Something that affects our community. I think it would be irresponsible for us not to report that story. I know some Muslims would turn around and say you are always portraying the Muslim community in a bad way but the stories we cover have to reflect what is going on in the communities and we don't just cover negative stories all the time. We do try to make an effort to cover positive stories, but it is a two-way process and I do think sometimes people forget the onus is also on them to communicate with us. (Reporter, Mya 2015)

What is interesting is that Mya emphasises her professional standards first but also places herself within the community of listeners despite the journalistic concepts of impartiality and objectivity. She uses the professional standards as a form of defence to create distance from any criticism. This replicates how media organisations defend themselves from accusations of bias. The concept of a two-way process is interesting. Mya points out that it is not the reporter or the media's burden to shoulder the representation of communities but that the communities also need to collaborate and cooperate. She also admitted in her interview that she struggles to convince Muslim contributors to take part in stories because they are "very wary of the media" because they believe the "BBC has an agenda and that the BBC is biased":

> Many people have come up to me and say, "Does someone tell you what to say?" Or "Are your pieces vetted?" They are actually quite surprised when I tell them that what you hear on-air is my work. I think this perception is perhaps created because they believe their views should be given complete airtime and I have to explain to people that we have to be unbiased and objective. (Senior Reporter, Mya 2015)

Mya's insight reveals that some parts of the audience are unaware of the BBC's values of impartiality, accuracy, balance, and independence, and thus they do not understand the way BBC journalists are expected to work. Flood et al. (2011) have questioned how the commitment to impartiality in the BBC can be reconciled with its public purposes, which include supporting learning for people of all ages, and to reflect and represent diverse communities. They argue that because the BBC coexists and functions in a similar business environment to other broadcasters its news values do not differ significantly from the competitors. Moreover, because Islam along with terrorism, conspiracy, conflict, anxiety, and insecurity or tensions in immigrant and host populations is perceived to have a high news values, this makes the stories compulsive journalism. Flood et al. (2011) also noted that news content on Islam has little focus upon British life in the UK and that the concentration of media content that presents this community to the audience within the context of "violence, destruction, political disorder, fanaticism, sectarian intolerance, threat, suffering and deprivation" necessitates balance in terms of positive coverage (Flood et al. 2011, p. 230). As a key cultural institution in the UK the BBC is positioned as a powerful entity to promote the opinions of British people, but it also articulates the dominant ideology which means Muslim audiences tend to mistrust the broadcaster (Harb and Bessaiso 2006). Kevin Silverton, former news editor, outlined that the Muslim coverage from the station is distinct:

> If you compare the Asian Network news coverage to other mainstream BBC outlets, then we are much more targeted towards different groups when we need to be. Sometimes you have to say this is really just that about this community and then break it down. The phone-in is good, when you start

talking about Muslim issues you can break it down to all the different sides. We do drill down but it's not easy it is hard, and sometimes we are probably guilty of taking an overarching view on matters rather than drilling down. (Former News Editor, Kevin Silverton 2015)

Here Silverton acknowledges that the station does on occasions adopt the same hegemonic stance on Muslim stories as the rest of the BBC. This creates a gap between the station and the listeners who have highlighted they expect the Asian Network to offer nuanced content that highlights their perspectives as opposed to Eurocentric views:

Sometimes when we do [Muslim stories] people get offended, and say, "Why are you doing a Muslim story again? Why are you doing Islam again?" (Former Senior manager Staff, Alia 2015)

The station is in a difficult position: it is part of the BBC, and therefore some stories either tacitly or overtly adopt the broadcaster's Eurocentric lens, and this naturally influences how British Asian listeners perceive the BBC Asian Network. It is worth noting that the communities who fear the media often do so because they have often been negatively portrayed (Poole and Richardson 2006; Hesmondhalgh and Saha 2013).

CONCLUSION

This chapter has demonstrated some of the challenges and tensions that are created through the organisational drive to share original journalism concerning the British Asian communities in the UK. It appears that whilst the wider institution accepts that the BBC Asian Network is the specialist centre of knowledge on British Asian audiences and is the originator of niche and original journalism, other parts of the BBC still imagine race, ethnicity, and religion within a restricted framework that tacitly promotes "otherness," conflict, and terrorism (Flood et al. 2011). Whilst the intention is that the BBC Asian Network contributes to the enhanced representation of British Asians across the institution, the in-depth interviews demonstrate ethnic employees continue to face similar issues to those outlined by Cottle's (1997) study 30 years earlier. Ethnic staff are still forced to cooperate with gatekeepers or commissioners who have fixed ideas on what can and cannot work. The insights from minority staff reveal that when they offer stories about the diverse communities in the UK to other departments, they do not necessarily want them. The interviews gathered for this research, therefore, provide an insight into the professional and production environment within the BBC Asian Network. Ethnic staff are aware that if they pitch stories pertaining to the Muslim community, they are more likely to be successful in getting commissioned. Subsequently, some journalists rationalise the prevailing economic and internal working norms to best position themselves and their career. There is also a suggestion that the journalists must prove themselves. Therefore, some ethnic staff feel undermined within the BBC and feel a "sense of exclusion and isolation" and believe there is a lack of opportunity for BAME (Black Asian and Minority Ethnic) staff development and progression (BBC 2018, p. 7). In response, the BBC set out plans in 2020 to make diversity at the heart of content for both TV and radio. Within the contemporary BBC, minority ethnic staff tend to be clustered in producer and journalism roles with fewer minority staff members in the decision-making roles (BBC Annual Report 2018/2019). This suggests that "class asymmetry" is evident in the media; the experiences of the people commissioning stories in the BBC do not concur with the audiences.

REFERENCES

Ahmed, Sara. 2012. *On Being Included*. Durham/London: Duke University Press.
Alia, 2015. (anonymised). Face to face interview, 16 June.
Ang, Ien. 1991. *Desperately Seeking the Audience*. London/New York: Routledge.
Banks, Mark. 2007. *The Politics of Cultural Work*. Basingstoke: Palgrave Macmillan.
BBC. 2018. Reflecting the Ethnic Diversity of the UK Within the BBC Workforce. A Report on Career Progression and Culture for BAME Staff at the BBC. http://downloads.bbc.co.uk/mediacentre/bame-career-progression-and-culture-report.pdf. Accessed 21 Oct 2020.
———. 2018/19. BBC Group Annual Report and Accounts 2018/19. https://downloads.bbc.co.uk/aboutthebbc/reports/annualreport/2018-19.pdf. Accessed 21 Oct 2020.
———. 2020. BBC Diversity Commissioning Code of Practice Progress Report. http://downloads.bbc.co.uk/aboutthebbc/reports/reports/diversity-cop-progress-1920.pdf. Accessed 21 Oct 2020.
BBC Media Centre. 2020. BBC – BBC Reveals Progress Through Its Diversity Commissioning Code of Practice – Media Centre. September 29, 2020. https://www.bbc.co.uk/mediacentre/latestnews/2020/diversity-progress-report

————. 2016. BBC Asian Network Service Licence 2016. BBC Trust. http://downloads.bbc.co.uk/bbctrust/assets/files/pdf/regulatory_framework/service_licences/radio/2016/asian_network_aug16.pdf. Accessed 21 Oct 2020.

Born, Georgina. 2004. *Uncertain Vision, Birt, Dyke and the Reinvention of the BBC*. London: Secker and Warburg.

Bourdieu, Pierre. 1993. *The Field of Cultural Production: Essays on Art and Literature*. Polity Press.

————. 1998. *On Television and Journalism*. London: Pluto.

Bowman, Paul. eds. 2010. *The Chow Reader*. New York: Columbia University Press.

Cottle, Simon. 1997. Television and Ethnic Minorities: Producers' Perspectives. Aldershot: Avebury.

Cottle, Simon. 2000. *Ethnic Minorities and The Media, Changing Cultural Boundaries*. Buckingham: Open University Press.

Curran, James, and Jean Seaton. 1997. *Power without Responsibility, the Press and Broadcasting in Britain*. 5th ed. London: Routledge.

Danish. 2016. (anonymised). Face to face interview, 10 February.

Flood, Chris, Stephen Hutchings, Galina Miazhevich, and Henri Nickels. 2011. Between Impartiality and Ideology. *Journalism Studies* 12 (2): 221–238.

Gerhards, Jurgen, and S. Mike Schafer. 2014. International Terrorism, Domestic Coverage? How Terrorist Attacks Are Presented in the News of CNN, Al Jazeera, the BBC, and ARD. *International Communication Gazette* 76 (1): 152–176.

Gunaratnam, Yasmin. 2003. *Researching 'Race' and Ethnicity: Methods, Knowledge and Power*. London: Sage.

Hall, Stuart, Critcher Chas, Jefferson Tony, Clarke John, and Roberts Brian. 2013. *Policing the Crisis: Mugging, the State, and Law and Order*. 2nd ed., 35th Anniversary edition. Basingstoke: Palgrave Macmillan.

Harb, Zahera, and Ehab Bessaiso. 2006. British Arab Muslim Audiences and Television After September 11. *Journal of Ethnic and Migration Studies* 32 (6): 1063–1076.

Harcup, Tony, and Deirdre O'Neill. 2016. What Is News? *Journalism Studies* 18 (12): 1470–1488.

Hesmondhalgh, David, and Sarah Baker. 2011. *Creative Labour, Media Work in Three Cultural Industries*. Abingdon: Routledge.

Hesmondhalgh, David, and Anamik Saha. 2013. Race, Ethnicity, and Cultural Production. *Popular Communication* 11 (3): 179–195.

Husain Hussaini. 2015. Skype Interview, 8 October.

Joy. 2015 (anonymised). Face to face interview, 14 December.

Kamlesh Purohit. 2015. Face to face interview, 17 March.

Kavya. 2015 (anonymised). Face to face interview, 25 March.

Kevin Silverton. 2015. Face to face interview, 15 June.

Malik, Sarita. 2002. *Representing Black Britain, Black and Asian Images on Television.* London: Sage.

———. 2013. "Creative Diversity": UK Public Service Broadcasting After Multicultur alism. *Popular Communication* 11 (3): 227–241.

Matsaganis, M.D., and V.S. Katz. 2014. How Ethnic Media Producers Constitute Their Communities of Practice: An Ecological Approach. *Journalism* 15 (7): 926–944.

Moylan, Katie. 2013. *Broadcasting Diversity, Migrant Representation in Irish Radio.* Bristol: Intellect.

Mya. 2015 (anonymised). Skype Interview, 10 July.

Nee, Victor. 1998. Sources of the New Institutionalism in Brinton, C, Mary., and Nee, Victor. (eds.). The New Institutionalism in Sociology. Stanford, Stanford University Press.

Poole, Elizabeth, and John E. Richardson, eds. 2006. *Muslims and the News Media.* Abingdon/New York: I B Tauris.

Sam. 2015 (anonymised). Face to face interview, 11 November.

Saha, Anamik. 2018. *Race and the Cultural Industries.* Cambridge: Polity.

Tracey, Michael. 1998. *The Decline and Fall of Public Service Broadcasting.* Oxford: Oxford University Press.

Virdee, Satnam, and Brendan McGeever. 2018. Racism, Crisis, Brexit. *Ethnic and Racial Studies* 41 (10): 1802–1819.

Yu, S. Sherry, and M.D. Matsaganis. 2019. *Ethnic Media in the Digital Age.* New York: Routledge.

CHAPTER 7

Language and Identity Politics

ROLE OF LANGUAGE PROGRAMMING

The BBC's digital radio station, the Asian Network, has been set a challenging task to serve all British Asian listeners equally with a singular service. The station is thus forced to try and appeal widely to the different communities, age groups, and different generations of British Asians, who occupy several socio-economic groups and have diverse lived experiences. Historically this was achieved through language-specific programmes in Hindi, Urdu, Punjabi, and Gujarati to appeal directly to linguist communities. Primarily, this chapter seeks to understand how the BBC Asian Network has evolved its language offer from singular language programmes to blended language—which is a hybrid of English and Hindi or Urdu—and how presenters try to connect with listener through the notion of shared culture and lived experiences. Through the study of language and culture this chapter tries to demonstrate how the BBC is responding to the changing listener.

Historically the language programmes on the BBC Asian Network tried to support and help immigrant communities to adjust and integrate utilising mother tongue programming for listeners who did not speak English. These programmes continued to extend the BBC's paternalistic and integrationist agenda that was evident in the early Asian programming on radio and television (Malik 2008). The early presenters on BBC Radio Leicester and later the BBC Asian Network were members of the Asian

G. Aujla-Sidhu, *The BBC Asian Network*, https://doi.org/10.1007/978-3-030-65764-2_7

communities; some were experienced radio presenters and others were simply volunteers (academics or lawyers) who had exceptional language skills. The BBC has a longstanding commitment to nurturing mother tongues and offers non-English output on radio through Radio Cymru, which broadcasts in Welsh, and BBC Radio nan Gàidheal, a Scottish Gaelic station. Through S4C, a Welsh-language British public service TV channel broadcast throughout the UK and Republic of Ireland, which is partly funded by the licence fee. Therefore, the BBC contributes to the maintenance and promotion of marginalised languages in the UK, and the broadcaster is able to promote British values by utilising mother tongue languages to encourage minority communities to integrate into British norms. Language is intrinsically connected to people's identity and culture. Caspi and Elias (2011) categorise ethnic media into three groups, media *about* which they characterise as being a mainstream model of media, media *for*, organisations where the primary focus is the majority group with some language content for minorities, and media *by* model which offers minority language for a minority audience. The BBC Asian Network can be understood to be shaped by the media *about* model because it is set up by a public service media organisation and it also includes elements of the media *for* model, because ethnic staff are recruited to create both linguistic content and specialist media content for listeners who speak English. Some of news stories pertaining to British Asians are shared with other departments within the BBC so that they can be seen or heard by mainstream audiences.

There has traditionally been an emphasis upon the maintenance of mother tongue language among the British Asian communities living in the UK. Gillespie (1995) found that some Indian parents viewed language-specific programmes on television as "essential language training for their children" (Gillespie 1995, p. 79). Her seminal ethnographic study concentrated on British Asians living in Southall, West London, and scrutinised how they viewed British content, *Bollywood* films and Indian programmes, and the impact this has on their identity. Gillespie (1995) suggests the process of watching ethnic content enabled British Asians to recreate and affirm their cultural traditions. Ethnic media is considered by minority groups to play a key role in maintaining and promoting language. It also contributes to creating a sense of community among ethnic minorities through the dissemination of culture and ethnic identity (Yu and Matsaganis 2019). However, ethnic media itself is often shaped and influenced by the diaspora it serves or targets, and as such this contributes to raising an awareness of diaspora among the community (Tsagarousianou 1999). This means that ethnic media and the community benefit, particularly in terms of broadening their knowledge by creating a support network.

The BBC implicitly accepts that many British Asians speak a South Asian language in addition to English. By using English as the main on-air language, it means the output is inclusive. However, the use of English as the principal means of communication also works to reinforce the articulation or promotion of British norms and values. The historic separate and specific language programmes on the BBC Asian Network acknowledged explicitly the different linguistic practices prevalent among the communities whilst also recognising differences in the listeners' heritage. There is debate over the relevance of mother tongue language for younger generations: one viewpoint is that mother language declines as younger generations of communities become further integrated (Wilson and Gutierrez 1995; Lay and Thomas 2012; Yu and Matsganis 2019). Wilson and Gutierrez (1995) have described foreign language ethnic media as being "transitional and generational serving the first generation of immigrants and having less appeal for the second and third" (Wilson and Gutierrez 1995, p. 225). Effectively they suggest that ethnic media's role becomes redundant; however, other research has documented that ethnic media is being revolutionised by younger generations of those communities (see Yu and Matsaganis 2019). Georgiou (2005) has highlighted that the manner and way people interact with ethnic media is complex; first- and second-generation communities tend to rely upon ethnic media as a source of information about their homelands and cultures, whereas the third generation may use media to connect to their grandparents and the fourth generation to learn about their heritage.

Whilst there has also been a documented growth in independent ethnic media in both the USA and Europe, the long-term future of minority language broadcasting is in doubt. Lay and Thomas (2012, p. 380) concluded that specific language content online or within broadcast media is likely to become "obsolete" because ethnic media organisations are forced to evolve to attract younger generations of users. However, ethnic media publishers and editors interviewed by Lay and Thomas outlined that mother tongue content is vital to "fostering and maintaining cultural unity and identity" (Lay and Thomas 2012, p. 376). Yu (Yu and Matsaganis 2019) notes that non-English media inevitably causes its own marginalisation from the border media ecology because it offers limited or zero access to the majority audience. This means that whilst ethnic communities can raise or discuss their issues and concerns, or in Husband's (1998, p. 143) words enact their "right to speak," the mainstream audience does not acknowledge it. Moreover, Yu (2016) has argued that, although first generations tend to rely upon mother tongue media, ethnic media has a role to serve both minority and majority communities in order to have the minority issues acknowledged. Husband (1994) has warned there is a danger that ethnic radio or television can offer a very narrow representation of minority communities, because they tend to reduce diverse and complex cultures to popular culture through an emphasis upon music or entertainment. Husband does recognise that ethnic media offers some public service content through the provision of news and information that helps and informs the listener. The growth and popularity of ethnic media is also blamed for aiding the fragmentation of audiences. Fragmentation of audiences poses huge worries for news organisations that offer essential information and play a key role as the "social cement of societies" because if people are turning to alternative sources then media organisations are not fulfilling their duties (Deuze 2006, p. 264).

COMMUNITY PROGRAMMING AT BBC ASIAN NETWORK

The BBC Asian Network remit originally required the language programmes to "connect listeners with each other, and with their cultural and linguistic roots" through a minimum of 20 hours of programming a week (BBC Trust 2016, p. 5). There was also a stipulation to offer opportunities for "informal learning" through linguistic content that "should be for listeners who may speak English as a first language" (BBC Trust 2016, p. 6). However, in the interviews a number of Asian Network employees highlighted that there is a "perception they are for older people" (Neeta, language problem) who want to connect to their cultural roots. The dominant view among interviewees was that language programmes primarily serve the first and second generations who are likely to want the nostalgia of their homeland and a connection to their identity. Kavya (*not her real name*), a former senior manager, outlined that the language programmes are important "for a particular type of listener who wanted that really strong cultural community connection."

> There was a real focus on purism for our Gujarati programme or Punjabi programme language purism, cultural purism. Now there is plenty of

English, on language shows, you want to connect with the audience, and we have lowered the purism of the language, colloquial language, slang its Punjabi as spoken or Sylheti Bangla as discussed on the streets of Tower Hamlets. (Former, Head of Programmes, Mark Strippel 2015)

The format of the language programmes remained unchanged until 2012. Kavya explained the presenters emphasised "puritanical" speech and attempted to engage listeners through notions of "cultural identity and through that came a religious identity." The presenters were not atypical BBC talent presenters were not atypical BBC talent.

They (presenters) were specialists in their field. A lot of them were academics and lot of them had really good intrinsic knowledge of their areas of specialism and that was great for then. The style of programme was for a particular type of audience who wanted that really strong cultural community connection. And these programmes fit into that raft. (Senior member of staff, Kavya 2015)

It is implied that a gap existed between the "expert" language programme presenter who tutored the listener and the other presenters who engaged and entertained the audience. The notion of "tutoring" is in keeping with the BBC's historical paternalistic inclination. This style made the programmes distinct from the main daytime schedule of the station. By reducing the emphasis upon language, the presenters are able to bond with younger listeners who identify less with the language but associate with the culture. Post 2016, the language programmes are no longer explicitly described as being specialist language shows. Mark Strippel, the former head of Programmes, described how they have evolved into new "specialist music programmes; they provide the best of that genre and language." The refreshed language programmes still seek to serve targeted specific linguistic communities, that is Punjabi or Urdu through the promotion of music and culture as opposed to the language alone. A significant change to the format is the introduction of blended language, meaning presenters no longer exclusively speak in a mother tongue language and instead mix English and the original tongue. The editorial strategy was implemented to mimic the manner in which many British Asians speak. The former Controller, Bob Shennan, described how he observed people switch between two languages with "incredible kind of deftness." This approach purposely tries to mimic a "more contemporary sense of what it's like to be young and of Asian descent in Britain today" (Former Controller, Bob Shennan 2015).

The new presenters are primarily third-generation British Asians, who may possess a strong social media fan base and have first-hand experience of the British Asian lifestyle to connect with the younger listener. Kavya explained there was a drive to recruit presenters who could speak "in the same way that someone in Brick lane would be speaking or Tower Hamlets. So, they can connect to them." The change in presenters also acknowledges that some listeners only speak English, whilst others speak in their mother tongue. Through this strategy it is clear that the BBC is trying to create a community of listeners through shared connections to music, culture, entertainment, and more loosely linguistics. In many ways the audience is "imagined" because programme makers try to find ways to unite disparate groups of people through the shared love of a music genre, similar backgrounds, or promoting a viewpoint or perspective. Thus, Fitzgerald and Housley (2007, p. 150) outline that the community is not only "bought into being" but also "maintained" through the interaction between the listener and the station. Individuals are invited to participate with the imagined community of listeners through the programme content, the language used by the on-air presenters, the music played, and the references to British Asian culture. Inevitably, this means because producers attempt to anticipate tastes and experiences since it is not possible to adequately reflect each and every one and, thus, they are forced to generalise. Blended language in some programmes enables the station to appeal widely. The number of specialist community programmes have been reduced to focus upon the Tamil-speaking community; Punjabi, Urdu, and Gujarati communities; and this content has been relegated to the weekend. This is similar to the move adopted by BBC Local Radio, which has also limited community language programmes for weekends.

Hybrid language has been woeven into the fabric of the station since 2012. Dipps Bhamrah, presenter of the Punjabi show, was one of the first presenters to embrace blended presentation at the station. His specialism is *Bhangra* music, and he explained that "I go for a 50/50 split if anybody can't speak Punjabi, it's great for them. If they speak English, they're still getting a flavour of what's going on." Bhamrah is also a music producer and DJ, which means some of his listeners come to the station to specifically hear him and the music he selects as opposed to the fact the music is packaged within a Punjabi community programme:

I can start a sentence in Punjabi, into English move back into Punjabi that's just how it is. No one speaks in full Punjabi unless you are in a situation you need to. So, I incorporate that what's happening in life, at home and just bring that to the show. I think it is authentic, I am not putting it on, that's me. (Presenter, Dipps Bhamrah 2015)

Bhamrah is able to appeal to more listeners through the use of blended language; he appears to imply that because he naturally does not speak in fluent Punjabi daily, this is also indicative of listeners the BBC is trying to serve. His former producer, Affie Jeerh, explained they have received positive feedback from listeners. She also emphasised that it is imperative that the BBC reflects real people's lives: "We live in the UK, I am a second-generation British Asian and on a daily basis ninety per cent of my conversation with people is in English" (Affie Jeerh 2015). Furthermore, Jeerh highlighted that blended language is inclusive and thus allows teams to reach more listeners, "one would assume they are for an older audience, but if you love music, regardless of what language it is presented in you can tune in" (Former Punjabi Programme Producer, Affie Jeerh 2015).

Blended language presentation is just one way that the Asian Network contributes to construction and reflection of "British Asian identity." Blended language is not unique to the BBC; other Asian commercial stations also adopt similar approaches for their daytime programmes. Former BBC presenter, Tommy Sandhu, emphasised in his interview that the BBC Asian Network sounds uniquely British Asian compared to commercial Asian radio stations:

I did feel a lot of the Asian presenters weren't like me. I felt like they didn't represent me, they didn't sound like me. They were very Asian in their way and I am not really, I am proud my roots and things like that. We [BBC] play house music, RnB, and things like that. (Former presenter, Tommy Sandhu 2015)

The reference to being "very Asian" is likely to refer to the use of formal language by presenters and a more serious tone. The suggestion is that some commercial radio presenters can appear to be overtly traditional and promote values that younger British Asians may not uphold. This may be, in part, because the presenters broadcast in mother tongue language as opposed to in English. Lewis and Booth (1989) do not agree with the idea that radio producers can construct a community (particularly geographical); instead they argue that radio and the media are able to reflect only common interests and express identity. Lewis and Booth focused upon geographical communities in the conclusion to their work, but they did urge radio stations to reduce the emphasis upon local and recognise identity, and interests can apply nationally and internationally. For example, the issues an ethnic group face in London will be replicated elsewhere in the UK; George Floyd's murder in 2020 evoked a reaction and response in UK communities and worldwide.

The Asian Network output acknowledges that the listeners are British first and foremost and that they have some interest in Asian music, entertainment, and culture. Therefore, programmes which emphasised South Asian language and South Asian news and current affairs have been reduced. As a consequence, it is unsurprising that some staff think that all language content ought to be removed from the schedule:

> I think it's a conflict of interests because the Asian Network's agenda is young audience and the listeners who tend to listen to language programmes are older. My mum used to love listening to Ray Khan because he did both Hindi and English. But when Mim Shaikh took over she didn't understand a word of it and switched off straight away. She watches the Asian channels because they are all in language the only thing, she will watch in English is the news. (Journalist, Mithra 2016)

Although this was a minority viewpoint, it demonstrates that individual listeners have different needs and interests due to their age, geographical location, and education. A range of media content is available via global satellite services in South Asian languages to appeal to diasporic communities worldwide. These services play a significant role in promoting language and culture to diasporic audiences. Deuze (2006) poses that although minority media has become an important part of people's lives, they do not necessarily replace mainstream media. Some of the BBC staff expressed concerns that South Asian languages will become obsolete if the BBC does not continue to promote them. Former journalist, Binali, explained language programmes can "educate our kids." In Binali's view, the BBC as a public service broadcaster has a role to play in maintaining and preserving South Asian language for the younger generations of British Asians. Safia, a reporter, also emphasised the language programmes play a significant role in preserving languages but was not optimistic about their survival.

I don't think there is a massive market with the next generation for an Asian Network, especially language programmes. I don't think our children listen to it like we did. I feel very sad that link to our heritage, our culture will die out. What are they going to teach their kids? So, the language is going to die out. (Reporter, Safia 2015)

Public service broadcasting is expected to embrace civic roles in society such as the maintenance of minority language. For example, the BBC funds S4C a Welsh-language free-to-air channel from the licence fee. However, Urdu and Hindi are not part of the UK heritage and history in the same way that the Welsh language is. The promotion of marginalised languages by the BBC offers a culturally diverse experience for all communities, which in turn helps to form "an educated and informed citizenry" (Born and Prosser 2001, p. 675).

Although some linguistic content remains the interviews revealed that the shows do not secure the same level of financial resource as the daytime programmes. They also have fewer production staff, fewer high-profile presenters, and historically have been moved around the schedule. Neeta described feeling "slightly alienated" working on specific language programmes. Which suggests there is also a division among the staff who produce the main daytime programmes and those who produce the lower-profile weekends and languages. Neeta did outline how the changes made to language content have resulted in younger listeners:

Because they (listeners) are using social media, they are younger, and they are engaging with Twitter. We are getting a younger listenership and the people approaching us to do interviews are younger and they are really into what we are trying to do. They recognise that Gujarati culture is not really out there, and they want to help. (Language Programme Producer, Neeta 2015)

Neeta's insight reveals the changes are gradual, but that among the listeners there is also a movement to support specific cultures as opposed to solely supporting the mother tongue of that group. The scheduling of these programmes causes problems because where they are placed denotes a switch from the main programming aimed at all listeners to specific communities attracting smaller numbers of listeners. The former news editor Mike Curtis described the schedule being "disjointed" but emphasised historically the language programmes were:

an appointment for people to listen. I speak Gujarati. I will listen into those two hours, but I am not terribly interested in the rest of it, it's a bit serious so I'll go back to commercial stations. (Former News Editor, Mike Curtis 2014)

Curtis's perspective shows that these programmes fulfilled different purposes for the listeners. It seems evident that different age groups come to the BBC Asian Network at different times of the day for their specific content as the friend of the family strategy envisaged (Chap. 4). The language spoken on-air needs to reflect the listeners' unique identities and their lived experience of the British Asian lifestyle. The move to incorporate blended linguistic practices in the "community" programmes allows the station to offer uniquely Asian "accented" content. Affie Jeerh pointed out it would be unusual to have no South Asian language presentation on the BBC Asian Network: "All the music is in language; how crazy would it be to have music played in a language and not speak the language?" (former Punjabi programme producer, Affie Jeerh 2015).

THE BRITISH ASIANS LISTENER

The BBC would like the listener profile for the BBC Asian Network to be younger. However, this demographic is also more likely to subscribe to streaming services such as Spotify for their music, thus making them a less natural radio listening audience (Sweney 2020). Alia, a former senior manager, had concerns about the strong commitment, on the part of the BBC, to pursue this age group. She acknowledged the reduction of the language-specific content was a purposeful attempt to target young listeners. The Asian Network is not alone in adapting; other Asian stations have been forced to innovate and change as they respond to the growing significance of British Asians in media production roles. The playlist for the Asian Network now emphasises non-*Bollywood* music in recognition that the listener is likely to be integrated into British life. Integration implies the maintenance of some aspects of a person's culture and a demonstration of contributing to the economy through employment and participation in civil society. However, although some of the staff consider the Asian Network as a music station first and foremost, a review of BBC stations in 2015[1] emphasised the unique music offered by Radio 1, 1Xtra, and Radio 2 but concentrated upon the news and current affairs content at the BBC Asian Network. This suggests that within the BBC the station commands authority for its unique news content which is selectively shared across the institution (see Chap. 6).

Although the majority of ethnic media organisations are founded by and targeted at first-generation migrants, they now recruit younger generations of their own communities who have a diluted, hyphenated, and hybrid identities (Yu and Matsaganis 2019). Moreover, Yu (2016) acknowledges that ethnic media produced by younger generations "operates under different conditions and on different scales compared with that of established diaspora, let alone that within a single diaspora" (Yu 2016, p. 2). This view underlines the differences of opinion that exist between the ethnic staff working at the BBC Asian Network. The experiences of third- and fourth-generation British Asians differ to the first and second generations. Therefore, the different points of view over whom the station should serve and how staff should address their listeners are emblematic of how media organisations attempt to find ways to remain relevant to the imagined core community of listeners whilst also responding to changes within those groups in a coherent manner.

> I think you're seeing this complete diversification of consumption. We've got all of the new means of communication that come with the internet. So, for all traditional broadcast platforms the challenge is to get a greater share of attention from those people whilst at the same time the levels of commercial competition are also increasing massively. It's a challenge for old media to connect with new audiences. (Former Controller, Bob Shennan 2015)

All media organisations are under pressure to secure audiences at a time when media consumption habits are changing. The growth of smart phone listening means that the act of listening is reducing into smaller periods of time, whilst the popularity of streaming services among younger generations poses serious competition for the primacy of radio. Although most of the interviewees understood or accepted the imperative to engage with younger listeners, they also identified problems with the strategy:

[1] http://downloads.bbc.co.uk/bbctrust/assets/files/pdf/our_work/music_radio/music_radio.pdf

> How do you say to an 18-year-old, 'I want you to listen to the Asian Network' when their grandmother and grandfather listen to that stuff? Some kids don't even have parents who listen to it. 'I want you to listen to the Asian Network,' well why would I? The brick wall is about culture, about links to mother cultures, and also actually just about who we are. (Presenter, Bobby Friction 2016)

Friction has outlined that some young listeners have fewer tangible links with British Asian culture, and Friction also alludes to a stereotype held among listeners that the station is intended for older audiences because its role is to showcase Asian culture. He seems to suggest that some third-, fourth-, and fifth-generation British Asians do not need media content about Asian culture and heritage because this is not a prominent aspect of their identity—instead, they have a deeper infinity to British culture, rap, or Grime music:

> We are talking 4th and even 5th generation British Asians now. A new generation of people who do not connect on a British Asian way to other British Asian's, and who possibly don't even connect to where they come from. Assimilation and integration and all those other words apply to this group. (Bobby Friction 2016)

The idea that younger generations do not affiliate on the basis of their shared British Asian identity is interesting. These young people seem to have looser connections to their faith, language, and culture in contrast to the shared heritage, which united Asian communities in the 1970s, as outlined in Chap. 2 by Kamlesh Purohit. Hirsch (2018) has also noted that second- and third-generation descendants of immigrants have less personal connection to the experiences of their forebears. Intergenerational change has been scrutinised by Dey et al. (2017, p. 789); they suggest the upbringing and education young British Asians are more attuned to British culture meaning that younger generations find meaning through "the concomitant and meaningful interactions with their cultural and ethnic heritage." In other words that their sense of identity is both informed and actively shaped by their heritage, traditions, faith, and their British values. Hence, Friction believes it is because the Asian Network attempts to appeal to all British Asians in contrast to specific groups, this creates the challenge:

The Asian Network is a glorious kind of extension of the BBC and also one of the hardest places to work if you're in management because you have to honestly sit there and consider 'how can I bring a Pashtun family who speak Pashto, who are nominally part of Pakistani culture and join them with this Gujarati family of lawyers in Wembley?' How do I hit both of those demographics and it's pretty hard! (Presenter, Bobby Friction 2016)

Economically the station needs to secure the largest audience possible, and the BBC Asian Network tries to achieve this by offering programmes in English which have a bespoke "accented" framing. The resillience of radio has been questioned for a long time, but the demand to focus on young ethnic mean listeners creates challenges for BBC Radio, becasue it has to find ways to unite disparate communities that are described as being "Asian."

Whilst Friction focused primarily on the challenges of intergeneration appeal, Alia emphasised the regional differences among the listeners:

I personally feel that because we are so diverse maybe it is better to use local radio, because if I say on the Asian Network that we don't need to do all this story as most Asians speak English then I will be alienating all my listeners up north. Totally alienating them. The woman there are still in purdah, women still don't work, they still have separate reception rooms. They are not backward, it just their way of life. They are still marrying abroad and bringing people over, so your Asian community there and here are completely different. I personally think that if the BBC really want to serve the Asian audiences then maybe they need to look at local ways. (Former senior manager, Alia 2015)

Both Friction and Alia underline that among the different groups that comprise the British Asian community, there exist huge lifestyle differences. These differences are not just about faith and language but are deeper and more nuanced, due in part to the individual community migration histories, their experiences, UK regions, education, and jobs (see Chap. 3). Alia underlined in Chap. 4 that ethnic staff need to possess cultural expertise and understand that the listeners are diverse and complex: "all the communities are different, so the Pakistani community in Manchester is different from the London Pakistani community. They want different things at different stages of their lives." In theory the employees should be cognisant of the differences and the similarities and reflect this in their work. Historically, the BBC was the only place for ethnic specific content on both television and radio; therefore, BBC programming was forced to appeal to everyone and not just specific communities. In 2020 the media ecology includes a growing number of Asian radio stations and community radio stations—which seek to serve specific linguist or faith groups regionally (e.g. Punjab Radio, Sanskar Radio and Desi Radio):

> Each community is catered for in their own town. One of my social worker friends says that we [the communities] are losing the 'Asian-ness', they are becoming more westernised and more integrated, so people don't rely as heavily on the Asian aspects. So as a station is it your agenda to go with the flow and become more integrated and more mainstream? or is your agenda to get to know that Asian community, to inform and educate people who are part of that community but maybe moving away and people who are still rooted in there. (Former senior manager, Alia 2015)

Chapter 3 looked at the divisions and similarities among the British Asian audience. According to Ali et al. (2006), the divisions between the Pakistani, Bangladeshi, and Indian (especially African Asian) communities are more apparent in terms of class and education. The north of England is often viewed by some BBC ethnic staff as having a "traditional" listenership; for example, the listener may marry partners from South Asia and work in factories or service sector roles. In contrast, Londoners and British Asians in the South East are conceptualised as being largely "professionals" or students. Alia recognises the differences are due to regionalism, but she also poses that the BBC requires a stronger understanding of the communities listening, and then serve and inform in a meaningful manner. Sam (*not her real name*) in contrast highlighted that station is able to engage the listener:

> We never had an issue of getting people on the phone-in. The presenter has to be the type of presenter that people want to talk to. The listener has got to feel as if their opinions are valid. We have to tap into those conversations, do they feel as if they're going to be listened to because they may have been having those discussions between their family and their friends and all of a sudden now it's on national radio and other people may feel the same as them. So, it's about reflecting those conversations, those thoughts, those feelings and also you know they want to react and where else can they do it? (Senior journalist, Sam 2015)

Sam believes the station makes an important contribution by reflecting British Asian identity and British Asian voices, and amplifying the concerns and discussions of this diverse audience to the BBC and the UK. By emphasising the notion of being British first and foremost it is evident that the BBC Asian Network does not promote Asian culture per se and instead aims to unite distinct ethnic groups who share similar post-colonial histories and the experiences of living in Britain. Mitchell (cited in Brunt and Cere 2010, p. 64) has argued that the significance of minority ethnic community radio is the fact that it is able to "broaden media representation with creatively useful definitions of communities." In other words ethnic radio is more organic and reflexive as opposed to public service broadcasting, which seeks to serve all listeners with a general approach. In this way, the BBC has managed to construct a distinct community of listeners for the BBC Asian Network. Yu (2016, p. 5) has outlined that ethnic communities have two identities: the identity that members of ethnic communities create themselves and a socially constructed identity, that is created and prescribed to them. It is evident that the BBC is juggling the requirement to reach out and connect with diverse audiences to minimise the risk of losing market share whilst also trying to enrich public service content across the organisation. Some BBC employees have a strong sense of direction and understand the BBC rationale to concentrate on younger ethnic listeners. By focusing on notions of Britishness, the BBC tries to enable a sense of belonging and seeks to offer information that is objective, offers clarity, and is presented in an inclusive manner, which inevitably means that the BBC is at times forced to ignore some groups. The drive to focus on British identity, lifestyle, and experiences is in contrast to the historic Asian radio programming, which aimed to appeal to all Asians through the use of Hindustani and sought to integrate viewers and listeners; therefore, the differences that existed between the minority groups were not recognised and were simply ignored. In 2020, there exist multiple generations of British Asians born in the UK, so now the BBC seeks to appeal widely to them by expressing the notion of British Asian identity and through that some British norms and values. Kamran a former producer at the BBC Asian Network explained that internally at the station some of the staff are not at ease with moving in a new direction, despite the huge changes to the radio sector:

> The majority of people have been here for a long time, so they always reminisce back to the days when and it was alright because we didn't have the competition, so you were in your own world, social media didn't exist. But look at radio stations around the world, India, Dubai, they've moved on and

doing all kinds of stuff where we [the BBC] are still making radio for 2005. (Former producer, Kamran 2015)

This appears to be the crux of the problem, although the BBC management has changed strategy due to obligations enshrined within the Royal Charter and its Diversity and Inclusion plan, but some ethnic staff do not necessarily agree with the management. This is not unusual in any organisation however; what is distinct at the BBC Asian Network is that some staff actively resist the drive to portray and focus upon young integrated British Asians in favour of wanting to serve older listeners. Which means some employees would like to continue showcasing a paternalistic agenda.

BUILDING A COMMUNITY OF LISTENERS AND CONNECTING WITH THEM

The radio producer is tasked with reflecting an imagined community of listeners on-air. Producers thus envision the listener and try and showcase the identity of the target audience through the music selected, the mode of address that is utilised, the speech content, and the perspectives articulated on-air.

> I feel as though you need experts to provide programming that nourishes every part of our audience. So, while it's entirely possible for any producer to make a program for our Asian audience, I think you need experts to make those programs with specialist knowledge, and I think that here at the Asian network we have that specialist knowledge. (Producer, Riaan 2015)

Riaan outlines that the ethnic staff have the specialist knowledge of the communities they serve. This view does contradict some of the perspectives expressed in Chap. 4, where some staff questioned the knowledge of the younger ethnic staff. An ethnic producer who possesses expertise knowledge of the listener thus ought to be able to create and shape content accordingly. There seems to be a difference of opinion from the bottom up among the staff and the manner in which staff are steered from the top down. The media producer in the age of social media is forced to engage with small communities in person or digitally, to find content that can be adapted and translated for the general or national audience. As indicated in Chap. 4, within contemporary media, the producer (in TV and radio) is positioned as a highly skilled and creative position, which appears appealing as a career choice. However, public service broadcasting is no longer as assertive or dominant as it once was. Young people are less likely to watch or listen to a BBC service, for example 60 per cent of the peak time audience for BBC1 is aged over 55 (Ofcom 2017, p. 11). Kavya outlined that Asian Network producers are acutely aware that the station is the only connection some listeners have with the BBC: "The Asian Network's role is perhaps as a vehicle to bring people into the BBC and to then push them around show them what else they might like." This suggests there is additional pressure on staff to encourage the listener to stay longer and make the rest of the BBC more appealing. It seems the burden is upon minority staff to implicitly appeal to listeners to increase their use of the BBC, as opposed to the BBC tailoring its schedules and content to better appeal to young and minority ethnic audiences. Problematically, British Asian viewers tend to spend half their time viewing non-UK public service broadcasters, such as Star or Zee (Ofcom 2018, p. 12). Therefore, the BBC Asian Network is strategically significant becasue it *appeals* to unique listeners and brings them to the BBC. The listeners that the station attracts contribute to the BBC's overall reach with ethnic minority audiences and, therefore, the audience as opposed to the station can be viewed as the primary product or commodity (Hendy 2000).

The BBC has been urged to take steps to appeal to young generations and other minority groups. It has decided to serve British Asian listeners through the BBC Asian Network, with music, news, and current affairs, and some blended South Asian programmes.

Gillespie (1995) has argued that younger generations of the Asian community do not believe their identity is exclusively British, Indian, or Pakistani, and that their identity is shaped by events and interaction with the new community. In contrast, McCrone (2002) found that people with Indian heritage are more likely to consider themselves to be English. The study does recognise that the majority of people do not understand the difference between "British" and "English," which appear to have different but interconnected meanings, which change in response to society and politics. One consequence of the BBC's inclusive British Asian mode of address is that some communities chiefly, Sikhs and Hindus, distance themselves from the Muslim community, to avoid being implicated in negative news, for example grooming cases (BBC 2012). Chapter 3 examined the usefulness of the term Asian Kamlesh Purohit highlighted that not everyone in the British Asian community identifies with it:

I used to hear people ringing in on Phone-In and debating this point saying, when it comes to for example child abuse why does the BBC use the word Asian? When actually it's a specific problem to a certain community. Rightly or wrongly people feel very strongly about that. The Indian communities have settled and integrated really well and do contribute in a very positive way but because the generic term Asian is used, they feel that they are being implicated in something. (Kamlesh Purohit 2015)

Identity is complex among the groups that comprise British Asian society. Recognising that identity also differs within groups according to age, region, or life experiences adds further complexity to the notion of a homogeneous Asian community (see Chap. 2). The BBC is often critiqued for showcasing a singular version of national identity through middle-class filters, which enables race to be illustrated in frames of "difference," "otherness," and judged by standards established by the West (Campion 2005; Moylan 2013; Shohat and Stam 2014). This move situates settled generations of minority communities as effectively "outsiders" to the dominant national culture. The station addresses the listeners as British and Asian and recognises they are likely to be integrated into British life. Sandhu, a former on-air presenter, explained he connected with the listeners through "our experiences of being British first and then having all this history of Asians roots, family, culture, religion all going through you." Sandhu positions his first-hand experiences within the wider context of the audience, and thus he makes tangible links by sharing his lived experiences. Friction admitted he can "became obsessed by" the need to try and appeal to the diversity of the British Asian listening community:

As a presenter, I try being everything to all people. I have learnt you don't have to kind of dumb yourself down because people expect a certain level of education and knowledge from their presenters. The way I have done it is through music, and how I joke about British Asian culture. (Presenter, Bobby Friction 2016)

Bobby Friction is also a DJ, and he is able to attract listeners with his specialist music knowledge; however, because he fronts a main daytime programme, he has less control over the playlist (see Chap. 8). He also addresses the listeners through notions of shared heritage and culture. The manner in which both Sandhu and Friction facilitate, discuss, and explore British Asian identity, and experiences, is thus a form of "accented radio" and contributes to cultural production in the UK (Moylan 2013, 2018). This type of production intrinsically incorporates characteristics of the transnational experience, alongside the British Asian experience and addresses the listeners in a manner they can relate to. This aesthetic enables the presenters to contribute to the construction of a community of listeners:

> I am quite fortunate in a sense that I've never really had to worry about it too much. I think once you start doing radio and you start to understand your audience you begin to understand what they like and don't like. I never felt like I needed to mould myself into somebody that the presenter likes. (Presenter, Noreen Khan 2015)

At the time of the interviews, Noreen Khan was the only female presenter on the main daytime schedule. Khan outlined that she was a listener before becoming a presenter at the station and felt the transition was fluid. She did concede that because her listeners watch Asian dramas (soap operas) on satellite stations she also began to watch them to discuss on the radio. The competition for British Asian listeners is fierce, over the last thirty years; the number of television satellite channels targeted at Pakistani, Indian, and Bangladeshi communities in the UK has grown exponentially. Access to Asian channels is offered in the UK by Sky, Virgin Media, and TalkTalk platforms that charge subscription fees for access. A huge proportion of the content is broadcast in South Asian languages such as Hindi, Punjabi, and Urdu, simply because the programmes are imported directly from India and Pakistan. These services specifically address "ethnic, linguistic and/or religious groups" residing in countries where they are considered to be a minority, and thus, they "have some connection (imagined or real) and share a sense of belonging within a larger community spreading beyond national boundaries (the diasporic element)" (Georgiou 2005, p. 483). Georgiou (2005) describes ethnic media as being media for the diaspora and suggests through the articulation of shared common cultural information on satellite television (e.g. Asian programming across Europe) this can lead to the (re)invention of shared identity and community. Malik (2010, p. 123) has argued the minority viewers simply want media content that links them to their homelands and a platform to articulate "common cultural concerns, such as a religion, language or ethnicity, to defend their collective interests." It does mean that minority viewers are treated as consumers by ethnic media opposed to citizens by PSB.

Chapter 5 outlined that the BBC Asian Network is using social media to appeal to younger audiences. The rationale for digital presence in this era is pressing, young people are less likely to consume live radio, and minority ethnic communities also are less likely to listen to radio in comparison to the general population (Ofcom 2013, 2017). Among ethnic audiences there are further differentials, for example just 28 per cent of Pakistani and Bangladeshi communities claim to listen to radio compared to a 42 per cent of the general population (Ofcom 2013). This poses huge challenges for the BBC. Whilst the fifteen- to twenty-four-year-old age group may not choose to listen to radio, they are more likely to listen to podcasts (RAJAR 2020, p. 6). The BBC's own internal research also revealed that the BBC Asian Network has "the highest proportion of smart phone listenership" (Strippel, former, Head of BBC Asian Network). A study by RAJAR (2020) also indicated that young people listen to radio as a cross-platform experience as opposed to using separate devices, for example, mobile, PC/laptops are the means through which a quarter of fifteen- to twenty-four-year-old listen to radio (RAJAR 2020, p. 8).

The Asian radio sector is dominated by the BBC Asian Network, Sunrise Radio, and Lyca Radio: all three have RAJAR listener figures. The BBC Asian remit demands that it is distinct from commercial and community Asian stations in terms of style, music, and speech content. The BBC therefore emphasises the journalism and enables commercial and community stations to fill the language programming gap. Kalia (2019) documents the main difference between Sunrise and the BBC Asian Network is the music played: the Asian Network showcases "left-field sounds of residents such as Nabihah Iqbal and DJ Manara's mix of contemporary Bollywood with dancefloor electronics," whereas Sunrise still places greater prominence upon *Bollywood* music. However, the achievements of the commercial Asian radio sector were largely unacknowledged by the BBC interviewees, who instead underlined how the Asian Network is distinct from them. Kamlesh Purohit, however, explained he has sympathy for independent Asian stations:

> I think they work under very tough conditions because the revenues from advertising aren't there. It's tough for them to survive and I think it's the BBC's role to support all other broadcasters as contradictory as that may

sound, because that competition is healthy competition. Commercial radio stations have a specific remit they serve their audiences in a different way. If the BBC replicates what commercial radio stations do then it's unfair competition in my opinion. How will those stations survive? Without them the Asian Network will be poorer for it. (Kamlesh Purohit 2015)

Purohit was a minority voice that supported the commercial Asian radio sector and the need for a plurality of Asian radio services. As indicated, many new community and commercial stations have concentrated upon specific Asian communities to serve either by age group or by different linguistic groups. The range and variety of ethnic media also means there is greater pool of minority talent to work across the various platforms and organisations. Concerns about the concentration of media ownership have always focused upon mainstream media outlets; more research is needed to examine the ownership of ethnic media.

CONCLUSION

The reduction of language programme content on the BBC Asian Network demonstrates the BBC's desire to pursue young British Asian listeners. Whilst the senior management of the BBC has directed the Asian Network to respond to changing tastes and intergenerational change, some of the staff firmly believe the BBC's public service goals mean the station is better suited to informing the first-generation Asian listener. It is evident that among some of the interviewees public service is understood to equate to giving information to those in greater need as opposed to serving audiences who are established or integrated. Thus, in many ways the public service ethos continues to have a paternalistic inclination. On the other hand, other employees have brought to light that connecting to audiences through accented production on the station brings unique audiences to the BBC. The BBC risks the future of the organisation if it continues to fail to connect with younger audiences, and it is clear that the BBC is responding to this imperative.

REFERENCES

Affie Jeerh. 2015. Face to face Interview, 14 September.
Ali, Nasreen, Virinder S. Kalra, and S. Sayyid, eds. 2006. *A Postcolonial People, South Asians in Britain*. London: Hurst & Co.
Alia. 2015 (anonymised). Face to face interview, 16 June.
BBC. 2012. Complaints over Use of "Asian" Label in Grooming Cases. *BBC News Website*, May 2012, sec. UK. https://www.bbc.co.uk/news/uk-18092605. Accessed 25 October.
BBC Trust. 2016. BBC Asian Network Service Licence (April) 2016. BBC Trust. http://downloads.bbc.co.uk/bbctrust/assets/files/pdf/regulatory_framework/service_licences/radio/2016/asian_network_apr16.pdf
Bob Shennan. 2015. Face to face interview, 11 November.
Bobby Friction. 2016. Skype Interview, 9 February.
Born, Georgina, and Tony Prosser. 2001. Culture and Consumerism: Citizenship, Public Service Broadcasting and the BBC's Fair-Trading Obligations. *The Modern Law Review* 64 (5): 657–687.
Brunt, Rosalind, and Rinella Cere. 2010. *Postcolonial Media Culture in Britain*. Basingstoke: Palgrave Macmillan.
Campion, Mukti. 2005. *Look Who's Talking Cultural Diversity Public Service Broadcasting and the National Conversation*. Oxford: Nuffield College.
Caspi, Dan, and Nelly Elias. 2011. Don't Patronize Me: Media-by and Media-For minorities. *Ethnic and Racial Studies* 34 (1): 62–82.
Deuze, Mark. 2006. Ethnic Media, Community Media and Participatory Culture. *Journalism* 7 (3): 262–280.
Dey, Bidit Lal, John M.T. Balmer, Ameet Pandit, Mike Saren, and Ben Binsardi. 2017. A Quadripartite Approach to Analysing Young British South Asian Adults' Dual Cultural Identity. *Journal of Marketing Management* 33 (9–10): 789–816.
Dipps Bhamrah. 2015. Face to face interview, 14 December.
Fitzgerald, Richard, and William Housley. 2007. Talkback, Community and the Public Sphere. *Media International Australia* 122 (1): 150–163.
Georgiou, Myria. 2005. Diasporic Media Across Europe: Multicultural Societies and the Universalism, Particularism Continuum. *Journal of Ethnic & Migration Studies* 31 (31): 481–498.
Gillespie, Marie. 1995. *Television, Ethnicity and Cultural Change*. London/New York: Routledge.
Hendy, David. 2000. *Radio in the Global Age*. Cambridge: Polity Press.
Hirsch, Afua. 2018. *Brit(Ish): On Race, Identity and Belonging*. London: Vintage.
Husband, Charles. 1994. *A Richer Vision*. London: UNESCO.
———. 1998. Differentiated Citizenship and the Multi-Ethnic Public Sphere. *Journal of International Communication* 5 (1–2): 134–148.

Kalia, Ammar. 2019. From Blaring Bhangra to the New Grime: 30 Years of Brilliant British Asian Broadcasting. *The Guardian*, January 23, sec. Television & Radio. https://www.theguardian.com/tv-and-radio/2019/jan/23/british-asian-30-years-of-sunrise-radio

Kamlesh Purohit. 2015. Face to face interview, 17 March.

Kamran. 2015 (anonymised). Face to face interview, 11 November.

Kavya. 2015 (anonymised). Face to face interview, 25 March.

Lay, Samantha, and Lisa Thomas. 2012. Ethnic Minority Media in London: Transition and Transformation. *Media, Culture & Society* 34 (3): 369–380.

Lewis, Peter M., and Jerry Booth. 1989. *The Invisible Medium Public, Commercial and Community Radio*. Basingstoke: Macmillan.

Malik, S. 2008. Keeping It Real, the Politics of Channel 4 Multiculturalism, Mainstreaming and Mandates. *Screen* 49 (3): 343–353.

———. 2010. From Multicultural Programming to Diasporic Television: Situating the UK in a European Context. *Media History* 16 (1): 123–128.

McCrone, D. 2002. Who Do You Say You Are? *Ethnicities* 2: 301–320.

Mike Curtis. 2014. Face to face interview, 1 December.

Mithra. 2016 (anonymised). Face to face interview, 10 February.

Moylan, Katie. 2013. *Broadcasting Diversity, Migrant Representation in Irish Radio*. Bristol: Intellect.

———. 2018. Accented Radio: Articulations of British Caribbean Experience and Identity in UK Community Radio. *Global Media and Communication* 14 (3): 283–299.

Neeta. 2015 (anonymised). Skype Interview, 15 May.

Noreen Khan. 2015. Face to face interview, 29 June.

Ofcom. 2013. Ethnic Minority Groups and Communication Services. Research report.

———. 2017. The Communications Market: Digital Radio Report. Ofcom's Eighth Annual Digital Progress Report. Research report. Ofcom. https://www.ofcom.org.uk/__data/assets/pdf_file/0014/108311/Digital-Radio-Report-2017.pdf

———. 2018. Representation and Portrayal on BBC Television, October, 48.

RAJAR. 2020. Audio Times. https://www.rajar.co.uk/docs/news/Audio_Time%20_FINAL_pages.pdf

Riaan. 2015 (anonymised). Face to face interview, 14 September.

Safia. 2015 (anonymised). Face to face interview, 15 June.

Sam. 2015 (anonymised). Face to face interview, 11 November.

Shohat, Ella, and Robert Stam. 2014. *Unthinking Eurocentrism Multiculturalism and the Media*. 2nd ed. Abingdon: Routledge.

Strippel, Mark. 2015. Face to face interview, 15 June.

Sweney, Mark. 2020. BBC Four Presenters Rally to Save Channel amid Closure Rumours. *Guardian*, May 14. https://www.theguardian.com/media/2020/may/14/bbc-four-presenters-rally-to-save-channel-amid-closure-rumours

Tommy Sandhu. 2015. Skype Interview, 17 June.

Tsagarousianou, Roza. 1999. Gone to the Market? The Development of Asian and Greek Cypriot Community Media in Britain. *Javnost the Public* 6 (1): 55–70.

Wilson, Clint C., and Felix Gutierrez. 1995. *Race, Multiculturalism, and the Media*. 2nd ed. Thousand Oaks: Sage.

Yu, S. Sherry. 2016. Ethnic Media as Communities of Practice: The Cultural and Institutional Identities. *Journalism* 11 (18): 1309–1326.

Yu, S. Sherry, and M.D. Matsaganis. 2019. *Ethnic Media in the Digital Age*. New York: Routledge.

CHAPTER 8

It's Not Just *Bhangra* and *Bollywood*! Mediating Music Genres at the BBC Asian Network

So far, this book has illustrated how the BBC tries to construct a distinct community of British Asian listeners for the BBC Asian Network, a digital radio station established in 2002. The various chapters have also demonstrated the impact of institutional frameworks in terms of recruitment and gatekeeping, political perceptions of race, immigration, and public service, and how this impacts the representation of minority audiences. This chapter concentrates upon how the music policies have been changing in response to changing tastes among the listeners. Music is used as a tool to not only imagine communities but also preserve and develop music-based communities by making genres accessible (Michelsen et al. 2019). The BBC Asian Network is tasked with offering a platform for new and emerging British Asian artists and to champion their music. Although this is clearly defined in the station's remit some staff have strong opinions over what music genres deserve airtime. There exists limited research about the BBC's music stations because there has been an emphasis upon Radio 3 and Radio 4, as the BBC is known to "elevate certain types of music over others"(Barnard 1989, p. 2). This means that some BBC stations have received limited attention from academic research, and the BBC Asian Network is an example of this. This chapter tries to offer an insight into the treatment of British Asian music on-air and contrasts this commercial Asian radio.

© The Author(s), under exclusive license to Springer Nature Switzerland AG 2021
G. Aujla-Sidhu, *The BBC Asian Network*,
https://doi.org/10.1007/978-3-030-65764-2_8

THE BBC ASIAN NETWORK PLAYLIST

All radio stations have a playlist which aims to reflect the target listener's interests and the style and tone of the station. Gallego (2015 in Bonini and Monclus) set out that radio stations define the identity of the listener through the music they choose to playlist. Whereas Hilmes (1997) has posed that music that reflects culture and heritage can erase some of the divisions among listeners, in other words that music can be used to unite disparate groups. The playlist is considered to be a musical "gatekeeper" because it narrows the range of music that can be played on-air (Negus 1993). Moreover, although listeners may imagine the act of listening to some genres means that they are contributing to trends, in reality, the music programming policies have limited the music that is offered in the first place. Whilst different genres of music have been studied within research such as jazz or pop, Lewis (2000) has suggested there has not been sufficient research to examine the impact that foreign language music, for example *Bollywood*, has in creating communities of listeners.

The BBC Asian Network is aimed at listeners aged under 35 years who are interested in British Asian music, culture, and news. It has an equal division of speech and music at 50:50 making it unique within the BBC. The remit specifies that 30 per cent of music played on-air must be produced by UK artists with a further 30 per cent of new music, which is translated as music released up to two months previously (this tends to be *Bollywood* music from India) (BBC Trust 2016, p. 3). Although the policy to promote and accentuate British Asian artists is contentious at the BBC Asian Network, it is not an unusual practice. Since April 2018, Radio 1 is required to play 45 per cent of music originating from UK artists and acts. There is also 10 per cent requirement to play specialist South Asian music such Qawwali or Ghazal (ibid). All BBC stations have defined licence agreements, which underscore the focus on British music and talent. Specifically, the Asian Network is required to make an important contribution to stimulating creativity by "providing a platform for new and established British Asian talent" and "cover a wide range of genres with an emphasis on new music and on nurturing and developing new acts" (BBC Trust 2016, p. 3). The station is also tasked "to find and develop new production and presentation talent" (ibid). This is achieved through high-profile talent searches that include Bhangra Star in 2019, Spoken Word artists in 2020, and Future Sounds, all schemes which seek out and elevate talent from the British Asian community.

The Asian Network playlist prominently features *Bollywood*, *Bhangra*, Grime, and RnB music. A number of weekend and evening programmes showcase specialist music replicating the friend of the family audience strategy outlined in Chap. 5. Wall and Dubber (2009) note that the BBC has positioned specialist music as a PSB (Public Service Broadcasting) commitment in order to appeal to "specific" groups of listeners as opposed to everyone at separate times of the day. This means that music genres in the BBC are selected to appeal to distinct, defined, and demarcated listener groups. There is an underlying implication within the BBC that specialist music is not considered to be mainstream popular music. The two dominant music genres played at the BBC Asian Network are *Bollywood* music, imported from India and aligned with the Indian film industry, and *Bhangra* either imported from India and/or produced in the UK by British Asian artists or Asian artists abroad.

Although radio listening figures in the UK reveal that people are listening for longer, radio's role as tastemaker has been profoundly impacted by technological changes pertaining to how music is distributed (Ofcom 2017, p. 97). Hendy (2000, p. 743) has argued that radio still plays a role in "shaping music tastes" in the digital age and that it attracts listeners. Radio has a long history of development and adaption and in many ways can be described as a chameleon platform that embraces new opportunities within audio to extend its reach and influence, for example being added into car stereos and more recently onto mobiles. Others have suggested that radio's tastemaker role has diminished and that radio is "more of a validator of the biggest hits often discovered on streaming platforms" (Hendricks and Mims 2018, p. 7). Music streaming services such as Spotify and Apple Music enable people to create their own playlist and they control what they listen to. Historically, music labels and radio stations would have wielded greater influence over listeners. Wall and Dubber (2009, p. 36) have argued that music streaming is best understood as "reshaping (rather than replicating or replacing) traditional radio broadcasting." In other words people use streaming services alongside live listening to radio. There are, however, concerns about the resilience of radio, with some suggesting that unless it adapts and competes strongly with streaming services it will become irrelevant (Hendricks and Mims 2018). It is also recognised that the growth in smart phones to listen to podcasts and music may ultimately weaken the appeal of live radio. Lacey (in Loviglio and Hilmes 2013) has observed that listening has become personal when people listen to radio via smart phones because it is through headphones. Moreover, Lacey has outlined that listening is a learned art, and the public has adapted to having a wireless in their home and to accept personalised content from the BBC (a formal institution), and now they can select exactly what they want to listen to. There are age differences; among younger and older age groups listening hours have decreased, whilst the middle group are listening on average for longer. One reason for this is as Hendricks and Mims (2018, p. 4) suggest "radio whether it be of the terrestrial, satellite, online streaming, or podcasting variety – continues to be one of the most pervasive media on earth." They do, however, acknowledge that the growth in the audio sector means radio stations must innovate in order to survive and recognise that radio is longer the sole source of music discovery and exposure. Berry (2006) has argued huge changes to the medium of radio mean that power dynamics have shifted from radio producers to listeners, who now make their own scheduling choices. Traditionally, radio stations commanded listeners by scheduling programmes and specific genres of music to reflect people's daily and weekly rhythms. For example, playing popular music or offering key news stories in the morning listening peak between 7 am and 8 am as people wake up. This poses challenges that are not insurmountable for the Asian Network, which is tasked with championing new talent and serving a heterogeneous listenership who have a range of musical tastes and linguistic needs.

BHANGRA MUSIC

Bhangra music is synonymous with British Asian heritage and identity; however, the genre belongs specifically to one community (Punjabi-speaking Sikhs and Muslims) as opposed to the entire Asian community. Therefore, some listeners, for example South Indians or Gujarati Indians, can find the prevalence of this genre of music problematic. *Bhangra* is considered to be a transnational genre of music because it enables the artist to incorporate their identity with traditional beats, instruments, and a sound that intrinsically connects the listener to India. Since the 1990s the UK has also become the home of *Bhangra* music through the incorporation of other styles such as jungle and soul, which has resulted in *Bhangra* becoming "quintessentially 'British' as it is 'Asian'" (Huq, in Sharma et al. 1996 p. 62–63). *Bhangra* has its roots in Punjabi folk music and is associated with the beat of the dhol drum. The music arrived in Britain with North Indian immigrants and was played at weddings and parties. It briefly crossed into the mainstream in the 1990s when Bally Sagoo was signed to Sony Records in the late 1990s and Apache Indian emerged during this same period. *Bhangra* has been exported across the world and back to India itself, and the Indian film industry has also incorporated it into its movies. Bennett (1997) has argued that whilst scholars have described *Bhangra* as being a "common form of counter-cultural expression for young Asians in Britain," this ignores the influence of communities in geographical regions and the social significance this has upon the development and promotion of the music scene (Bennett 1997). Roy (2010) has defined three types of *Bhangra* music: *Punjabi Bhangra*, which originates from India, *Vilayeti Bhangra* from the UK, which mixes folk rhythm with reggae, hip-hop, and rap; and *Desi Bhangra*, which is featured in *Bollywood* movies.

The 1990s' British Asian music scene allowed for a distinct British Asian identity to emerge that challenged notions that the term "British" exclusively applied to non-minority groups because the music drew from both cultures and expressed a uniquely British sound. Saha (2020) has argued this crossover of British Asian cultural production into mainstream was enabled by the changes to cultural policy in the 1990s by the New Labour ideology and the politics of multiculturalism, which have become largely redundant after multiculturalism was blamed for causing segregation of minority communities (see Chap. 4). Moreover, Anamik Saha outlines how the policy changes offered independence and autonomy to British Asian artists, musicians, actors, and directors to "self-represent and self-define" their identity event though this conflicted with the way these communities were presented in the media (Saha 2020, p. 13). Within the dance scene British Asian identity depicted "a sense of Asianness that is not necessarily in opposition to notions of being black, and though more problematically, even British" (Sharma et al. 1996, p. 40). In other words, the music was inspired by multiple cultures and as such uniquely showcased a distinct version of British Asian identity. This crossover was brief, and this chapter will discuss how British Asian music artists remain marginalised within the music sector. The predominance of *Bhangra* as the "diasporic South Asian music" has to some extent prevented British Asian artists from participating or receiving acclaim for their contribution to grime, soul, punk, and jungle genres (Sharma et al. 1996, p. 8, 26).

Bhangra remains a marginalised genre in mainstream British music (Dudrah 2002a). The genre draws on British urban experience and combines notions of traditional Indian cultures and as such enables a type of identity formation among British South Asians that is not in opposition to notions of being black and British (Dudrah 2002a). Thus, *Bhangra* has become synonymous with British Asians in the same way that reggae and soul music became the main way in which Caribbean migrants constructed their identity as black Britons (Wall and Dubber 2009). However, despite the popularity of *Bhangra* in India, which has been amplified by its use and association with *Bollywood* (Roy 2010), in the UK the genre remains marginalised because it has been unable to break into British mainstream music charts despite the success of artists such as Punjabi MC and the track *Mundian to Bach ke* (beware of the boys) originally released in 1998. There are a few reasons for this; this chapter considers the idea that British Asian artists are primarily offered airtime only on the BBC Asian Network and that they struggle to access the playlists on Radio 1 or 1xtra. Roy (2010, p. 114) has suggested that *Bhangra* is marketed in India, through an emphasis upon cultural difference, and as exotic, this is seen by the emphasis upon the turban and the beard and glittering costumes. In the UK, the image of *Bhangra* has evolved, but it is still marketed as "exotic." This branding does not correlate with the image of young British Asian music artists in the UK who are British.

Bollywood

Hindi film music more commonly referred to as *Bollywood* by the interviewees emerged from the big screen and has become a popular genre of music in its own right. Hindi-language movies have a huge appeal across the world, especially in the UK, Germany, parts of South America, and Indonesia. The genre is not just popular among diasporic audiences but also among non-Hindi-speaking communities abroad. Dawson (2005) has suggested that Hindi films offer the second generation a "visual and aural archive" from which they can develop their identity, but there is also acknowledgement of the fact that "many of the images produced by mainstream Hindi film remain relatively alien" for younger generations of British Asians (Dawson 2005, p. 162). *Bollywood* movies are viewed by the South Asian diaspora to maintain links and connections with India and simply for entertainment. Simultaneously since the 1990s Hindi film makers have tried to depict wealthy middle-class Non-resident Indians (NRI) in *Bollywood* movies, in response to the huge worldwide appeal for *Bollywood* films and music. Dudrah (2002b) has suggested that *Bollywood* films are best viewed as global cultural texts because they transcend national borders in terms of production and distribution and examine issues within the films that also cross borders. Elsewhere scholars have explored the exertion of Indian soft power through *Bollywood*, with particular reference to the elevation of middle-class Hindu aspirations which are predominantly showcased in movies. These aspirations align with the right-wing Hindu Nationalist Party, which is in power (Thussu 2013).

Bollywood soundtracks are the main music genre played on most Asian radio stations, meaning it is often played for several hours each day. The *Bollywood* film industry is considered to be an influential and powerful entity within Asian music. Asian Network presenter, Bobby Friction claimed: "We [Britain] will always be the servants to the masters that are the Bollywood industry and the media conglomerates in India."

Anindya Raychaudhuri (2018) examined the concept of nostalgia for Asian heritage and history through the study of media texts such as *Bollywood* movies and music to examine British Asian history in the West. Raychaudhuri concedes that each subsequent generation has their own nostalgia and that is evident in the way the BBC Asian Network tries to cater to multiple Asian generations on-air.

> Noreen Khan, Harpz Kaur and the BBC Asian Network demonstrate that diasporic nostalgia is able to make the case 'that the culture of diasporic immigrants is central to British national identity,' and thus is able to articulate a demand that 'South Asian cultural forms be recognised by mainstream culture in ways that do not quite so easily resolves into mere absorption or appropriation. (2018, p. 169)

What is striking about Raychaudhuri's perspective is the manner in which people feel connected to the BBC Asian Network is individual and unique due to their attachment or nostalgia for their childhood, cultural history, or music; due in part to their education and upbringing; and due to the ease with which they can mix up aspects of their heritage. Raychaudhuri (2018) recognises that South Asian culture has not simply merged into British culture, meaning Asian music remains distinctive and on the fringes of society in the UK. The former head of Programmes Mark Strippel underlined that Hindi music offers listeners the "perspective of looking back whilst also looking forward in Britain," and as a result music from the *Bollywood* film industry plays a significant role in maintaining popular culture within the Asian diaspora worldwide.

PROBLEMS WITH THE MUSIC POLICIES

Strippel outlined in this interview that it is important the station's playlist promotes a range of music genres as opposed to just *Bhangra* and *Bollywood* in recognition that British Asian listeners have diverse musical tastes and different languages, arts, culture, and music. However, the production staff offered the opposite perspective in their interviews, and they worried about an over-emphasis upon British Asian music. A minority of the interviewees worried about the exclusion of other genres of music:

> It's almost like a BBC Trust thing where we've got to show that we are supporting British Asian music to keep getting our money and to make sure we are still a station on the BBC. I am not entirely sure though if putting such strictures on a playlist is the best thing for the growth of listeners. (Presenter, Bobby Friction 2016)

It is clear that Friction feels British Asian music is imposed upon the BBC Asian Network regardless of its standard or appeal, and as a presenter he is expected to "forcefully push British Asian music" on his shows to meet metrics imposed upon the station. Friction's underlying concern is that the music quotas remove flexibility for presenters like him who are specialist music experts who would like to innovate and showcase other artists. Dubber (2013) suggests radio stations opt for familiar music to appeal to the listeners as opposed to innovating with new or specialist music. The BBC actively promotes music created by UK artists across all its radio stations in line with its public service remit, including on Radio 1 and Radio 2. According to Wall and Dubber (2009) the promotion of British music enables the BBC to defend itself from criticisms that BBC radio stations offer the same listening experience as commercial radio stations. Traditionally, the BBC Asian Network also pushed *Bollywood* music in line with its competitors. Under Strippel's leadership *Bollywood* music has been reduced and the station is viewed as the eminent platform for British Asian music (Baddhan 2017; Kalia 2019). The contemporary British Asian music scene in the UK is small and less influential than the 1990s. Friction agreed that British Asian music "is unique" and deserves nurturing he did not agree with the quota method. The BBC Asian Network is unique in that the representation of British Asian communities is offered by a public service provider as opposed to the communities themselves. This means the producers within the BBC must decide what type of identity and image will be portrayed on-air, and this is influenced in part by the decision to select specific genres of music to reflect this community of listeners. Turino (2008) has argued music and dance are the principal ways in which people showcase their group identity, language, or heritage, and sustain them. Husain Husaini, former head of Programmes and News at the station, underlined that the outreach work the radio station undertook with British Asian artists had profound impact on improving listener engagement with the station.

> The content involving musicians from the London Mela, or when we did a concert, meant we created content for people get involved with. Listeners like music, they like musicians, they get associated with that. (Former head of News and Programmes, Husain Husaini 2015)

This meant that the BBC made unique connections with potential listeners through the involvement in big community music events (melas). The station could also market itself by collaborating with organisers and offering their on-air presenters as hosts. Former language programme producer, Affie Jeerh, proposed the key contribution the station makes to British culture is through the platform that is offered to new and emerging artists; "people like Raghav, people like Jay Sean, these people were nobodies, and the Asian Network gave them a platform. They are big stars now." Furthermore, she defended the station against claims that it plays the same music as commercial Asian stations, commenting that you cannot stop championing musicians "just because they are big stars."

Historically only music in South Asian languages was played on-air, which meant the inclusion first in 2005, and later again in 2012, of music in English was controversial. The move to playlist chart music clearly shows the BBC shift towards younger listeners aged between fifteen and thirty years, who are likely to be integrated into British society and listen to non-Asian music. Priya *(not her real name)* a music producer at the station explained they are aware that different generations of listeners have different musical tastes: "it is the music that brings people to the station as well as the presenters and the content." However, despite the emphasis upon promoting British Asian music within the BBC she was not convinced by the value it added:

> Asian music isn't getting as much of a buy in. Probably due to lack of knowledge and probably the lack of British Asian artists. People basically question

me to say who the big artist is. Like this year name one person and it is so difficult. I don't know if the platforms are not there for them or if they're trying to get into the mainstream and the mainstream aren't looking so much. (Music producer, Priya 2015)

Priya appeared to be frustrated by the condition of the British Asian music industry and also by the malaise surrounding British Asian artists within the BBC. Her perspective underlined the need for deeper engagement with British Asian talent external to the Asian Network. Moreover, she further indicated that at the station's listener forums people outlined contradicting viewpoints on the playlist:

> Basically, there was two rooms, one had people aged 18 to 25 and other 25- to 35-year-olds. The difference in the two rooms was huge. I went into the younger room first and I am not that old myself, but the younger people were all about Grime and the beats. The older listeners were like bit more kind of oldskool and they wanted to hear Bollywood. (Music producer, Priya 2015)

All radio stations have to find ways to unite listeners who differ for many reasons. This issue is not isolated to the BBC Asian Network. Moreira's (2019 in Michelsen et al.) case study of Radio ALFA, a station based in Paris broadcasting to the Portuguese community in the area, reveals that it has also grappled with serving multiple generations of Portuguese communities. The historic mission of the station was to help the new immigrants to learn about France, but now it has a broader strategy to illustrate Lusophone culture, through the inclusion of, for example Brazilian music and programming to appeal to younger listeners who have integrated into the French way of life. The station directors recognise that their younger listeners want and need different things to older listeners: "the great challenge is keeping the Luso descendants interested, particularly those who have married a non-Portuguese wife for instance" (Michelsen et al. 2019, p. 40).

In addition to the different music needs among the age groups, there is also greater competition for the attention of the listeners, "it is a lot more difficult now to have people tune in for longer and I think that's why Asian Network have started to play mainstream music so that listeners do not feel they have to switch over" (Priya 2015). Priya describes music in English as being mainstream, and it is now part of the playlist in order to keep listeners tuned in for longer periods of time in recognition that the listeners like both Asian and other genres such as rap or RnB. Kamran (*not his real name*) noted that although the BBC ought to "champion" British Asian music, this should not mean that the playlist is comprised of "mediocre stuff which the listeners are not that interested in." Kamran voiced concerns that the playlist is compromised when music that is not strong, or popular, is included for the sake of metrics as opposed to its quality. Alia (*not her real name*) a former senior manager was worried about the precarious nature of British Asian music: "there is no British Asian music anymore. It's like at its lowest level at the moment. You can't rely on Bollywood music because it is international. Radio 1 does not rely on American music it relies on British music." Tommy Sandhu a former presenter also supported the need to champion British Asian music but questioned the visibility of this music in British culture "I would love to see more British Asian artists, just making music regardless of them being Asian. Making great 'whatever' music. We been there long enough." It is implied that the contribution of Asian artists is not adequately recognised within mainstream music and that Asian artists are actively marginalised by the BBC's music policies:

> If you are making British Asian music, with the kind of twist of your cultures and, yeah, the Asian Network is there for that. If you are making straight up Hindi music or Punjabi music, that is what the Asian Network is there for. If you are making crossover music, we got Yasser and Candyman. But even if you are just making dance, hip-hop, R&B, garage underground music and you are British and Asian, then your music should be played on any platform. That's almost like positive discrimination, almost like box ticking. They're just giving them Asian Network as a platform. It shouldn't matter that you're Asian, the music has to hold its own on Radio 1 and anywhere else. (Former Presenter, Tommy Sandhu 2016)

Sandhu suggests that the existence of the BBC Asian Network facilitates the side-lining of British Asian artists and thus their ability to access mainstream stations such as Radio 1 or KISS. The BBC has traditionally emphasised "music that can be relied upon" in other words, music that will have a wide appeal in the key daytime programmes across all its stations (Dubber 2013, p. 86). Hendy (2000, p. 750) has argued that new artists who feature in specialist programmes often lack sufficient exposure on the radio and "remain 'trapped' in the cultural ghetto of 'specialist' minority programming, even when played by a high-profile station." Sandhu also revealed that due to quotas imposed upon the station that music is selected to conform to the remit:

> Timbaland probably uses more British Asian samples than Naughty Boy. But we can play Naughty Boy's music because he is a British Asian artist. It's great we should champion him, and we should be proud that an Asian Pakistani guy from North London is making mainstream music with Beyoncé. (Former Presenter, Tommy Sandhu 2015)

Sandhu encapsulates the crux of the issue with reference to BBC music policies: the station is forced to playlist artists who are British and Asian over other genres of music which may have greater appeal among the listeners the broadcaster is actively targeting. Thus, artists such as Timbaland can be played, but not as frequently as other artists who happen to be British Asian. This means that British Asian artists are at risk of being relegated solely to the BBC Asian Network if they are viewed as being explicitly "Asian artists" regardless of the genre of music. Saha (2012) suggests that British Asian identity is limited to marginal spaces in British society—which means it becomes trapped in a cultural ghetto—something which Sandhu fears the BBC Asian Network has become. Moreover, Saha contends that despite the efforts of Asian artists to display a mainstream identity, they are commoditised by the cultural industries to "reproduce Indophilic representations of exotica," which means they are forced to showcase normative versions of Asian identity as envisaged by British society (Saha 2012, p. 737).This means their identity is reconfigured to conform to stereotypes of British Asians in order to sell a familiar image to the wider general population. Saha singles out the artist MIA (Mathangi "Maya" Arulpragasam) as someone who has managed to avoid this marginalisation because she has control over her representation and because her music is considered political and global. MIA, Naughty Boy, Jay Sean, and Zach Knight are just some of the contemporary British Asian musicians whose work fuses *Bhangra* with R&B, rap, and Western music. Zayn Malik (formerly of One Direction) and Naughty Boy (producer) and MIA are prominent figures within the UK music industry and not just the British Asian music sector and get airtime across all stations, whereas Zack Knight is mostly confined to the BBC Asian Network.

Music is a cultural text which means it undergoes a systemised production process to make it appealing for the intended consumer, a process that is comparable to the production of a programme or news summary. Chapter 6 outlined how most news content is produced, framed, and packaged to appeal to the desired audience (chiefly, white middle classes) in the hope it will appeal to all. Saha (2012) contends more attention needs to be paid to the cultural-political potential of music and that there needs to be a scrutiny of the production process and how that influences the cultural meanings that can be identified. Sharma et al. (1996) also offers a similar perspective; they oppose the notion of Asian identity that is either absolute or essentialist and outline that identity in this way is managed by the state or media. Moreover, they also argue that South Asian cultural representation continues to be theoretically undeveloped, and as such remains marginalised within cultural studies. Their work examines the crossover of Asian artists into the mainstream music cultures of 1990s which they suggest disrupted the normative stereotypes of second-generation British Asians because it challenged the imposed Asian identity. Furthermore, the Asian dance, hip-hop, and *Bhangra* genres enabled artists to represent through music the "non-exhaustive identification of British and Black and Asian," meaning the music showcased a unique version of Asian identity(Sharma et al. 1996, p. 40).Critically, they acknowledge British Asian artists who opt to produce music that foregrounds an Asian identity—for example, *Bhangra* can mean they are not able to access to mainstream music platforms (Sharma et al. 1996, p. 748).Subsequently a sizeable proportion of British Asian musicians are relegated to peripheral spaces defined by the music industry and radio stations as "Asian music," and within the BBC they can be heard upon the BBC Asian Network. Consequently, Sharma et al. (1996) recognise that the signing of the 1990s' artist Bally Sagoo to mainstream record label Sony was not an attempt to capitalise upon *Bhangra* or to create a global *Bhangra* market but, instead, was an attempt by the label to exploit the bigger Hindi music market on a global scale.

Hindi/*Bollywood* music is popular and played by all Asian commercial stations. Historically, the early Asian programmes featured *Bollywood* music on local radio programmes because Asian listeners wanted to be entertained and reconnected to their cultures as opposed to being informed (see McCarthy 2018). Sandhu believes the well-resourced Indian film industry is attractive for international music producers including British Asians who lack opportunities in the West and are welcomed in the contemporary *Bollywood* industry. As a consequence of the international collaboration the tone of Hindi music has changed: "they got rappers, and really cool sounds, modern sounds, great production on it, so there's more of a fusion happening there then a British Asian music scene" (Former presenter, Tommy Sandhu 2015). This means some *Bollywood* songs may have been produced by British Asians in India, but that music is likely to be on the *Bollywood* playlist as opposed to the UK British Asian artists' playlist. Whilst Sandhu accepted the need for a mix of genres, Kamran firmly believed Hindi music deserved greater attention by the BBC:

> A film is releasing tomorrow, and we have only played two tracks out of the ten on the album so far. That's where I think Asian Network doesn't connect with our listeners because Sunrise Radio and Lyca Radio will have played most of the tracks. People don't come to Asian Network to listen to the latest Bollywood tracks because they know it's very formulaic. (Former Producer, Kamran 2015)

It is plausible that *Bollywood* fans would expect to hear more than two songs from new music albums, and, therefore, they are likely to seek this music through streaming services or on commercial Asian stations. However, Ishani a former senior manager argued that because the genre is popular that does not justify its inclusion on the BBC playlists:

> Bollywood is big, so the treatment of the content is very different on the BBC Asian Network. Just because it is popular, it does not mean the network should not to go anywhere near it. Instead, the producers focus on the different ways they can produce this content. (Ishani, former senior member of staff, 2015)

Ishani has alluded to the internal drive within the BBC to be distinctive. Therefore, in her view the manner in which *Bollywood* music is treated, played, or discussed ought to differ from how commercial Asian radio utilise the genre. The 2016 *Royal Charter* underlined that the BBC should ensure it is "sufficiently distinctive– discernibly different in approach, quality and content to commercial providers – is a central objective of this Charter Review" (Department for Culture, Media and Sport 2016, p. 27). However, the definition of distinctive is ambiguous; commercial media often define it to mean that the BBC ought to provide content for narrowly defined groups that are not catered for. The implication of this rationale is that distinctive content should not have popular appeal or formats. Born (2004) has argued that the BBC is forced to juggle competing and conflicting goals—to be popular and secure viewers in order to justify the licence fee whilst also providing a broad range of programmes and serve minority audiences. In essence the BBC is tasked with doing far more than other media organisations and to justify its existence in part, because it is a "revered organisation" (Department for Culture, Media and Sport 2016, p. 1). In his interview Strippel, the former head of Programmes, underlined that the station is in fact individual:

> We are wholly distinctive in every measure from any Asian commercial radio competitor. We had a service review recently which was for all the BBC Radio Music stations. They found us to be wholly distinctive. Why are we distinctive? Because the music we play is absolutely distinctive if you compare the level of South Asian music that isn't Bollywood, we are absolutely distinct. There is a real contrast between what we do. At the core we are a British Asian station for a younger audience. (Former head of Programmes, Mark Strippel 2015)

The British Asian emphasis does make the service unique because the competitors such as Sunrise seek to provide the Asian community in Britain with a connection to South Asia. Kalia (2019) acknowledges that the early Asian radio stations were entrenched in the immigrant experience and naturally appealed to those who had migrated as opposed to their children whose connections to South Asian were less apparent in their identity. BBC Local Radio and Asian programming on TV similarly used the same immigrant framing (see Chap. 3). Since 2012 the Asian Network has focused upon third- and fourth-generation British Asians who are likely to be aged under 25. The major difference between the BBC and commercial Asian radio is the music. Whilst the BBC emphasises British Asian music which includes contemporary *Bollywood*, dancefloor electronics, and Grime, commercial Asian stations tend to stick to the *Bollywood* and *Bhangra* formulae. Therefore, whilst Kamran advocates greater impetus upon *Bollywood*, the BBC can meet the charter obligations to be distinctive and its public service goals by emphasising British Asian music. Priya pointed out that *Bollywood* music plays a unique role within Asian cultures:

> I have always thought that Bollywood is a bit more universal because I think everyone regardless of background, if you are Bangladeshi or Sri Lankan or

Indian, from whatever part of India or South Asia that everyone kind of does have a bit of Bollywood in them (Music Producer, Priya 2015)

Priya is suggesting that *Bollywood* music has a generic appeal across the British Asian communities. Research by Wolock and Punathambekar (2014, p. 666) has suggested that, because there has been a tendency within Western media to "privilege cinema, Hindi-language films from Bombay, and English-language diasporic films," this genre is naturally popular, and as such, *Bollywood* has played a dominant role in the Indophile interest in the UK media. The different perspectives offered by the BBC members of staff reveal a common thread: that music is vital to attract listeners, and they are worried about music is selected. The role of music within a radio station is important in attracting the listener, and the choice of music played on-air influences people's musical tastes.

ASIAN RADIO COMPETITORS

The UK has a thriving independent ethnic media sector. The first radio licences were issued in 1989, to Sunrise Radio. In 2019 it marked its thirtieth birthday, making it the longest running Asian radio station in the UK. Sunrise initially launched as a cable station and in 1989 was given a spot on the medium wave. It later developed national broadcasting through DAB. Sunrise is the first 24-hour Asian radio station and continues to offer music, news, and entertainment from South Asia, broadcasting in English, Hindi, Urdu, and Punjabi. It has signed up to RAJAR[1] and nationally has 372,000 listeners (RAJAR Q1 2020) and in London 192,000 (RAJAR Q1 2020).There is a concentration of Asian radio stations in the capital, all of them competing for a share of the same audience. They include Lyca DilSe (Greater London), Lyca Radio (Greater London), Punjab Radio (Greater London and North London), Sunrise Radio (Greater London), and community stations: Asian Star (Slough), Betar Bangla Radio (Stratford), Desi Radio (Southall), and Radio Minhaj. The BBC Asian Network faces intense competition for listeners in London because listeners can choose from several ethnic specific stations. Lacey (in Loviglio and Hilmes 2013) suggests that listeners do not tune into one

---

[1] RAJAR—Radio Joint Audience Research Limited was established in 1992 to operate a single audience measurement system for the radio industry in the UK. RAJAR is jointly owned by the BBC and Radio Centre.

station consistently and instead look for a few radio stations to identify as either listeners, users, or contributors.

Lyca Radio broadcasts across Greater London reaching 92,000 listeners (RAJAR, Q1 2020). It is described in application to Ofcom as a music service with "particular emphasis on British Asian urban artists within a music mix that also appeals to young and older British Asian listeners" (Ofcom 2017b).This means the station is a potential competitor to the BBC Asian Network's distinct British Asian claim. Punjab Radio, described as a faith and cultural radio service, has 75,000 listeners (RAJAR Q1 2020). The station predominantly plays Punjabi music, including *Bhangra* and folk music, classical music, and devotional music for both Sufi Muslims and Sikhs, and provides news in Punjabi specifically for first- and second-generation British Asians. Other mid-sized commercial Asian stations include Sabras Radio in Leicester, which was launched in 1995; it does not subscribe to RAJAR and claims to have the largest Asian audience in the Midlands. The name Sabras means "all tastes," and the station caters for its audience by offering something for "all tastes" by playing *Bollywood*, *Bhangra*, Gujarati, and Indian pop genres (Sabras Radio 2018).[2] Sanskar is a community radio station owned by Sabras, the commercial arm of the company. Sanskar caters specifically for the Hindu community by playing religious music across all its shows. Other notable commercial Asian stations include Asian Sound Radio in Manchester and Radio XL in Birmingham, none of which subscribe to RAJAR.

Community stations are growing in significance and numbers in the UK since their licensing began, and they tend to serve geographical and language communities such as Sanskar Radio and Desi Radio. They are designated as non-profit-making organisations and as such offer a space for diverse cultures, alternative narratives, and media discourses which make them appealing for minority ethnic communities, both settled and more recent refugee and migrant communities. Mitchell and Lewis (Follmer and Badenoch 2018, p. 35) outline that community stations are participatory because they are owned by the community, and thus their voices are articulated by the communities and they are involved in the production of programmes. Haydari's (2018) case study of Desi Radio, a community station in Southall, West London, highlighted that female volunteers found that spending time at the station, producing programmes, and speaking in Punjabi (the presentation is solely in Punjabi) encouraged them to be more conscious of their identities and history:

---

[2] Sabras Radio webstite – what is Sabras https://www.sabrasradio.com/advertise/about-sabras/.

Music and language also play an important role to claim and promote a Panjabi identity beyond the divisions of caste, gender, politics, and religion. The physical location of the radio in the midst of Southall, continuous training activities, and the process of radio production also facilitate connection and communication among all communities. (Haydari 2018, p. 40)

Community stations operate in a narrowly defined space in broadcasting with a specific remit to engage the listener in the output whilst also providing a public space to articulate a social and political identity with music that asserts specific cultures. What is apparent is that Asian-specific broadcasting in the UK offers information and a counter-narrative to dominant hegemonic media messages. During the Covid-19 pandemic Asian radio stations turned to the government for financial help and to request that the government increase advertising on commercial radio to Asian audiences—so that vital updates on coronavirus could be provided in mother tongue languages. It became apparent in the local lockdown of Leicester in early July 2020 that a lack of translation of vital information about coronavirus into minority languages had been overlooked (RadioToday n.d.; Triggle 2020).

Measuring Engagement

Since 1992 radio listening is measure by Radio Joint Audience Research (RAJAR) through a retrospective listening diary. Respondents are required to complete a one-week diary listing all the stations they listened to, in quarter-hour time blocks. A total of 130,000 respondents are used each year to compile listener data for 340 radio services, making it one of the largest audience research surveys in the UK. Each station is required to pay for the option to join the service; consequently, a number of independent and community stations do not opt into the survey. The survey method is contested because respondents are required to retrospectively fill in a diary, and ethnic and niche media argue that minority respondents are under-represented in the survey (Starkey 2004, p. 9). In addition, the increased use of digital tools by media organisations means stations can evaluate the number of clicks a story or content has generated or which social media platform received the most engagement. Consequently, this makes retrospective listening diaries, filled in by people invited to participate, a dated concept.

It is evident that radio has evolved and has incorporated visual elements epitomised by Radio 1's Newsbeat strategy, which has called on people since 2014 to "listen, watch, share," as a means by which to tackle the reduction in listening hours among younger people by getting them to engage with Radio 1 via its YouTube channel. Loviglio and Hilmes (2013, p. 44) describe contemporary radio as "a screen medium: we access it through screens both mobile and static, using tactile visual and textual interfaces... Radio crosses platforms." The modernisation and extension of New Broadcasting House in London meant that Asian Network, Radio 1, and 1Xtra had the radio studios fitted with cameras, lights, and a control room, which allows radio content to be filmed, streamed live online, or edited quickly. Radio 1 has utilised the internet to extend the brand visually. These changes demonstrate the medium's resilience and innovation taking place in the sector. However, it is also clear the BBC does not believe that radio is immune or insulated from changes taking place across the media industries. Former Controller of Radio 1, 1Xtra, and BBC Asian Network Ben Cooper set out that "young audiences are key to the future of the broadcasting industry and if we don't adapt, we will die" (Radio Times 2016). This perspective has been echoed by Ofcom, and other leading media figures include former BBC Director General, Mark Thomson:

> Does it count if someone views our content on iPlayer? Yes, it does. It is engagement with the Asian Network. They are watching content that's linked to radio and it's linked to our core values. So, it's really important. I am more than comfortable with that, and Radio 1 and other networks approach it with the same way. (Former, Head of Programmes, Mark Strippel 2015)

Strippel underlines here that he studies digital engagement alongside listening figures to see how the station is doing in terms of attracting the listener. He outlined that within the BBC editors scrutinise brand touchpoints, which includes social media engagement on Instagram or Twitter alongside video views. Other members of staff also highlighted that social media interaction is helpful and plays a role in influencing the topics and subjects they cover on-air.

Conclusion

Under Mark Strippel's leadership, the BBC Asian Network has made significant changes to the music played in order to better appeal to younger listeners. Strippel took over the management of programme content on

1Xtra in 2017 so it is not coincidental that the music at the BBC Asian Network has evolved and that there has been greater movement of staff and presenters between the two stations, demonstrating a degree of joined-up thinking and a sharing of resources. This chapter set out to look at the music policies and see how they help the BBC to build a cohesive community of listeners for the BBC Asian Network. The significance of music radio is the ability to build communities of listeners through genres of music that unite people together and evoke nostalgia or a connection to heritage and culture. This skill in creating imagined communities also erases differences that exist among listeners due to age, class, or ethnicity (Hilmes 1997). However, the BBC appears to promote the journalism generated by the BBC Asian Network as opposed to the music it supports and nurtures. The BBC's reputation for its journalism being balanced and objective far outweighs its reputation for music, with the exception of Radio 1. In many ways, the BBC is demonstrating resilience and innovation in its strategic attempts to evolve the music offered on the BBC Asian Network in order to match the changing audience tastes and experiences. The BBC has changed how it addresses British Asian listeners by explicitly focusing upon young listeners and their British lived experience, but crucially remains committed to serving all young British Asians. These changes are likely to mean that the station can continue to air for the foreseeable future.

The music metrics set for the BBC Asian Network are likely to be broadly correct because they enable the station to remain distinct from Asian commercial radio. However, one deep contradiction remains as acknowledged in Chap. 4: although the station accepts the listener is likely to be young and integrated, the BBC demands that the listener has some interest in Asian music and entertainment. Similarly, the music policies recognise a wide range of genres appeal to the target listeners, but the two dominant genres of music are *Bhangra* and *Bollywood*. The other issue identified in this chapter is the marginalisation of Asian music artists within the music industry. This has another unintended impact that most British Asian music is deemed to be "foreign" and is consigned to the BBC Asian Network or specialist programmes on Radio 1 and 1Xtra. Thus, the influence of British Asian music is limited to small audiences. Wall and Dubber (2009) suggest that the BBC has utilised specialist music, for example, British Asian music, and its prominence on the playlist at the BBC Asian Network, as a way to present itself as a public service broadcaster. What is implicit in the ordering of music into social groups or genre is a distinction between a majority mainstream and a series of minority "taste groups." Further research is required to clarify if young British Asians prefer a less Indophile genre of music. If this is the case, then the BBC needs to reduce the airtime *Bollywood* music receives further.

REFERENCES

Baddhan, Lakh. 2017. Mark Strippel's Position Signals New Changes at BBC Asian Network? *Biz Asia*, 2017. https://www.bizasialive.com/mark-strippels-new-position-sign-new-changes-bbc-asian-network/. Accessed 25 October.

Barnard, Stephen. 1989. *On the Radio*. Milton Keynes: Open University Press.

BBC Trust. 2016. *BBC Asian Network Service Licence 2016*. BBC Trust. 2020http://downloads.bbc.co.uk/bbctrust/assets/files/pdf/regulatory_framework/service_licences/radio/2016/asian_network_aug16.pdf. Accessed 25 October.

Bennett, Andrew. 1997. Bhangra in Newcastle: Music, Ethnic Identity and the Role of Local Knowledge. *Innovation: The European Journal of Social Sciences* 10 (1): 1351–1610.

Berry, Richard. 2006. Will the iPod Kill the Radio Star? Profiling Podcasting as Radio. *Convergence* 12 (2): 413–162.

Bobby Friction. 2016. Skype Interview, 9 February.

Born, Georgina. 2004. *Uncertain Vision, Birt, Dyke and the Reinvention of the BBC*. London: Secker and Warburg.

Dawson, Ashley. 2005. Bollywood Flashback. *South Asian Popular Culture* 3 (2): 161–176.

Department for Culture, Media and Sport. 2016. *A BBC for the Future: A Broadcaster of Distinction*. CM 9242. Government. https://www.gov.uk/government/uploads/system/uploads/attachment_data/file/524863/DCMS_A_BBC_for_the_future_linked_rev1.pdf. Accessed 25 October.

Dubber, Andrew. 2013. *Radio in the Digital Age*. Cambridge: Polity.

Dudrah, Rajinder K. 2002a. Drum'n'dhol 1: British Bhangra Music and Diasporic South Asian Identity Formation. *European Journal of Cultural Studies* 5 (3): 363–383.

Dudrah, Rajinder Kumar. 2002b. Vilayati Bollywood: Popular Hindi Cinema-Going and Diasporic South Asian Identity in Birmingham (UK). *Javnost – The Public* 9 (1): 19–36.

Follmer, G., and A. Badenoch, eds. 2018. *Transnationalizing Radio Research. New Approaches to an Old Medium*. Bielefeld: Verlag.

Haydari, Nazan. 2018. Desi Radio by and for the Panjabi Community: Citizens' Media, Gender, and Participation. In *Transnationalizing Radio Research*, ed. Golo Föllmer, Alexander Badenoch, 65–72. Bielefeld: Transcript Verlag.

Hendricks, John Allen, and Bruce Mims. 2018. *The Radio Station Broadcasting, Podcasting, and Streaming*. 10th ed. New York: Routledge.

Hendy, David. 2000. Pop Music Radio in the Public Service: BBC Radio 1 and Music in the 1990s. *Media, Culture & Society* 22 (6): 743–761.

Hilmes, Michele. 1997. *Radio Voices American Voices 1922–1952*. Minneapolis/London: University of Minnesota Press.

Husain Husaini. 2015. Skype Interview, 8 October.

Ishani. 2015 (anonymised). 9 September.

Kalia, Ammar. 2019. From Blaring Bhangra to the New Grime: 30 Years of Brilliant British Asian Broadcasting. *The Guardian*, January 23, sec. Television & radio. https://www.theguardian.com/tv-and-radio/2019/jan/23/british-asian-30-years-of-sunrise-radio. Accessed 25 October.

Kamran. 2015 (anonymised). Face to face interview, 11 November.

Lewis, Peter M. 2000. Private Passion, Public Neglect the Cultural Status of Radio. *International Journal of Cultural Studies* 3 (2): 160–67.

Loviglio, Jason, and Michele Hilmes, eds. 2013. *Radio's New Wave Global Sound in the Digital Era*. New York/London: Routledge.

Mark Strippel. 2015. Face to face interview, 15 June.

McCarthy, Liam. 2018. BBC Radio Leicester in 1976: Kick Starting British Asian Radio. *Journal of Radio & Audio Media* 25 (2): 269–283.

Michelsen, Mortem, Mads Krogh, Steen Kaargaard Nielson, and Iben Have, eds. 2019. *Music Radio Building Communities, Mediating Genres*. New York/London: Bloomsbury Academic.

Ofcom. 2017a. *The Communications Market: Digital Radio Report. Ofcom's Eighth Annual Digital Progress Report. Research Report*. Ofcom. https://www.ofcom.org.uk/__data/assets/pdf_file/0014/108311/Digital-Radio-Report-2017.pdf

Ofcom. 2017b. Radio Broadcast Update December 2017. https://www.ofcom.org.uk/manage-your-licence/radio-broadcast-licensing/monthly-updates/radio-broadcast-update-december-2017

Priya. 2015 (anonymised). Face to face interview, 9 December.

Radio Times. 2016. Radio Must Adapt to Young Britain – or Face Death. June 29. https://www.radiotimes.com/news/2016-08-04/radio-must-adapt-to-young-britain-or-face-death/. Accessed 26 October.

RadioToday. n.d. UK Asian Radio Stations Call for Government Support. *Radio Today*. https://radiotoday.co.uk/2020/04/uk-asian-radio-stations-call-for-government-support/. Accessed 26 October.

RAJAR Q1. 2020. retrieved from https://www.rajar.co.uk/docs/2020_03/2020_Q1_Quarterly_Summary_Figures.pdf

Raychaudhuri, A. 2018. *Homemaking: Radical Nostalgia and the Construction of a South Asian Diaspora. Critical Perspectives on Theory, Culture and Politics*. Lanham: Rowman & Littlefield International.

Roy, Anjali Gera. 2010. *Bhangra Moves from Ludhiana to London and Beyond.* Farnham: Ashgate.

Saha, Anamik. 2012. Locating MIA: "Race", Commodification and the Politics of Production. *European Journal of Cultural Studies* 15 (6): 736–752.

———. 2020. Funky Days Are (Not) Back Again: Cool Britannia and the Rise and Fall of British South Asian Cultural Production. *Journal of British Cinema and Television* 17 (1): 6–23.

Sharma, S., John Hutnyk, and Ashwani Sharma. 1996. *Dis-Orienting Rhythms, The Politics of the New Asian Dance Music.* London: Zed Books.

Starkey, Guy. 2004. Estimating Audiences: Sampling in Television and Radio Audience Research. *Cultural Trends* 13 (1): 3–25.

Thussu, Daya Kishan. 2013. *Communicating India's Soft Power Buddha to Bollywood.* New York/Basingstoke: Palgrave Macmillan.

Tommy Sandhu. 2015. Skype Interview, 17 June.

Triggle, Nick. 2020. Why Has Leicester Had a Coronavirus Spike? *BBC News,* July 1, sec. Health. https://www.bbc.com/news/health-53235709. Accessed 26 October.

Turino, Thomas. 2008. *Music as Social Life: The Politics of Participation.* Chicago: University of Chicago Press.

Wall, Tim, and Andrew Dubber. 2009. Specialist Music, Public Service and the BBC in the Internet Age. *The Radio Journal: International Studies in Broadcast and Audio Media* 7 (1): 27–47.

Wolock, Lia, and Ashwin Punathambekar. 2014. Race and Ethnicity in Post-Network American Television: From MTV-Desi to Outsourced. *Television & New Media* 16 (7): 664–679.

CHAPTER 9

Future of the BBC Radio and the BBC Asian Network

INTRODUCTION

This book has used the testimony of minority ethnic staff who work in the BBC to offer an insight into the operations of the BBC Asian Network, the BBC's specialist radio service for British Asian listeners. The chapters have evaluated working practices, internal processes such as gatekeeping in journalism, recruitment, career progression of minority ethnic staff, music policies, representation of British Asians in the media, and linguistic programmes and their evolvement. There has been an emphasis throughout the book upon how the producers imagine and construct a cohesive community of listeners for the broadcaster. It is evident that minority ethnic listeners are not homogeneous, and neither are the ethnic producers who are recruited by the BBC to produce the distinctive media content. Differences of opinion among the staff have been explored in relation to the music played on-air, the recruitment of young ethnic staff who lack knowledge of the lived experiences of British Asian listeners, linguistic policies and the target listener determined by the BBC. Considering the challenges interviewees face in their roles, what is the future of the BBC Asian Network? This discussion is positioned within a wider consideration of the challenges facing BBC Radio and public service broadcasting, because they influence and impact how the BBC Asian Network operates.

© The Author(s), under exclusive license to Springer Nature   197
Switzerland AG 2021
G. Aujla-Sidhu, *The BBC Asian Network*,
https://doi.org/10.1007/978-3-030-65764-2_9

Future of the BBC Asian Network

The interviews with BBC staff took place during a controversial charter renewal in 2015 and 2016, so they framed their responses about the relevance and future of the BBC Asian Network accordingly. A public consultation about the future of the BBC was launched amid claims that the government wanted to weaken the BBC (Mance and Brown 2016). Commercial media had strongly argued that the licence fee is unfair and that the BBC ought to focus on underserved audiences, the market failure argument. In response, the BBC has restructured its operations to respond more robustly to economic imperatives. The 2016 *Royal Charter* demands that the BBC is measured by its distinctiveness; this ought to ensure that the broadcaster cannot crowd out commercial news organisations. At the BBC Asian Network distinctiveness is demonstrated through the original news journalism, the music played, and content that reflects the lived experiences of British Asian communities.

> It educates, it informs, and it entertains. Now the entertainment factor can be got from anywhere. By entertainment we mean fun, features, quizzes, competition, and music. Music is streaming, it's like everywhere. In terms of quizzes and competitions we don't do that anymore, as BBC we don't indulge in that kind of stuff. What we do is find a thread of Asian-ness in a story and try and sell it to people who you think may not be leading an Asian life, you can try and educate them, at the same time, people who are living it, you can inform them of about it, so it's a careful balance. (Former manager, Alia 2015)

Chapters 3 and 4 outlined the problems with the media representation of minority communities, particularly where broadcasters have tried to showcase diversity within mainstream programmes to appeal to all audience. The Asian Network stands out among the BBC radio stations because it brings unique minority listeners to the BBC. Alia notes that it must be done in a "careful" way so that they do not patronise listeners:

> This radio station is the best cost-effective way of serving British Asians, and half of the people who listen don't consume anything else from the BBC. So, they get value for money from the licence fee, which everybody must pay, through the Asian Network which shows how important it is to the BBC. (Former Controller, Bob Shennan 2015)

Whilst the BBC Asian Network may be an efficient way to serve a distinctive audience, there were concerns over its relevance moving forward and naturally its future role. Georgiou (2005) has suggested that the first and second generations use ethnic media as a source of information and as a link to their homeland. Whereas the third generation may utilise ethnic media to open a dialogue with parents or grandparents, the fourth generation may wish to learn about their heritage or culture through ethnic media. Therefore, some of the producers were concerned about the future purpose and role of the BBC Asian Network. Kevin Silverton, former head of News, questioned how long the station could operate:

> You could argue that you would hope that British society would become so much integrated and multicultural that you wouldn't need something like the Asian Network. What you can't argue with at the moment is the Asian Network audience is large, larger than it's ever been. Its news output is seen and read by more people than ever before and whilst we are in that healthy position it seems difficult to argue against it. When there is a demand you feel like that you need to satisfy that demand.
>
> It's just whether you feel all the richness the BBC Asian Network has and whether its ability to serve these various kinds of audience could be done elsewhere on the BBC or whether it could be done in a separate way to a radio station. (Kevin Silverton 2015)

Silverton casts doubt on the idea that radio station is the best means to serve British Asian audiences. The debate over how the BBC serves minority audiences has been taking place inside the BBC for decades. The Immigrants Unit was initially set up to serve minority audiences; it was later separated into the Asian and African-Caribbean Units. In 1991 the departments were united in the BBC Multicultural Programmes Department until 1995. The Asian Programmes Department was axed in 2009 because the BBC outlined it wanted to "reach those audiences through all of our output" as opposed to specific targeted programmes (Hundal 2009). Simon Cottle (1998) has described the process whereby the producers balance institutional and cultural constraints and rationalise their programme-making activities accordingly as "professional pragmatics." Silverton acknowledged that the internal discussion within the BBC about the role of minority services such as the BBC Asian Network, and ethnic television programmes, is still ongoing. It is clear that despite the BBC's long history of diverse programme production, the broadcaster is still unclear where ethnic content belongs and, more problematically, its long-term future.

Malik (2013) suggests that public service providers such as the BBC and Channel 4 have re-positioned themselves to enact creative diversity actions, which means, diversity is embedded into content created for mainstream audiences, as opposed to specific content for targeted groups. This incentivises diverse employment policies to recruit staff to achieve this objective. However, there is an unintended impact: the quality of the representation offered is ignored in favour of the recruit drive. Therefore, Malik (2018 in Freedman et al.) argues the emphasis upon diversity is financially driven, in the hope that media organisations can attract greater audience figures.

If the BBC Asian Network is to survive then it must align its goals and purposes to contribute to creative diversity policies. This implies that the staff who want greater independence to showcase a non-integrated British Asian identity may not secure it. The former head of Programmes Mark Strippel outlined that the BBC needs the station to serve British Asians:

> Is there an absolute need for the Asian Network in modern Britain? Absolutely it's needed more than ever to ensure that British Asians are woven into the discourse of the BBC. We plug British Asian audiences into the BBC and help the rest of the BBC understand this audience and there are few things more important than that for the future of BBC. The BBC needs to be more relevant to all audiences more than ever. The strategic drive across the BBC is to push toward youth audiences, BAME audiences, C2D audiences – well we cover all three. (Former Head of programmes, Mark Strippel. 2015)

Strippel indicates that British Asian audiences are not enmeshed within the media discourse offered by the BBC. This contradicts Silverton's concern that potentially the BBC Asian Network will not be required if the target listeners become deeply integrated into British culture as anticipated. Strippel also highlighted that the BBC Asian Network performs a fundamental purpose in attracting ethnic listeners to BBC services. This audience, according to the BBC, is difficult to reach; in fact, research has found that just 32 per cent of subcontinent Asian viewing is directed at public service providers (Digital i 2017, p. 8).

There have been notable calls by Sir Lenny Henry to ringfence funding, which can be used to increase the portrayal of diversity on-screen and better reflect minority communities in the UK (Press Association 2016). In 2020 the BBC's Creative Diversity Unit led by June Sarpong set out a £100 million investment to not only accelerate diversity and inclusion of employment strategies, but also require all new commissions to adhere to a 20 per cent diverse talent target from April 2021 (BBC Media Centre 2020c). Approximately 33.54 million people listen to BBC Radio each week (Q1 2020, RAJAR). BBC Radio is managed by Radio and Music, which similarly now requires independent audio production companies to meet the 20 per cent diversity target. These measures infer an element of box ticking because statistical metrics alone do not solve the "problem of diversity." Whilst the BBC has committed funds to ensure diverse content is commissioned externally, internal BBC structures and processes within the institution privilege economic metrics, which means original ideas about diverse communities are often diluted to make them appealing. The employee interviews also revealed that some Asian Network producers lack the autonomy to use their knowledge to craft robust authentic representations and stories about British Asian, and this frustrated them. At present the BBC Asian Network is positioned as a centre of expertise on British Asians within the BBC, a resource that can be used by the rest of the organisation. Alia outlined that this ought to justify its existence within the public service broadcaster:

> I would like to believe that it does have a place. It is rated, because it provides a window on British Asians for the rest of the BBC, it also now provides the rest of the BBC with the Asian stories. (Former senior manager, Alia 2015)

The sharing of diverse content has gained a greater impetus within the BBC because it is being forced to evidence that PSB does serve all audiences and not just some groups. It is widely accepted that the BBC is better able to serve older middle-class audiences and articulate notions of a common culture or common values of Britain (DCMS 2015). The stipulation in the 2016 Royal *Charter* to offer an accurate and authentic reflection of minority communities in the UK exists because all households are required to pay the licence fee, and therefore, they should see themselves reflected within the media. The Asian Network's unique role within the organisation prompted Safia *(not her real name)* to speculate if the Asian Network will turn into a specialist news department within the BBC:

We are now focusing more on original stories that you can get from the heart of the community out. So, they might just set up a department that specialises in Asian Affairs across the BBC. I don't think there is a massive market with the next generation for an Asian Network. I love it because I love Bollywood, but I don't think our children are listening to it like we did. (Reporter, Safia 2015)

Safia recognises that changes will naturally occur—but her suggestion that the radio station will cease and change into a new department would mark a radical departure from the current status quo. She recognised that as the target listener becomes younger, the influence of *Bollywood* and Asian culture will decrease. Therefore, she accepts that the target listener will inevitably influence the scope of the BBC Asian Network. However, Bela (*not her real name*) a daytime producer posed the future target listeners could be new immigrant communities:

I feel like we're so integrated but then I think the other argument is that actually there are other Asian communities who feel less integrated ie the Muslim community maybe, they probably feel quite isolated. Maybe our future listenership is going to be a specific minority. (Producer, Bela 2015)

Whilst Bela sees a role for the BBC Asian Network, in the light of further integration and audience fragmentation, she also suspects that the service will evolve and change to reflect UK society. The Former Director General, of the BBC, Mark Thomson has expressed that the organisation faces huge challenges in delivering its core purposes, which includes serving all audiences during a period of digital change and transformation. The BBC's lack of success in this area has meant that young and minority audiences are accessing the broadcaster less (Freedman et al. 2018, p. 26). Matsaganis and Katz (2014) and Husband (2005) have outlined that ethnic media is forced to appeal to large communities to be commercially successful. For example, Sunrise Radio targets all Asian listeners in London and whilst it may command, respectable RAJARs (Radio Joint Audience Research) the station is not well known among Mainstream media. Therefore, ethnic media services are relegated to the fringes of the media ecology because mainstream organisations dominate the public sphere.

Joy (*not her real name*) also accepted that the BBC Asian Network service will evolve and adapt but suggested Asia-specific content could be delivered by different mediums as opposed to radio:

I think if the BBC don't keep the Asian Network and nurture it, they are making a big mistake, because the BBC as a whole doesn't even have adequate understanding of the different Asian cultures and what they mean to British society and how they interact. It is at risk. I think I wouldn't be surprised if they made it into a more multimedia centre. (Producer, Joy 2015)

Joy's suggestion echoes the discussion in Chap. 3, which outlined how minority audiences are often seen as being a homogeneous group, and consequently, their portrayal in the media is often poor, emphasises difference, or is based on stereotypes. Radio 1 offers multimedia content alongside radio programmes, and BBC 3 was moved online only in 2016 to better engage with young audiences it served. However, in March 2020 it emerged that BBC 3 could return to television after viewing figures showed it only reached 8 per cent of the intended sixteen- to thirty-four-year-old audience each week in the online format (Waterson 2020). During the 2020 coronavirus lockdown the BBC 3 show "Normal People" was accessed over sixteen million times on the iPlayer, prompting further discussion about the future of channel. Strippel also highlighted that the Asian Network's original multi-platform content reaches a wide audience, "I think the modern-day reality is there will be sections of the audience whose only engagement with the Asian Network, is with our visual content online." All the content the station creates, on-air or online, is distinct because it highlights diversity, albeit in broad or ambiguous terms. However, this book has tried to illuminate the difficulties of creating distinct diverse content for both ethnic and mainstream listeners. Within this climate where diversity is showcased in ambiguous broad-brush tropes to appeal widely, the role of a specialist service focused on British Asian listeners is perhaps in doubt:

To be honest I think the days of Black and Asian programmes and perhaps to some extent the BBC Asian Network are numbered. As we get to a point where there are more and more Black and Asian employees at the BBC working in mainstream programmes, they will start to bring in those stories which truly reflect what is going on in the communities and reach out to the underserved audiences. Then I think the need for specialist programming will become less and less in the long term. (Reporter, Mya 2015)

Mya's perspective mirrors the prevailing diversity and inclusion strategy within the organisation, that greater recruitment of diverse employees will naturally improve the on-air content and reflection across all programmes. Although this viewpoint is positive because ethnic-specific content is not "ghettoised" in the schedule, there are concerns that diversity remains portrayed in limited ways (see Malik 2013; Saha 2018). The emphasis on employment policies does not take into account that other changes need to be enacted to organisational behaviours, cultures, and structures, to empower ethnic minority journalists to create original diverse content. The BBC's focus groups with Black, Asian, and minority ethnic (BAME) staff found that "mainstreaming is confused for inclusion. This cuts right across all diversity, not just BAME" (BBC 2018, p. 7). In other words, commissioners and editors whilst being aware of diversity do not have sufficient understanding of how this affects the story, event, or action, they are covering because they are more conscious of conforming the issues to standardised production processes to make them appealing. Malik (2013) has argued initiatives such as this ignore the distribution of power in broadcasting and works to minimise the fact that "race remains real and persists as a salient factor in identity claims and ongoing demands for fairer representation" (Malik 2013, p. 238). In other words, Malik suggests that the media tries to gloss over inequality and issues such as racism or prejudice within their programmes. Therefore, although public service broadcasters try to strengthen their reflection, the diverse media policies they use allow them to portray "culturally unspecific tropes of diversity through a unifying diversity frame" (Malik 2013, p.237). Against this context it is apparent that the future of BBC services such as the BBC Asian Network and BBC Radio depends upon how diversity policies are enacted across the organisation. The success of the BBC is measured by how the organisation can serve all audiences.

ALTERNATIVE AND DIVERSE VIEWPOINTS AND THEIR ABSENCE IN PUBLIC SERVICE BROADCASTING

The future existence of the BBC Asian Network is tied to the fortunes and future direction of the BBC. It is an institution that is vulnerable to interference particularly at a time when the underlying public service goals of the BBC are being questioned. Lord Puttnam has put forward the argument that a "well- resourced and fully independent public service television system free of political coercion offers our most reliable means of rebuilding public trust and accountability" (Freedman et al. 2018, p. 4).

The threat to the public service broadcasting has largely come from external media organisations who seek to narrow the BBC remit. Thoday (2018 in Freedman et al.) has explained that the "BBC is being squeezed by myriad forces," meaning managers worry less about media content and spend more time examining finances and perceived threats. Moreover, he outlines that because the BBC is spending less on programme content creation, this results in lower-quality programmes and affects the creative risk that producers are prepared to take and simultaneously the risk that the organisation can sanction. In other words, original PSB content has become risk averse. The frameworks that public service broadcasters are forced to work with are incompatible and contradictory, for example pre-determined schedules even though technology allows on-demand viewing, and creative risk juxtaposed with the need for high ratings. This means that all media content is created to comply with schedules which strike to supply programming aimed at a specific group at a specific time whilst also trying to attract a main general audience for rating purposes (Freedman et al. 2018). Ofcom has also recommended that the BBC should make a greater effort to produce distinctive content which includes a range of genres and to continue support for specialist services where no direct comparable competitor exists, for example the BBC Asian Network (Ofcom 2018, p. 10). The report noted that the BBC has been spending less money on UK-originated content, and to remain distinct, it needs to create original material that reflects the experiences of UK audiences. More urgently, the BBC is being urged to attract young audiences who are described as being critical to its future success. This group, however, increasingly do not watch live content and are more likely to listen to commercial radio as opposed to BBC Radio. The BBC is also facing intense competition from on-demand music streaming services such as Spotify and Apple music, which account for around 12 per cent of all audio listening, but this grows to almost 50 per cent of all listening among fifteeen to twenty four year olds (Ofcom 2018, p. 20).

In response to the continuing marginalisation of non-mainstream perspectives, a range of alternative media exist. Increasingly minority groups are producing their own self-representation online—thus bypassing the requirement for public service organisations to frame and establish the agenda on the issues they wish to explore. Vrikki and Malik (2019) suggest podcasting is an emerging space where marginalised communities can create a "counterpublic" to dominant racialised narratives presented in the mainstream press. Hendricks and Mims (2018) suggest in the USA 40 per cent of the podcasting audience is non-white. They outline that a low barrier to entry, for example the low cost, reduced equipment, and ability for anyone to publish their content, means that increasingly non-white podcasters are able to disseminate their message. It is difficult to suggest the same situation is occurring in the UK. Research reveals a mixed picture with some noting that white men dominate the sector (Markman and Sawyer 2014). Although the BBC as an organisation has produced podcasts from as early as 2004, the early content lacked innovation primarily, because a huge proportion were simply programmes produced for Radio 4 that were labelled as a podcast on BBC Sounds. Thus, the innovation and experimentation in podcasting has taken place external to mainstream media organisations. Vrikki and Malik (2019) outline that this is because the dominant cultures and frameworks in the creative industries work to prevent minority ethnic staff from taking part in the first place. They also suggest that algorithms are the new gatekeepers in social media and at Spotify and that they contribute to the maintenance of existing race and class inequality (Vrikki and Malik 2019). The majority of podcasters and their content exist on the fringes of mainstream media; therefore, their influence and message remain restricted to their target audience.

In the light of George Floyd's murder in May 2020, and the subsequent Black Lives Matter protests in the UK, James Purnell, Director of BBC Radio and Education, set out how BBC Radio will improve its representation and reflection of diverse listeners. BBC Radio has been directed to commission "more diverse stories, voices and experiences on air, and from 2021 and 2022, over three years we'll commit £12 million pounds of our existing commissioning money to new diverse content" (Purnell 2020). The aim of funding is to support staff to pursue innovative ideas and create diverse teams. The announcement was part of larger plans to create diverse teams and correspondingly representative content across BBC Radio and Music department. Other commitments include setting up the 50/50 project to include ethnicity and disability in 50 programmes by end of 2021, a commitment to including diverse staff in commissioning teams and editorial plans to showcase diverse music genres and stories on-air. Writing in Radio Today, James Purnell outlined that:

> One thing is crystal clear to me – the importance of a diverse workforce to making great programmes. The parts of the BBC that were diverse got the importance of this [George Floyd] story and responded quickly and effectively, more so than the rest of us. (Purnell 2020)

This quote underlies the BBC's commitment to employment policies and guidelines to improve the representation of race on-air. The strong commitment to employing staff from a range of diverse background is based on the idea that a broader range of staff will naturally offer varied ideas and solutions. However, conversely post the coronavirus pandemic in July 2020 the BBC announced plans to cut 450 regional and online journalism roles and reduce on-air presenters on BBC Local Radio (BBC 2020). The cuts in local radio impact the programmes with two presenters on key programmes, which were introduced to place more women into on-air roles across the regions. It was followed by the New Voices scheme, which first ran in 2018 to find new talent and offer opportunities on new evening programmes on local radio. Whilst the BBC has been trying to address diversity in radio, job cuts and the reduction of opportunities in radio specifically for women and minorities will adversely impact any gains achieved.

Chapter 6 juxtaposed the key restrictions imposed upon the broadcaster, for example the need to maximise audiences whilst also serving distinct ethnic communities in the UK and showcase their experiences. Often this results in media content that illustrates issues relating to diversity and race within a restricted framework that promotes so-called British values through the process of "otherness," conflict and terrorism (Flood et al. 2011). Ethnic journalists also illuminated that they are forced to navigate gatekeepers, internal cultural norms, and the maintenance of the political position on immigration and race whilst trying to meet the needs of their ethnic listeners. Their views outlined in Chaps. 4 and 6 also show that they feel marginalised in the newsroom and lack the autonomy to be creative and robustly serve their community of listeners because they feel pressured to conform to internal journalism norms.

CREATING AND REFLECTING A COMMUNITY OF LISTENERS

The manner in which BBC producers actively construct a cohesive and distinct community of listeners has been key theme throughout the book. The young British Asian listener profile has been imposed upon the BBC Asian Network and more lately on BBC Local Radio (Ofcom 2017). The BBC needs to attract younger viewers and listeners because they are critical to the future success of the organisation. However, the BBC faces tough competition for their attention from streaming services and YouTube. It is fundamental that the BBC is able to justify its claims to universality—that everyone is offered something in a genre or format that is appealing to the demographic or minority group. The BBC management is thus trying to craft a community of British Asian listeners, specifically third- and fourth-generation listeners into a rationalised audience. The BBC tries to connect them through the portrayal of culture, heritage, shared lived experiences, and a shared post-colonial history. The former Controller at the station described the connection between the individual listeners in Chap. 7 as "Britishness not Asian-ness, its Britishness" (Former Controller, Bob Shennan). What can be explicated from this is that the BBC is not focused on promoting Asian music and languages but is focused on trying to reflect a version of British Asian lifestyle as experienced by some third- and fourth-generation British Asians. This version of identity that the BBC tries to articulate is broad so that they can appeal widely to capture a greater number of British Asians, but this vision of identity has been envisioned and bought to life by BBC producers. Yu (2016, p. 5) has demonstrated that there are usually two identities for minority communities: the identity that members of ethnic communities self-identify with which can be described as authentic and reflexive, and the identity that is socially constructed and prescribed to them—in this instance, by the BBC.

Striking differences were evident among the BBC staff interviewed: the older staff, from the first- and second-generation groups, oppose the top-down BBC agenda to concentrate on young assimilated British Asian listeners. They described this listener in their words as being "westernised" or "mainstream," and what could be drawn from this was that they believe these groups do not need an ethnic-specific service. However, they feel older listeners deserve a dedicated radio service that has a stronger focus on promoting Asian culture, news from South Asia, and related music rather than content that appears to be in their view "whitewashed." The younger staff comprising some second- but largely third-generation British Asians did not appear to oppose the drive to secure younger listeners. They are also able to successfully pitch story ideas that are shared across the BBC and more likely to appeal to the listener through digital and social media. The older staff appear to have internalised the BBC's paternalistic tendencies with reference to minority programming and appear to want young generations of staff and listeners to learn and connect with their culture. This is symptomatic of the struggle all migrant communities face at some point, when they feel their distinctive heritage is becoming unacceptably diluted. This is one of the key differences that characterises the way the older production staff at the BBC Asian Network perceive the different generations that comprise their British Asian listener; they inherently want to create material that bonds the listeners to their faith, heritage, and culture. They accept, grudgingly, that their young listener does not require this type of content because they are "integrated" or "westernised" and the specific use of this terminology implies that this is negative or undesirable. Therefore, they lack the autonomy to produce content for listeners who are more likely to want to gaze back to their countries and cultures.

Chapter 2 explored how the identities of immigrant communities change in response to interaction with the host nation (Gillespie 1995). As such, third and fourth generations of British Asian communities increase their acceptance within youth cultures, employment, and education through familiarity with other cultures and, thereby, dilute their distinctive identity. In the early years of Asian radio programming the BBC through the regional radio programmes and television programming sought to provide communities with information to support their settlement into Britain and to conform them to British values and standards (Hendy n.d.). However, in contemporary society British Asians play a more prominent role in employment and education. This is also reflected in the staff composition at the BBC Asian Network, where increasingly third- and fourth-generation journalists who have attended university secure entry-level journalist roles. What was also revealed is that some new journalists are hired even if they lack knowledge about British Asian communities. It is significant that former senior manager Alia claimed a balance must be found to manage the social differences that are evident between staff, because it was insinuated that this is a difficult task.

The differences among the ethnic staff are the consequence of intergenerational change within the British Asian community: the younger generations are more likely to be invested in Britain in contrast to the first generation who may not speak English. Presenter, Bobby Friction, described the desired listener as likely to be assimilated and integrated. What is also striking is some staff feel pressured to chase listeners who do not strongly identify with their Asian heritage simply because they are members of the imagined community of listeners. This reveals a complex paradox, first, the listener is presumed to be integrated into British life, but the BBC appear to stereotype the listener by also expecting them to consume *Bollywood* films and like *Bhangra*. The BBC as a broadcaster and cultural institution in the UK appears to mandate that Asian culture is promoted through tropes that emphaise Hindi movies and Asian music.

The way the target listener is addressed by the staff can lead to confusion over whom the content is directed at. Whilst the music policies focus on reflecting genres that appeal to young listeners the news and current affairs content appears staid in contrast. It is plausible younger listeners do not require three-hour debate programmes and that they have a greater appeal among older listeners who fought to make a space for themselves in society or have struggled against inequality. Subsequent, British Asian generations have grown up during a period of multiculturalism where different faiths and communities were an accepted norm, but their voices and experiences have been side-lined in the media, education, and society. Due to the complex struggles to own and control media, content that highlights the lived realities of some British Asians remains marginalised due to the existence of a rigid gatekeeping system that enables the commodification of diverse content (Saha 2018; Hesmondhalgh 2019). Therefore, minority communities are often featured within the media due to their difference. Audiences often lack the power and influence to change the representation of their groups because the audience is viewed either from above, or from the outside, or from an institutional perspective (Ang 1991).

Chapter 2 scrutinised how the term "Asian" has been socially constructed to describe a group of people who collectively form the largest minority group in Britain. Whilst the station recognises that the listener is integrated into the British way of life, the news agenda directly conflicts with the message disseminated because on issues such as terrorism it tends to promote the dominant narrative about communities (mostly Muslim) that are segregated (Parekh 2000; Poole and Richardson 2006; Virdee and McGeever 2018). This implicates the BBC Asian Network into promoting British Asians in the terms prescribed by the dominant majority culture.

RECRUITMENT AND GATEKEEPING

Chapters 4 and 6 focused upon recruitment and gatekeeping practices within the BBC. The BBC is trying to improve the numbers of BAME journalists, producers, presenters, and editors, recruited to the organisation to improve the on-air reflection of diverse audiences. The evidence suggests that despite the existence of diversity and inclusion strategies across media organisations to increase the numbers of ethnic staff, these groups are still under-represented in radio, including Bauer Media (Ofcom

2019a). Ofcom's diversity in television report sets out that Channel 4 and Viacom have greater numbers of minority ethnic staff compared to BBC (Ofcom 2019b, p. 6). However, the interviews with ethnic staff highlighted need to recruit a range of diverse staff in terms of class as well as ethnicity; some interviewees indicated that BBC recruitment policies favour middle-class, integrated, or assimilated minority ethnic staff, educated to at least degree level. It was suggested that they are hired for roles at the BBC Asian Network, even if they may have little lived experience of British Asian culture. Some staff were also concerned that senior ethnic staff within the BBC are not representative of the audiences because many are Oxbridge graduates. The BBC published details about the socio-economic diversity of its workforce in 2018 after employees were surveyed about their parents' occupations. It revealed just 39 per cent of the BBC employees are from low- and intermediate-income households compared to the UK average of 67 per cent (BBC 2018b, 5). Hesmondhalgh (in Deery and Press 2017) has argued class differences lead to "class asymmetry" between the staff at audience.

Academic studies of production have proposed that the producer is able to convey their knowledge, views, and identity through their work; therefore, their views contribute to the sum of knowledge and information circulated within the public sphere and society (Hesmondhalgh and Baker 2011; Mayer 2011). This study reveals that the mode of address used by ethnic staff is reflective of the generation and demographic to which they belong to. For example, some staff try to create content that evokes a connection to South Asia, whereas others craft material that articulates a diluted or hybrid British Asian identity.

The differences between how producer address the target listener is most apparent when they attempt to get commissioned by other BBC departments. Staff are expected to share their journalism to reach a bigger mainstream audience. However, the interviews revealed in Chap. 6 that journalists are keenly aware that stories that include Muslims/Islam are more likely to be selected by commissioners. This has a direct consequence upon innovation and creativity because ethnic staff stifle ideas about other Asian communities to focus on plans that will sell and allow them to progress in their careers. Saha (2018) has outlined that when ethnic staff change their practices to conform to the dominant internal cultures and norms, they have rationalised conventions and thus contributed to the reproduction of content that fails to address racial inequality or racism. Thus, he argues that diversity strategies enable the media to "sustain the institutional whiteness of the cultural industries even while they claim (often genuinely so) to do something more inclusive" (Saha 2018, p. 107). The interview material echoes Cottles (1997) study, which also found that staff are forced to work with gatekeepers and commissioners who may have rigid ideas on what can work and what won't. This insight sheds a light on the professional and production environment within the contemporary BBC Asian Network. Ethnic staff across the BBC revealed to their employer in internal focus groups that they feel a "sense of exclusion and isolation" with some staff believing there is a lack of opportunity for BAME staff development and progression (BBC 2018a, p. 7).

Race is a social construct and as such society can prescribe behaviours, and historical frames onto minority groups in most fields. The Black Lives Matter protests in the UK 2020 highlighted that some histories have been erased from the education and media discourses at the expense of a dominant Eurocentric understanding of the world. The BBC as elite institution has the ability to disseminate the hegemonic perspective, and this explains why some ethnic groups are critical of their limited representation by the public service provider (Mills 2016; Freedman 2019). Gutsche (2015) explains that the press is:

> As an institution of white domination that recalls histories and explanations of the world that come from western/Anglo/white perspectives with the intention of maintaining a status quo that benefits future generations of white folk, which involves the function and act of violence to enforce submission. (Gutsche 2015, p. 36)

As a consequence, the knowledge that is shared and circulated within society by the media is filtered and interpreted by journalists who work in a system of control and power. Therefore, the BBC as a public service broadcaster tasked to promote British values, and the idea of a British nation decides the depth and variety of representation that British Asian communities receive. Meaning, the parameters of representation are defined by the media, government, and other elite organisations—and not the audience. Within the BBC ethnic staff who pitch and propose ideas may need to demonstrate or prove their credibility or skills to be successful. To improve the internal culture, the BBC has committed to itself to having at least two members of staff from BAME backgrounds on senior leadership groups and launched further commissioner development role programmes (BBC Media Centre 2020a, b).

Managing Race and Diversity in a Public Service Remit

A key aim of this book was to examine how the BBC as a public service broadcaster manages race and ethnicity within the staff composition of the organisation and on-air. It is evident that several diversity and inclusion strategies are being enacted to improve the diversity of staff and address how internal cultures impact the experiences of their employees. One shortcoming of such initiatives is that they tend to place the burden of representation upon minority staff, and therefore, there is little imperative for non-minority journalists to improve media content. Within the contemporary BBC, minority ethnic staff tend to be clustered in producer and journalism roles with fewer minority staff members in the decision-making roles (BBC Annual Report 2017/18). Several diversity schemes aimed at disabled people or minority ethnic groups offer the incentive to join the BBC on short-term contracts, with the promise of being trained, but there is no clear evidence if these employees are retained by the organisation. Therefore, such schemes window-dress diversity as opposed to addressing underlying barriers that prevent access to the organisation or career progression. What also emerged from the interviews is that some staff feel that internal hierarchical structures impede their creativity. This resonates with Hall's (in Morely and Chen 1996) words that ethnic staff are recruited to be visible but lack autonomy to influence editorial policies.

Some employees also felt that the target listener, the mode of address, the British Asian identity, and other practices are imposed upon the Asian Network, meaning the BBC is not as "responsive" to ethnic staff as perhaps it ought to be. What was also conveyed through the interviews, although not explicitly, was a sense that the BBC Asian Network remains marginalised within the institution despite efforts by management to move it to the heart of radio operations. This may not be the fault of senior BBC leadership. It is more likely to be a consequence of the fierce internal competition that exists between the different stations and programmes within the BBC who individually have to illustrate their success through listener or viewing figures. Historically, journalism has been characterised by competition: the need to break news, the need for the key guest on a story, the need for the stronger angle; therefore, internally, the News at Ten will fight for the eminent guest as opposed to letting Radio 1 or the BBC Asian Network have them first. There is also an underlying suggestion from the material gathered that the BBC leadership is out of touch with their ethnic staff and the minority audiences.

The existence of a rigid internal gatekeeping system that encourages employees to generate ideas they believe will appeal to the commissioners as opposed innovative ideas shows a lot of work still needs to be done to achieve culture change. All the interviewees agreed that whilst the representation of race and ethnicity on the BBC has increased, they worried that if the Asian Network were closed, the original content about British Asian would vanish from the media discourse. When the station was launched it was set up to challenge dominant media stereotypes of the Asian communities and offer a unique national public service platform for them to articulate their views. However, Chap. 5 outlined that the listeners are highly managed by radio producers and that listener participation is permitted within parameters set by the producers. Meaning, radio is perhaps not as democratic or open as it would seem.

This study has concentrated specifically upon radio to shed light on the experiences of ethnic production staff working in the BBC. The proposed closure of the Asian Network in 2010, to making financial savings, indicated at that time British Asian audiences were not important. However, in the last ten years issues relating to race and diversity in the media have gained greater dominance, and therefore, the BBC has come under further pressure to showcase how it will meet its goals of universality, diversity of programming, and the mission to represent and serve diverse audiences (regional and ethnic). There is clearly a gap between the top-down policies enacted by the BBC Board and senior staff and how they are received by ethnic producers at the other end. This is where the process of in-depth interviews with BBC journalists, editors, and controllers was fruitful; a wealth of material was gathered, which revealed different perspectives on the production process, depending upon the interviewee's role. Thus, this book shines a light on internal cultures, behaviours, and practices from the perspective of minority ethnic producers who work to a public service remit.

CONCLUSION

This book has looked in detail at the challenges ethnic staff face producing content for minority listeners. Over the last decade the Asian Network has sought to attract the younger listeners, and consequently changes have been made to the station's playlist, specifically the genres of music selected, linguistic policies, and the move to blended language-specific instead of mother tongue-specific shows, the on-air presenters, and the journalism.

The key aim of this book was to outline the experiences and perspectives of minority ethnic producers who work in the BBC. Production studies often focus upon mainstream film or media, and therefore, less is known about the conditions under which ethnic media producers labour under and the unequal power distribution and consequently the impact this has upon the media that is created. Hesmondhalgh and Saha (2013, p. 180) recommended that "theories of cultural production need to make the intertwined oppression associated with race and ethnicity far more central than they have been until now" and that the oppression should be explored with reference to power dispersal and class to better understand why some groups are not properly heard in the media, despite the plethora of diversity strategies and initiatives that exist to address the situation.

This book uses the BBC Asian Network as a case study to examine diverse radio production within a public service remit. Therefore, the different chapters have scrutinised the editorial and audience strategies enacted by the BBC, music policies, career progression within the broadcaster, the structure and organisation of the BBC itself, and the impact this has upon the content produced. A minority of staff at the BBC Asian Network outlined concerns over what they described as restrictive music policies in Chap. 8. Journalists also described how they experienced the internal gatekeeping in terms of news story ideas and suggested that BBC editors and commissioners select stories that conform with familiar or "other" stereotypes in Chap. 6. Chapter 4 looked at the recruitment and the skillset that ethnic staff ought to have. This revealed tensions and differences of opinion between minority ethnic staff due to intergenerational change which in turn influences how staff represent British Asians on-air. Chapter 7 looked that the reduction of language content on-air as the station has tried to better reflect young British Asians. Against this context the book has also outlined how the public service goals that form the basis of the BBC influence how it serves audiences and scrutinised if this hinders or enables diverse content.

What has been identified is that minority ethnic producers face a number of challenges when they create media content for their listeners; they lack the autonomy to offer nuanced variations of British Asian identity, they believe their ethnic expertise is marginalised and as such they feel their ideas are stifled within the wider BBC, and some staff profoundly oppose the imposition of third- and fourth-generation British Asians as the target listener. What also emerged is that these issues have deeply divided employees leading to internal divisions among the staff over whom they ought to serve and what identity is articulated on-air. Whilst these discussions are expected in any media organisation that is trying to remain relevant, it does indicate that the way staff at the BBC Asian Network tries to imagine and construct an audience is best described as haphazard. This research thus contributes to the study of ethnic media, radio studies, and public service broadcasting because it has offered a behind-the-scenes insight into the production of radio content for British Asian listeners. This study is also timely: all media organisations are under pressure to improve the recruitment of minority staff and correspondingly enhance the representations of minorities on-air and on-screen. Furthermore, whilst the numbers of British Asians working in both mainstream and ethnic media organisations have increased, what has also emerged is that perspectives and experiences of third- or fourth-generation Asian communities inevitably differ from first and second generations. This study has bought to fore the intergenerational differences between older and young British Asian staff working at the BBC.

REFERENCES

Alia. 2015 (anonymised). Face to face interview, 16 June.
Ang, Ien. 1991. *Desperately Seeking the Audience*. London/New York: Routledge.
BBC. 2017. *BBC Annual Report and Accounts 2017/18*. London. http://downloads.bbc.co.uk/aboutthebbc/insidethebbc/reports/pdf/bbc_annualreport_201718.pdf#page=244. Accessed 25 Oct 2020.
———. 2018. *Reflecting the Socio-Economic Diversity of the UK within the BBC Workforce*. A Report on Career Progression and Culture at the BBC. http://downloads.bbc.co.uk/mediacentre/socio-economic-diversity.pdf
BBC Media Centre. 2020a – BBC Sets out Plans to Transform Its Local Services – Media Centre. https://www.bbc.co.uk/mediacentre/latestnews/2020/bbc-sets-out-plans-to-transform-local-services. Accessed 14 Aug 2020.
———. 2020b. BBC – BBC Radio & Music Boosts Its Diversity Commitments with £12 Million of Dedicated Funding and New Targeted Initiatives – Media Centre. July 2020. https://www.bbc.co.uk/mediacentre/latestnews/2020/bbc-radio-diversity-12m-funding
———. 2020c. BBC – June Sarpong Sets out Her Vision for Creative Diversity at the BBC – Media Centre. May 20. https://www.bbc.co.uk/mediacentre/latestnews/2020/creative-diversity-vision
Bob Shennan. 2015. Face to face interview, 11 November.
Cottle, Simon. 1997. *Television and Ethnic Minorities: Producers' Perspectives*. Aldershot: Avebury.

Cottle, S. 1998. Making Ethnic Minority Programmes Inside the BBC; Professional Pragmatics and Cultural Containment. *Media Culture and Society* 20 (2): 295–317.

DCMS. 2015. *BBC Charter Review Public Consultation.* CM9116. https:// assets.publishing.service.gov.uk/government/uploads/system/uploads/ attachment_data/file/445704/BBC_Charter_Review_ Consultation_WEB.pdf

Deery, June, and Andrea Press, eds. 2017. Media and Class, TV Film and Digital Culture. New York and London: Routledge.

Digital I. 2017. Mind the Viewing Gap. https://www.digital-i.com/wp-content/ uploads/2017/11/Mind-The-Viewing-Gap-Compressed.pdf.   Accessed 29 Aug 2020.

Flood, Chris, Stephen Hutchings, Galina Miazhevich, and Henri Nickels. 2011. Between Impartiality and Ideology. *Journalism Studies* 12 (2): 221–238.

Freedman, Des. 2019. "Public Service" and the Journalism Crisis: Is the BBC the Answer? *Television and New Media* 20 (3): 203–218.

Freedman, Des, Trine Syvertsen, Vana Goblot, Mark Thompson, Jon Thoday, Amanda D. Lotz, Tess Alps, Patrick Barwise, Jennifer Holt, and Matthew Powers. 2018. *A Future for Public Service Television.* Cambridge: Goldsmiths, University London.

Georgiou, Myria. 2005. Diasporic Media Across Europe: Multicultural Societies and the Universalism, Particularism Continuum. *Journal of Ethnic & Migration Studies* 31 (31): 481–498.

Gillespie, Marie. 1995. Television, Ethnicity and Cultural Change. London and New York: Routledge.

Gutsche, Robert E. 2015. *Media Control: News as an Institution of Power and Social Control.* New York: Bloomsbury Academic.

Hendricks, John Allen, and Bruce Mims. 2018. *The Radio Station Broadcasting, Podcasting, and Streaming.* 10th ed. New York: Routledge.

Hendy, David. n.d. One of Us? Make Yourself at Home In 1965, the BBC Launched Its First Programmes Specially for Immigrants. What Were They Like? And Did They Deliver? BBC Website. https://www.bbc.com/ historyofthebbc/100-voices/people-nation-empire/make-yourself-at-home

Hesmondhalgh, David. 2019. *The Cultural Industries.* 4th ed. London: Sage.

Hesmondhalgh, David, and Sarah Baker. 2011. *Creative Labour, Media Work in Three Cultural Industries.* Milton Park: Routledge.

Hesmondhalgh, David, and Anamik Saha. 2013. Race, Ethnicity, and Cultural Production. *Popular Communication* 11 (3): 179–195.

Hundal, Sunny. 2009. Differences over Diversity. *The Guardian*, January 12, sec. Media. http://www.theguardian.com/media/2009/jan/12/bbc-asian-programmes-unit

Husband, Charles. 2005. Minority Ethnic Media as Communities Of Practice: Professionalism and Identity Politics in Interaction. *Journal of Ethnic & Migration Studies* 31 (3): 461–79.

Joy. 2015 (anonymised). Face to face interview, 14 December.

Kevin Silverton. 2015. Face to face interview, 15 June.

Malik, Sarita. 2013. "Creative Diversity": UK Public Service Broadcasting After Multiculturalism. *Popular Communication* 11 (3): 227–241.

Mance, Henry, and John Murray Brown. 2016. BBC Pushes Back Against Government Plans. *Financial Times*, May 12. https://www.ft.com/content/3d7dd5a0-182e-11e6-b197-a4af20d5575e. Accessed 9 December.

Mark Strippel. 2015. Face to face interview, 15 June.

Markman, Kris M., and Caroline E. Sawyer. 2014. Why Pod? Further Explorations of the Motivations for Independent Podcasting. *Journal of Radio & Audio Media* 21 (1): 20–35.

Matsaganis, Matthew., and Vikki Katz. (2014). How Ethnic Media Producers Constitute their Communities of Practice: An Ecological Approach. *Journalism* 15 (7): 926–944.

Mayer, Vicki. 2011. *Below the Line Producers and Production Studies in New Television Economy*. Durham: Duke University Press.

Mills, Tom. 2016. *The BBC Myth of a Public Service*. London: Verso.

Morely, David, and Kuan-Hsing Chen. 1996. *Stuart Hall Critical Dialogues in Cultural Studies*. London: Routledge.

Mya. 2015 (anonymised). Skype Interview, 10 July.

Ofcom. 2017. Operating Licence for the BBC's UK Public Services. https://www.ofcom.org.uk/__data/assets/pdf_file/0017/107072/bbc-operating-licence.pdf. Accessed 25 Oct 2020.

———. 2018. Ofcom's Annual Report on the BBC 2018.

———. 2019a. Diversity and Equal Opportunities in Radio Monitoring Report on the UK Radio Industry. https://www.ofcom.org.uk/__data/assets/pdf_file/0022/159421/diversity-in-radio-2019-report.pdf

———. 2019b. *Diversity and Equal Opportunities in Television – Monitoring Report on the UK-Based Broadcasting Industry. Research report*. UK: Ofcom. https://www.ofcom.org.uk/__data/assets/pdf_file/0028/166807/Diversity-in-TV-2019.pdf

Parekh, Bhikhu. 2000. *The Future of Multi-Ethnic Britain*. London: Profile Books.

Poole, Elizabeth, and John E. Richardson, eds. 2006. *Muslims and the News Media*. London: I B Tauris.

Press Association. 2016. Lenny Henry Repeats Call for Ringfenced Funding to Boost TV Diversity. *The Guardian*, January 19, sec. Media. https://www.theguardian.com/media/2016/jan/19/lenny-henry-ringfenced-funding-tv-diversity-tony-hall-channel-4

Purnell, James. 2020. Building a Creative, Diverse Future for BBC Radio & Music. *RadioToday* (blog), July 22. https://radiotoday.co.uk/2020/07/building-a-creative-diverse-future-for-bbc-radio-music/

RAJAR Q1. 2020. Retrieved from https://www.rajar.co.uk/listening/quarterly_listening.php

Safia. 2015 (anonymised). Face to face interview, 15 June.

Saha, Anamik. 2018. *Race and the Cultural Industries.* Cambridge: Polity.

Virdee, Satnam, and Brendan McGeever. 2018. Racism, Crisis, Brexit. *Ethnic and Racial Studies* 41 (10): 1802–1819.

Vrikki, Photini, and Sarita Malik. 2019. Voicing Lived-Experience and Anti-Racism: Podcasting as a Space at the Margins for Subaltern Counterpublics. *Popular Communication* 17 (4): 273–298.

Waterson, Jim. 2020. BBC Three Could Return to TV Four Years After Online-Only Switch. *The Guardian*, March 6, sec. Media. https://www.theguardian.com/media/2020/mar/06/bbc-three-could-return-tv-channel-broadcast

Yu, S. Sherry. 2016. Ethnic Media as Communities of Practice: The Cultural and Institutional Identities. *Journalism* 11 (18): 1309–1326.

INDEX